SYSTEMIC INTERVENTIONS FOR COLLECTIVE AND NATIONAL TRAUMA

Systemic Interventions for Collective and National Trauma explains the theoretical basis for understanding collective and national trauma through the concept of systems theory, and gives ways of implementing systems theory in interventions at the micro, mezzo and macro levels. Particular attention is given to the use of socio-political and cultural aspects of interventions with victims, as well as to the ethical codes that social workers and other mental health professionals need to integrate in their work with collective/national trauma. Separated into two distinct parts on theory and practice, this volume is appropriate for practitioners as well as students in advanced courses.

Michal Shamai, Ph.D. is Associate Professor in the School of Social Work in the University of Haifa, Israel.

SYSTEMIC INTERVENTIONS FOR COLLECTIVE AND NATIONAL TRAUMA

Theory, Practice and Evaluation

Michal Shamai

Routledge
Taylor & Francis Group

NEW YORK AND LONDON

First published 2016
by Routledge
711 Third Avenue, New York, NY 10017

and by Routledge
2 Park Square, Milton Park, Abingdon, Oxon, OX14 4RN

Routledge is an imprint of the Taylor & Francis Group, an informa business

© 2016 Taylor & Francis

Library of Congress Cataloging in Publication Data
A catalog record for this book has been requested

ISBN: 978-1-138-89245-3 (hbk)
ISBN: 978-1-138-89244-6(pbk)
ISBN: 978-1-315-70915-4(ebk)

Typeset in Sabon
by Swales & Willis Ltd, Exeter, Devon, UK

This book is dedicated to the memory of my late husband Dr Shalom Shamai, who did not live to see its publication, but was a constant source of love and support throughout every stage of the process.

CONTENTS

ILLUSTRATIONS

Figures

Tables

INTRODUCTION

Collective and national traumatic events have occurred throughout human history. Over the past two decades, however, the degree of awareness of these events has greatly increased, mainly due to major media developments, which have turned the world into a "global village." Alongside this awareness is the growing recognition of the important role played by mental well-being in coping with trauma. Therefore, social workers and mental health professionals have become key figures in dealing with impacts of the traumatic events. Notwithstanding the hundreds of articles and studies on collective trauma, very few have dealt with its impact on systems as units, such as families, communities and nations, and on referral to systemic psychosocial/mental health interventions following the traumatic event.

To fill the knowledge gap in this area, this book has two main objectives: first, to conceptualize the term "collective and national trauma" by describing the types of traumatic events that fit this description; and second, to propose a theoretical framework and specific techniques for psychosocial or mental health interventions that consider both the special characteristics of collective and national trauma and the system as a unit.

The first two chapters in this book focus on conceptualizing the term "collective and national trauma." They describe different aspects of the phenomenon in the attempt to reach a clear definition. In so doing, they highlight the similarities between collective and national trauma, as well as the difficulty in distinguishing between them. A suggestion is made for an analysis that conceptualizes collective and national trauma according to the phenomenology approach (space, time and significant others). Specific attention is given to: a) the role of the context in which the collective or national traumatic event occurs; and b) the specific impact of collective and national trauma on systems, such as family, community, ethnic group, society, or nation, as units rather than as groups of individuals.

The third and fourth chapters propose a theoretical framework and specific techniques for systemic interventions. Special attention is given to the use of socio-political aspects in systemic interventions with victims

1

of collective or national trauma and to the ways in which these aspects can be used in the intervention process. Socio-political aspects of trauma refer to the collective or national experience as a framework for constructing and interpreting traumatic events.

The fifth chapter describes the impact of the help on the mental health helpers, and suggests systemic principles that can prevent possible negative impacts and to heal the effects if they occur. The final chapter deals with the reasons for the lack of evidence-based systemic practices relevant to situations of collective and national trauma. Some "imperfect" directions are suggested to deal with the challenge of evaluation of emergent, short- and long-term systemic interventions provided to the victim population.

Throughout the book, the theoretical analysis is followed by examples and illustrations from various national and cultural contexts, in which collective and/or national traumatic events occur. Thus, the reader is exposed to the social, cultural and national elements to be considered in understanding the impact of national trauma and in working with its victims. For the illustrations, I draw on traumatic events that occurred all over the world—in the United States, the United Kingdom, Former Yugoslavia, Sri Lanka, Palestine, South Africa, and more. However, as an Israeli living in Israel, many of the examples are taken from my extensive experience with research and practice with the Israeli population. If this focus appears unbalanced to readers, it should be noted that the examples and illustrations are based on system theory principles, which, with certain changes, can be implemented in other cultural and social contexts.

Writing about collective and national trauma, even from a mental health perspective, includes many ideological and political aspects. For example, the use of the term "terror attack" might be open to criticism. One perspective might ask who decides what is defined as a terror attack, rather than an act of freedom fighting against a regime that invaded a land or a culture. From another perspective, it can be argued that such a deconstruction of the term might justify cases such as 9/11, if the perpetrators felt that Western culture, led by the United States, had invaded their culture. Both perspectives need further exploration and analysis, but exploring the complexity of the term "national terror" is beyond the scope of this book, and I leave this to researchers in the fields of political science, law, philosophy, or history. My intention is to suggest a framework in which to understand the systemic impact of collective trauma on mental health and to implement appropriate interventions. Therefore, I use the term "terror" from the perspective of the victims, when a violent act is perpetrated against non-combatants, who are neither directly nor indirectly involved in the armed conflict.

One might ask what led me to write this book and to describe so many situations in which I was deeply involved. The answer might seem a little

2

odd: I did not choose the topic, but the topic chose me. I am Jewish and have lived in Israel since birth. From early childhood, I was directly exposed to wars and terror events. I heard my parents' stories about their extended families who were murdered in the Holocaust. I heard my father's stories about his service in the Jewish Unit (Auxiliary Military Pioneer Corps (AMPC) in the British Army during World War II and about his experiences in a Nazi prisoner-of-war camp. In Jewish history lessons at school, I learned about the repeated traumatic events in which the Jewish people suffered through the ages. I read many books about the Zionist pioneers' ongoing fight for a Jewish state. Later, I learned that the Palestinians experienced our War of Independence as a traumatic event, and that the pain of each nation is a source of ongoing conflict, characterized by war and terror. This complicated history and painful present have taught me about the importance of systems (families, communities and nations) in the process of resisting and coping with various traumatic events. Belonging to a system is more than just a source of social support; it is also a source of strength resulting from the sense of togetherness, commitment, beliefs, and more. Many participants in my studies have indicated that their sense of belonging to a system gave them strength to cope with loss and pain. I could easily differentiate between people with and without such a sense of belonging. When working directly with families and communities, who were coping with collective trauma, I encouraged them to search for this togetherness and this sense of belonging to empower them as individuals and to strengthen the systems as units. I hope that the presentation in this book of the importance of systems in coping with traumatic events will convince its readers of the importance of systemic interventions in situations of collective and national trauma.

I have a naïve and irrational wish: that this book will be irrelevant. This could happen if human-made traumatic events, such as wars and terror would cease, and if global policy would succeed in preventing or reducing the effects of natural disasters.

As this is unlikely to happen in the foreseeable future, meanwhile, as a social worker and researcher, I am committed to my role of helping victims of collective and national trauma and to developing knowledge that might improve the understanding of the special characteristics of collective trauma, its impact and directions for help. I hope that this book will contribute to the implementation of my mission.

Part I

THEORY OF COLLECTIVE AND NATIONAL TRAUMA

1

EXPLORING COLLECTIVE AND NATIONAL TRAUMA

Defining Collective and National Trauma

I was once at an international conference, where an African American man gave the keynote speech about the impact and legacy of slavery. In response to his question to the audience as to which of them had experienced slavery, most of the African Americans stood up. Much to everyone's surprise, one white person stood among them, and in answer to the looks of astonishment, he said: "I am Jewish. My ancestors were slaves in Egypt and some were enslaved by the Romans, too." He was right. African Americans and Jews have a painful history of slavery. Both collectives consider these periods to be an essential part of their past, which has colored their collective and/or national identity, as well as their ongoing existence. Furthermore, both Jews and African Americans perceive this slavery as an evil attempt by others designed to endanger their physical and cultural existence.

I assume that many of my readers will be familiar with the Holocaust, Darfur, 9/11, the 2004 Indian Ocean tsunami and Hurricane Katrina. Although referring to different events, all these names describe catastrophes shared by many people, which, like African American and Jewish slavery, frequently remain as lacerations in the historical narrative of the victims' collectives. Several terms are used to refer to these catastrophic experiences, each emphasizing a different aspect of the event, but pertaining to similar characteristics. Among these terms are "cultural trauma" (Pastor, 2004), "historical trauma" (Brave Heart & De Bruyn, 1998; Brave Heart, 2004), "mass trauma" (Wieling & Mittal, 2008) and "disasters" (Weaver, 1995).

Before describing the meaning of each term, it is important to ask to what extent the events mentioned above may be defined as cultural trauma, historical trauma, mass trauma, or disaster. An interesting attempt to answer this question illustrated the near impossibility of obtaining a definite, clear response (Quaranteli, 1998). Quaranteli quoted a statement made by a United States Supreme Court judge: "I cannot define pornography, but I know it when I see it" (p. 236). Quaranteli claimed that most people who study disasters, mass traumas, or cultural traumas have somewhat similar opinions regarding their definition. However, a summary of some of the attempts to deal with defining an event as a disaster shows that most answers focused on its consequences. "Mass trauma" was used to refer to a large group of individuals who were exposed to a potential traumatic event, and "cultural trauma" was used to refer to systems such as communities, nations, or cultures. Social and cultural variables often play a part in the consequences of the disaster, and it is, therefore, difficult to differentiate between the nature of the reality and the way it is constructed by the victims, helpers and society (which might, in some cases, be the entire world, researchers, media, etc.).

I agree with the claim that it is difficult to develop a precise definition for an event that can be described as a disaster, cultural trauma, mass trauma, etc., and that, while the event is happening, people are sometimes unaware that it can be defined as such. I agree that the lack of a comprehensive formulation can hinder the study of this phenomenon, but I believe that even in its absence, sufficient knowledge exists to allow us to address different events according to these definitions. Throughout this book, I will present some of the existing knowledge, while emphasizing my view of the formulation of these events thus defined, as well as their impacts and methods of intervention used in these situations. First, however, I will share my perception of those events referred to as disasters, cultural trauma, mass trauma, etc. In conceptualizing the term, I integrate the search for reality—What actually happened? How did it happen? What are the damages?—with the way it is constructed by different systems. Although the search for reality might be difficult, it should not be ignored, as lack of knowledge may lead to the denial of catastrophes due to various political interests, such as the denial of the Nazi Holocaust (Lipstadt, 1994), or of the Armenian Holocaust (Taner, 2006). I also follow Carr's (1932) claim that a catastrophe becomes a traumatic event when the sense of cultural protection collapses.

Due to the difficulty in formulating the catastrophic event, the various names used reflect some differences in conceptualization and emphasis. Some that are relevant in constructing the subject matter of this book are listed here.

Cultural Trauma

According to Pastor (2004), trauma can be perceived as a "cultural trauma" when people who have the sense of belonging to a collective, such as a state, or an ethnic or religious group, feel that they have been subjected to fearful and painful events, which have left their mark on their collective consciousness and memory. Pastor (2004) claimed that a cultural trauma is a socially constructed process that has an impact not only on the past, but also on the future identity of the collective. Sztompka (2000) identified four characteristics of cultural trauma:

- it occurs suddenly;
- it has particular substance and scope (i.e., it is radical, deep and comprehensive, and touches the core of the culture);
- its origin is clear and is perceived as imposed and exogenous, and
- it is characterized by a specific mental frame (i.e., it is unexpected, surprising, unpredicted and shocking).

Among the events that Sztompka described as potentially creating cultural trauma are: political and social revolutions, terrorists attacks, genocide, extermination, mass murder, forced migration, ethnic cleansing, political assassination, wars, lost wars, the collapse of empire, collapse of a market, or radical economic reform.

Historical Trauma

Brave Heart (2004), who studied the mental health of Native American Indians, named traumatic events that impact a collective or a nation as an historical trauma. She defined historical trauma as cumulative emotional and psychological wounding over an individual's lifespan and across generations, emanating from massive group trauma experience. According to Brave Heart, the historical trauma response is the constellation of features in reaction to this trauma, which may include depression, self-destructive behavior, suicidal thoughts and gestures, anxiety, low self-esteem, anger, and difficulty in recognizing and expressing emotions. Historical trauma response evolves from unresolved grief that may be considered fixated, impaired, delayed and/or disenfranchised.

Mass Trauma

Landau, Wieling and Mittal (2008) conceptualized mass trauma as an event involving multiple persons, who simultaneously experience, witness, or are confronted with the actual and/or the threat of the death of self or others. Most mass traumas are created by wars, political violence, terrorist attacks and natural disasters.

Disaster

Weaver (1995) suggested the term "disaster" to describe emergencies and crises that involve many people and are considered to be social rather than individual occasions. Weaver claimed that to define an event as a disaster, there must be public agreement regarding the observable damage, social disruption, official disaster declarations and demands for action. As can be seen, the definition of disaster includes an official element, an "official disaster declaration," which is based on the conceptualization of the Federal Emergency Management Agency (FEMA). FEMA has been operating in the United States since the Congressional Act of 1803 and was the first disaster legislation, formulated in response to an extensive fire in a New Hampshire town (Halpern & Tramontin, 2007). According to FEMA, disasters are

> unforeseen and often sudden events that cause great damage, destruction and human suffering. Though often caused by nature, disasters can have human origins. Wars and civil disturbances that destroy homelands and displace people are included among the causes of disasters. (Halpern & Tramontin, 2007, p. 4)

However, the need for an official disaster declaration (Weaver, 1995) is an example of a definition constructed within the Western developed countries, where formal institutions are involved in providing emergent and long-term help for the victim populations. It is important to note that declaring some events as disasters, either by national or international institutions, often depends on irrelevant political factors. Many disasters still leave their mark on populations even though they were not declared as disasters. Some disasters occurred many years before such national and international institutions existed; even today, in many places around the world, such institutions do not exist. Furthermore, in some disaster situations, even the existing national or international institutions cannot offer the necessary help, due to political or organizational issues. Therefore, the non-declaration of an event as a disaster does not mean that it did not happen.

Although some people make the following distinction between disasters and collective trauma—that disasters describe natural catastrophes whereas collective trauma describes the outcome of human-made catastrophes—most of the examples of natural disasters and human-made catastrophes in the literature are placed under the same umbrella (Walsh, 2007); they are referred to as disasters by some authors (Halpern & Tramontin, 2007) and as collective trauma by others (Ainslie, 2013; Pastor, 2004). For example, in their book on disaster mental health, Halpern and Tramontin (2007) mentioned the Holocaust, 9/11 and various natural disasters, whereas Erikson (1978) defined the Buffalo Creek Flood of 1972 as collective trauma. Abramowitz (2005) used this same definition in his article describing the attacks on Guinea by the Sierra Leone Armed Forces, in which war was referred to as collective trauma. The use of both terms to describe similar phenomena does make sense because some of the immediate and long-term results may be similar. I suggest that collective trauma is a more comprehensive term, and is the outcome of a situation that begins with some level of catastrophe (disaster), which may develop into collective trauma. This is based on the severity and duration of the catastrophe and on the available resources of collective coping and rehabilitation, but one of the most important elements is the way it is constructed in the narrative of the specific collective. In this book, I integrate the conceptualization and emphasis described by the different terms into the single term "collective or national trauma."

Collective or National Trauma

Collective or national trauma is developed through a process that begins with a catastrophic event, such as disaster or mass trauma that causes loss, physical and psychological damage and pain, which have an impact on the entire group and on individuals within the group. The impact creates emotional and psychological wounds that become keystones in the group's narrative, set of beliefs and identity, as well as those of individuals within the group, across generations. The national and/or collective trauma is a socially constructed process and has an impact not only on the past, but also on the future identity of the group and its individuals. Events that develop into collective or national trauma may have an impact on groups by remaining part of the group narrative, even if the members of the group are coping well with the physical and psychological damage.

According to this definition, the event can be human-made, such as war, terror, or genocide, or caused by nature, such as earthquakes, tsunamis, hurricanes, etc. The group of people can be defined by religion, race, ethnicity, nation, community, or people living in the same geographical area. Since the terms "collective" or "national" trauma are not operationalized according to diagnostic criteria, as is individual trauma, most studies that explored the impact of collective or national trauma used individual post-trauma measures (Cohen-Silver et al., 2002; Kupelian, Kalayjian & Sanentz, 1998; Pfefferbaum et al., 2005). As defined previously, the nature of collective trauma goes beyond loss and damage, and extends to the entire collective or to the nation as a unit. Thus, when studying a collective trauma, it is important to look for aspects of impacts that also consider the relationships between the subsystems within the collective or nation, and the impact on both present and future collective or national narratives. Observing a collective and national trauma is sometimes difficult, especially among collectives that have the resources and resiliency to cope effectively with the traumatic event. However, the mark left by the event, which might be symbolized by collective or national strength and resilience rather than pain and loss alone, is part of the collective historical narrative and constructs some of the future collective beliefs and decisions.

Some people might ask whether every collective or nation that experiences natural disaster, war or terror attacks will be traumatized. The answer to this question is somewhat complicated. If a collective trauma is conceptualized as individual trauma, it is possible to assume that only a small percentage of the collective's members will experience it, and most of them will recover after less than a year (Bonanno & Mancini, 2008, 2012). However, collective trauma does not refer only to "symptoms" resulting from a specific event. Collective trauma is an outcome that includes both the collective response to the catastrophic event and the way it is constructed and incorporated within the collective set of beliefs, decisions and behaviors, and the collective narrative. Thus, it is possible to conclude that every potential traumatic event leaves its mark on the collective, to some extent, but the method of coping with the damage caused, and the way it is constructed within the collective narrative—whether it emphasizes coping and resiliency vs. emphasizing only the painful aspects—determines whether the potential traumatic event will develop into collective trauma.

This answer may be followed by another question referring to the use of the word "trauma." Why it is considered a collective or national trauma and not just an historical event? The use of the word "trauma" implies that specific decisions and sets of beliefs of a collective have evolved from traumatic events. Let us take as an example President Obama's decision against attacking Syria in 2013 after the Syrian Army used chemical weapons against Syrian non-combatants. This decision seems to contrast the United States' human rights policy: in 1999, NATO, led by the United States, bombed Serbia for killing Bosnian and Kosovar civilians. Since then, however, the United States has been involved in two wars—in Iraq and in Afghanistan—of which the outcomes were worse than had been expected. Although the entire nation appeared not to feel as traumatized as in the immediate aftermath of 9/11, the polls indicated that more than 50% of the population opposed taking military action against Syria. The opposition was based partially on the high cost of the wars in Iraq and Afghanistan, including deaths of soldiers, as well as physical and mental injuries, and the high financial cost involved. Another source of opposition was strong support of the United States' isolationist policy, which historically evolved from traumatic events. Some of the opposition came from people who believed that the military action suggested would not be strong enough to end the fighting in Syria. They based this view on past wars in which the United States had been involved. I believe that these types of opposition are indicative of a narrative on which collective trauma has left its mark, despite the collective and national resilience and the ability to cope with past traumatic events. It is possible, therefore, to perceive the intensity of collective trauma on a continuum. One end symbolizes collectives that do not have the necessary resources to cope with traumatic events. The middle of the continuum symbolizes communities that cope well with the consequences of the traumatic event but in which the event remains mostly as a painful part of its narrative. This sometimes leads to collective and/or national beliefs and decisions that are based on a past and sometimes irrelevant reality. At the other end of the continuum are the collectives that have the resources to cope well with the traumatic event and who constructed a narrative that emphasizes resiliency. As there is a lack of empirical studies that evaluated collective resilience and recovery processes of collectives, it is not possible to define the exact types of collectives or the percentage of the collectives that are close to each end of the continuum, as was possible with individual responses (Bonanno & Mancini, 2008, 2012).

Another question that may be asked before presenting a detailed discussion of different aspects of collective and national trauma refers to the similarities and differences between collective and national trauma. Both terms are very similar, since a nation is a type of collective. In cases of national trauma, however, its causal events are targeted against a specific nation due to overt or covert conflict with that nation's existence. Thus, the Holocaust or other cases of genocide, the ongoing conflict between the Palestinians and Israel, the terror attack of 9/11, and other wars around the world are considered national trauma.

Pastor (2004) used four different aspects to analyze cultural trauma as a way of understanding collective trauma. Unlike most of the writing on collective trauma, which focuses either on the reasons for its occurrence or on its results, Pastor presented a means of assessing why some situations are constructed as collective trauma and others are not. Pastor's view is systemic, but he did not refer to it as such, as he addressed the victims, the perpetrators, and the relationships between them within the wider social context. The four aspects are as follows: the nature of the pain, the characteristics of the victims (Pastor, 2004), the relationships between the victims and the surrounding society, the cause of the pain (e.g., human-made vs. natural disaster), and a single vs. recurring or ongoing event. Let us explore what characterizes each one of these aspects and how these characteristics contribute to the construction of the event as a collective and/or national trauma.

The Nature of the Pain

Pain is always an integral part of collective and/or national trauma and is related to the type of loss resulting from the traumatic event. Hobfoll (1998), who developed the Conservation of Resources (COR) theory, which describes factors contributing to the impact of stressful and traumatic events, perceived the level of stress and the ability to cope with it as an outcome of the quality and quantity of resources that were lost in the traumatic or stressful event. According to Hobfoll (2001), all human beings have various types of resources, including physical, psychological and social ones, and some of these resources include more than one type. Home, salary and property can be considered physical resources. High self-esteem, beliefs and sense of control can be considered psychological resources, and a sense of belonging, commitment and social relationships can be considered social resources. However, home has more than merely physical aspects, property may include psychological elements, and salary may be a basic source of self-esteem and social status. Furthermore, the death of someone close can be a psychological loss for some, but for their families, also a physical loss, due to loss of income and contribution to home chores.

In addition, the resources include individual and collective aspects, since individuals do not live in a vacuum, but are nested within a family, which is nested within a community, which is nested within a larger society. Thoughts, perceptions, behaviors and emotions evolve and develop from the society or collective in which the individual exists, through interactions between individuals and other members of society. Thus, the perception of the loss depends on the norms and values of the collective. In addition, as individuals are part of collective loss, it can be perceived as an individual loss of resources on the collective level, even if the individuals did not lose their personal resources. The 9/11 terror attacks had a strong impact on the entire population of the United States, even those outside of the vicinity of New York or Washington. The general sense of security was severely damaged. The nation, or more specifically, the citizens, who had experienced wars only from a distance, suddenly felt very vulnerable to terrorism, and questions were raised regarding the present and future safety of the nation as a unit. Thus, individuals' and families' loss of loved ones became a collective loss.

Different kinds of loss can occur as a result of collective or national trauma: loss of life, ambiguous loss, loss of physical or mental health, loss of property, security and beliefs. This confronts the individuals and the collective with strong feelings of sadness, fear and anxiety, which often affect individual and collective assumptions about the world and life, and challenge self- and collective identity.

The death of someone close is always considered a stressor event. However, this loss can be experienced differently, depending on the circumstances. The loss of an old person at the end of the life cycle is very different than losing someone at a young age, or even in middle age. An expected death due to illness is different than a sudden, unexpected death in an accident. The circumstances surrounding the death echo the impact

14

of stress. A death of one person might be different from a mass death due to natural disaster, war or genocide. Although loss of life always evokes sadness and mourning, different circumstances might evoke different emotions.

I would like to share another type of collective loss to which I was exposed as a young girl in Israel at the beginning of the 1950s, through the radio program, "Looking for Missing Relatives." In those days, Israel had only one radio station, and when we arrived home from school in the early afternoon, the radio was always on. For 15 minutes, I would hear the radio not only in my own home, but in all the other apartments and stores in the neighborhood. When visiting school friends in another neighborhood, the radio was playing there, too. Everyone tuned in to this program. None of the adults I knew would stop their regular activity, but they all listened, just in case they might know someone. I remember the long list of names: "Mr Isaac Abramovitch is looking for Mr Ya'aqov Abramovitch and Mrs Golda Abramovitch from the city of . . . in Poland . . . Your brother/sister/uncle/cousin is looking for you. Please contact . . . ." Sometimes, additional information was given: "Last seen at . . . ." People were searching for their relatives who were lost during the Holocaust, a situation that was common to a large percentage of the Israeli population at that time. Many had no definite information as to whether these loved ones were really dead, or had managed to escape and were living somewhere around the globe. I was reminded of this fifty years later, two weeks after the terrorist attack on 9/11, when walking around Greenwich and the East Village and Union Square in New York. Hundreds of notices were displayed, mostly with the names and pictures of people who had been in the World Trade Center and who had been missing since the day of the attack.

People around the world following wars and natural disasters have been exposed to different kinds of searches for missing people. The uncertainty of whether a close family member is alive is a common phenomenon in situations of collective trauma. Boss (2007) called this "ambiguous loss," referring to the physical absence yet psychological presence of the lost person. In other words, when clear evidence exists that the person has died, a place is left for mourning. Even if one thinks, feels, or even behaves as if the person is still alive, it is with the knowledge that the person will not return and that the mourning process will continue. In cases of ambiguous loss, however, when people do not really know whether or not the person has died, the mourning process becomes much more complex. It may overlap with trauma, attachment problems and symptoms similar to those of posttraumatic stress disorder (PTSD). The experience of ambiguous loss may include depression and/or anxiety and/or feelings of guilt; intrusive memories regarding the missing person or thoughts regarding the cruel circumstances of the death, and difficulty with transitions or changes and with decision making, especially when making life choices. When a significant number of people lose their lives in situations of collective and/or national trauma, the individual loss becomes a collective loss, evoking collective pain, which might be characterized by a collective sense of anxiety, depression and guilt that contributes to the ways in which the collective or the nation copes with daily challenges (Possick, Sadeh & Shamai, 2008).

Loss and pain as a result of collective or national trauma are associated not only with loss of human life, or of physical and mental health, or of property. The sense of losing beliefs and of harm to identity is often a part of the consequences of national or collective trauma. This was clearly illustrated at a conference organized by the International Family Therapy Association (IFTA) that took place in Slovenia about twelve years after the wars in the region ended, in the presentation given by mental health professionals from the different states that belonged to former Yugoslavia. L., a mental health professional living in Kosovo, described her experience during the war in former Yugoslavia. At the beginning of her story, she explained her nationality: she was originally Serbian, was married to a man from Croatia, and was living in Kosovo. "We are considered the worst," she said. Why she defined herself as "the worst" was unclear, but the Serbian and Croatian combination was evidently considered to be the "worst" kind of national identity. In spite of this, she chose to remain in a place where she was considered to belong to a "bad" collective. Her colleague, who was also Serbian, had emigrated to New Zealand shortly after the outbreak of war in former Yugoslavia, claiming that she could not bear to live among people in a nation responsible for terrible acts against other human beings. She was ready to undergo the painful process of immigration simply to avoid her national identification as a Serbian. However, even after living in New Zealand for nearly fifteen years, she was still having to cope with her national and collective identity:

in New Zealand, I am a minority within a minority. I am a Serbian among immigrants from former Yugoslavia. Among the former Yugoslavian minority, I am considered as part of the "bad". . . I still come to Serbia to see my friends and I like so many things in Belgrade, but I am a human being, and this is my identity. When another Serbian woman heard this, she was furious: "What does she mean by describing herself as a human being, as if other people in Serbia are inhuman?" A Slovenian man responded, saying that if he was Serbian, he would also leave the country, because the Serbs were responsible for all the bad things that happened in former Yugoslavia.

Analyzing the responsibility for the war and cruelty during the conflict in former Yugoslavia is beyond the scope of this book, yet it is noteworthy that the traumatic experience caused significant damage to the entire collective in Serbia, as is apparent from these quotations. Many Serbians could not bear to be defined as aggressors; many felt that they could not be part of a nation that is responsible for cruel acts perpetrated by other Serbians. Some, who had the opportunity to emigrate, did so, but most of the population continued their lives as part of Serbia, while looking for ways to account for their Serbian identity. Among these accounts were disengaging from the Serbian regime that initiated the war, focusing on the difficulties and pain experienced by the Serbian population when they were bombed by NATO, or expressing their loss of identity as Yugoslavians. All these accounts are a sign of damage to the collective and their national identity.

Many Holocaust survivors, especially those who were children during the war and were hidden in churches, in monasteries, or by religious Catholic or Pravoslavie families, perceived the atrocities perpetuated against the Jews as a sign that their Jewish identity was a bad thing. Some reacted by converting to Christianity. Some performed Christian rituals in secret after the Holocaust, when they were returned to Jewish organizations; and others simply continued to live with a damaged sense of national identity. In general, the Jews, as a nation today, still live with a sense of the need to be on guard and to prevent any possibility of a future Holocaust. This sense of fear is shared by Jews around the world, as well as by those who did not directly experience the horrors, including the second and third generations who were born after the Holocaust.

African Americans in the United States are still left with the trauma of the evil that was done to them as slaves; being taken by force from their African homelands to America and facing inequality for many years after their release from slavery. The African American community is still dealing with many questions, such as: can black be as beautiful as white? Can we be as successful as the white people? These experiences are expressed both overtly and covertly.

Staub (1989) claimed that most people prefer to align themselves overtly or covertly with those in positions of power. In a survey by Wuthnow (1991), it was found that 54% of the participants felt that people deserve the suffering that comes their way. Thus, if a collective feels deserving of its suffering, this sense of "badness" will color the collective identity, as well as the individual identity of people within this collective, i.e., "I am part of the badness." This can lead to different types of activities. At one extreme, groups within the collective might behave "badly" and will account for this by projecting the responsibility for these activities onto others. Post-World War I Germany was held responsible for the war and some difficult sanctions were imposed upon it by the Treaty of Versailles. The way the treaty was formed and the manner in which it was imposed upon Germany negates its legal and moral worth. The Nazi Party made use of this in their election campaign in 1932. They projected the responsibility for the economic crisis in Germany and the damage to their sense of national pride onto other nations, which could be a partial explanation for their electoral success. Projecting responsibility onto others served as justification for breaking the Treaty of Versailles and led to World War II.

Sometimes, the damaged identity can cause anger toward another collective inside and outside the nation, or between nations. The anger might be expressed through violent behavior, perceiving the others as "deserving" of revenge. This behavior may be conscious, but in many cases, is unconscious and can last for generations. This can be seen by the relatively high number of African American prison inmates in the United States and the relatively high number of Jews in Israeli prisons whose families had immigrated from Arab countries, who claimed having suffered humiliation at the hands of Jewish immigrants from Europe, because of their cultural differences. In her study of Native American Indians, Brave Heart (2004) pointed out that such anger and damage to identity can last for generations and is often accompanied by behavioral problems that are rooted in depression and anger resulting from the collective or national traumatic history. Such negative acts, ranging from less damaging violence (theft), through extreme violence (murder) to very extreme violence (genocide) often cause additional damage to the collective or national identity.

At the other extreme, the sense of internal "badness" may lead some groups or individuals to "reparation" (Klein, 1975), as a cleansing process. Such behaviors can range from individuals' motivation for success, to group activities targeted toward the collective or nation that is perceived as being hurt by the "badness" of their own collective or nation. One example of this is the groups from Germany who come to Israel to work with needy populations, in an attempt to atone for the sins of their parents' and grandparents' generation against the Jews in the Holocaust. Although these reparation activities often relieve the sense of damaged identity to some extent, they sometimes increase it. Let us imagine that the strong motivation for achievement does not work and that the individual cannot "prove" that he or she is not "bad." This might increase these individuals' sense of "badness" and might add to the damaged sense of "bad" collective or national identity. It might also turn into anger toward others who are perceived as putting obstacles in the way of this attempt at success, or to a sense of depression (Klein, 1946). Criticism of the victim's collective or nation might develop during the reparation activity, and act as a psychological defense mechanism that helps reduce the "bad" identity—i.e., if those considered as our victims are "bad," then we can't be so bad after all . . . .

Yet, although most people with damaged identity will not be located at one of these extremes, they will easily identify with one extreme or another, usually from the position of their own damaged sense of identity. Thus, it is the wounded sense of identity that unites these two extremes, which, according to Klein (1946), will be characterized by the intensive use of splitting as a defense mechanism, dividing the world into good and bad, black and white. Splitting is considered a primitive defense mechanism, used by healthy adults in crisis situations when they feel a threat to their existence. The intensive use of splitting is accompanied by a sense of paranoia, according to which the others (individuals, collectives, or nations) are considered as threatening, and thus legitimizing all methods of self-protection (Geron, Malkinson & Shamai, 2005). Furthermore, in many situations, the intensive use of splitting and the behaviors that follow create an interactive process in which the sense of "bad" is projected toward the other collective or nation. Thus, specific activities are required for protection, including aggressive acts. These acts might arouse fear of the other's revenge, which in turn, increases the need for protection, which might also lead to aggressive acts. Since the "other" nation or collective is usually part of this interaction, it is possible that to protect themselves, both sides take action against the other, thus increasing the level of mutual hurt. Therefore, this process can last for generations. Many collective or national trauma events around the globe can be explained according to this split worldview. Figure 1.1,

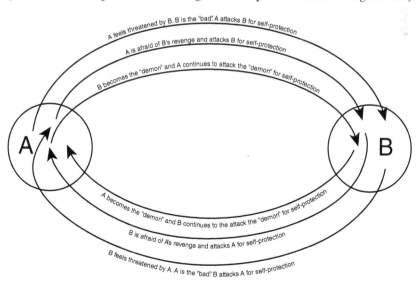

Figure 1.1 Demonizing the other: The cycle of aggression.

which is based on Klein's theory (1946) and further develops Geron, Malkinson and Shamai's (2005) work illustrates the interactive process that continues the violence circle.

Whereas Klein's theory did not center directly on trauma, Janoff-Bulman (1985, 1989, 1992) focused on the nature of pain that is the outcome of trauma. According to Janoff-Bulman, a traumatic event always damages people's assumptions about themselves and the world. The world becomes an insecure place, and people start questioning why this has happened to them (or to the collective or nation). According to Janoff-Bulman, the pain can linger for years and can impact cognitions and behaviors, including the sense of collective or national identity, or collective or national worth. The level of pain is related to the ability to bounce back to a sense of collective or national worth and trust in others. Thus, the pain resulting from collective or national trauma includes physiological, psychological, sociological and philosophical elements. This notwithstanding, the nature of the pain is not the sole aspect according to which a collective or national trauma is constructed. The construction of a collective or national trauma is also associated with the nature of the victims.

The Nature of the Victims

Who are the victims of collective or national trauma? The answer is very simple: they can be anyone. People of different ages: babies, children, teenagers, adults and older persons. People of different genders, people of different ethnicity and race, people with different formal status: citizens, immigrants, refugees. People with different roles: combatants and non-combatants, and people with different socioeconomic backgrounds. Yet, does the society's perception of the collective or national traumatic event differ depending on the victims? Is there a difference in the help given to victims, depending on their status? Are there differences in the legitimacy given to a collective or nation to define their experience as a collective or national trauma depending on the identity of the victims? These questions need to be asked when analyzing why similar events that could be defined as collective or national trauma are perceived differently by society; or how the nature of the victims impacts our perception of specific collective or national trauma.

I will start with an example that may shed some light on these questions. In the summer of 1999, during the Balkan War between Serbia and Bosnia, many Bosnians from Kosovo and elsewhere became refugees and sought shelter in a NATO refugee camp. Various countries took responsibility for facilitating their basic needs, including youth organizations from Israel, who volunteered to organize activities for children and teenagers in the camp. The war received intense media coverage,

20

addressing, among other things, the impact on Bosnian refugees, including those who stayed in the camp. Even U.S. President Bill Clinton visited the camp and met the children, an event followed extensively by the media worldwide. However, several days after the ceasefire, while many refugees were still in the camp, the media attention dramatically decreased. About two weeks later, while people were still in the camp, most of the activities stopped and the camp was preparing for closure. The media showed hardly any interest in the plight of the people who remained in the camp. An Israeli youngster, who had taken part in organizing the children's activities, said:

> Well, it was like in many other places around the world. The first to leave the camp were the wealthiest families, then the less wealthy, then those of middle socioeconomic status, leaving only the poorest and most needy families behind. But then—I don't know who made the decision—we were told that our activities were no longer needed, as not so many children were left in the camp . . . I don't know when these families left or when the camp was closed, but I was sure that these children and their parents were still in need of our activities.

This example sheds light on several issues and raises a number of questions, the first being what is the role of social variables that define the status of a national trauma? The answer to this question needs to take two perspectives into consideration. The first is the viewpoint of those who were damaged by the collective or national trauma. The second is that of the outsiders, namely, those who are not part of the collective, but who encounter the consequences of the damage, either as helpers, journalists, or researchers, as well as the entire society surrounding the damaged collective. The first perspective will be widely discussed in the second chapter of this book, which will focus on the impact of collective or national trauma on those who experienced it. The second perspective is a core issue in this chapter, as it is essential to the social construction of an event as a collective or national trauma. Gilbart (1998) claimed that the social vulnerability of the harmed population is the basic paradigm for understanding an event as collective trauma. Gilbart (1998) followed the long-term discourse regarding the role of social variables, especially socioeconomic conditions, in the outcomes of various kinds of disasters (O'Keefe, Westgate & Wisner, 1976). Thus, the nature of the victims, based on their social and political status, is associated with the attitude toward the event as collective or national trauma and with the way it is studied and analyzed. This attitude determines the kind of help provided to the victims by formal and informal organizations. Thus, society may relate to children, women and elderly victims differently than toward male adults. The attitude toward the death or injury of combatants will be different than that toward non-combatants. Harm to privileged collectives might receive greater media coverage than harm to lower socioeconomic groups; and as a result, more resources and attention might be available for the privileged collective to overcome the physical and psychological damage. Today, a collective or national trauma occurring in a developed Western country, or to its citizens, will receive greater attention, often followed by acknowledgment of the suffering and the provision of more means for recovery.

Let us try to imagine the coverage that would have been given to the consequences of the tsunami that occurred in the Indian Ocean in December 2004, if there had not been many Western tourists among the victims. The news of a distant disaster would have been broadcast, helpers from around the world would have come to assist the local victims, and the phenomenon would have fascinated seismologists. However, we can still assume that "the voice of the trauma" would have been much less intense. The level of modern technology that has created the global village has allowed the immediate sharing of information from all over the world. It can be assumed, therefore, that nowadays, we have far more information about catastrophes around the world than in the past. However, the impact of such knowledge is different when the catastrophe occurs in New York as opposed to a less central location. Compare the locations of the 9/11 terror attack within people's cognition with that of Hurricane Katrina. Let us go even further and compare the place of the war in Iraq to that of other ongoing wars in Africa and the Middle East, such as the wars in Darfur and in Syria, in which even greater numbers of people, including women, children and non-combatants are being killed than in Iraq. Or consider whether immigrant victims of 9/11 and their families received as much attention as non-immigrant groups. Thus, although we do have information at our disposal regarding catastrophic events that become collective or national trauma, our evaluation of their severity may depend on the nature of the victims and their public status. The impact of the catastrophic event, namely, its definition as a collective trauma, the amount and type of help given to the victims and to the collective, the recognition and acknowledgement of their pain, as well as the public, academic and professional interest all create the "voice of the trauma" and are associated with the local and national centrality or marginality of the victims. It is possible to claim that the existing knowledge regarding the impact of marginalization (Mullaly, 2007; Young, 2000) is relevant also in the effort to understand an event of collective or national trauma.

Marginalization can be understood in light of the social structure of globalization. The development of technology alongside strong capitalist ideology has increased the gaps within society and the number of marginalized groups (Alphonse, George & Moffat, 2008). Sewpaul (2006) claimed that globalization has had an impact also on language and discourse in such a way that the dominant global discourse, which is influenced by the Western world, has the "potential to dilute or even annihilate local cultures and traditions and to deny context specific realities" (p. 421). Therefore, it could be assumed that a catastrophic event might be defined or described as collective or national trauma, not necessarily due to its reality, but to the way it is constructed by society; and sometimes by the discourse that is being constructed according to the globalization processes, which includes a certain set of beliefs that might stigmatize specific collectives, cultures and nations. It is important for researchers and helpers from different academic and professional fields, and for policy makers, to take into consideration the "voice of the trauma" and to be aware how social processes, such as globalization, impact the volume of this voice. Furthermore, it is crucial to be aware of how the dominant discourse regarding the responses to a traumatic event might impact the type of help and attention given to the victims. In certain cultures, feelings such as sadness, anxiety and anger are not expressed, but does this mean that the event is experienced as less traumatic? Or at the other extreme, will these victims be pathologized as excessive users of a denial mechanism? It is the responsibility of researchers, helpers and policy makers to understand and analyze the specific nature of the traumatized collective and to be aware of the impact of this specific nature on the type of studies they conduct, the type of help they provide and the type of policies they choose to deal with the collective or national trauma.

As mentioned before, the age, gender and role of the victims within the traumatized collective or nation is significant, as the differential attitude toward these groups is constructed by society's attitude toward them. The Holocaust memorial museum in Jerusalem, Yad Vashem, has a separate section to memorialize the children murdered in the Holocaust. One might ask why a special section exists for children and not for adults. Both children and adults were murdered in the Holocaust purely because they were Jews. Both children and adults were helpless in the face of the powerful evil; but society tends to perceive children as innocent, "not responsible" for the evil and unable to take care of themselves without the aid of adults. Part of this claim might be relevant to situations of collective or national trauma. However, in most cases of such trauma, this claim is not necessarily relevant, as neither Jewish children nor adults were responsible for what happened to Jews during the Holocaust. Nor were African or Native American children or adults responsible for the slavery and control imposed by the white men who destroyed their culture. Both children and adults from the poor neighborhoods in New Orleans were helpless and in danger during and after Hurricane Katrina. Neither the children nor the adults were responsible for the flooding, and for the lack of short-term and long-term help from the governmental authorities. However, the public tends to be emotionally moved by the effects of catastrophic events on children, women and elders, who are perceived as weaker and less able to cope. This special attitude results in the way the catastrophic event creates "emotional moving" in the public and as a result, contributes to the attention and help given to the victims. Although the relevance of emotional moving to the actual outcomes of a catastrophic event can be questioned, I join other researchers (Porfirieu, 1998; Hewitt, 1998; Quaranteli, 1998) in my main claim that collective or national trauma is socially constructed. Therefore, values and attitudes toward the victimized collective modify the definition of the catastrophic event as collective or national trauma, the attention given to the event and as a result, the type of help given to the victims.

Natural vs. Human-Made Collective/National Trauma

Human-Made Disasters

Human-made collective or national trauma usually occurs as a result of war, terror attacks, genocide, or due to technological advances such as through exposure to toxic chemical or biological materials, nuclear accidents and fires. Whereas war, terror attacks and genocide can be defined as both collective and national trauma, accidents due to technological advances tend to fall only into the collective trauma category, as they do not generally threaten the physical existence and values of a nation. This does not mean that behind many catastrophes that occur due to technological advances, there are no political interests and even political ideology. Imagine and compare the collective response to an attempt to build an industrial area involving harmful chemical materials or nuclear energy, in an area with a low-income marginalized population as compared to one with a high-income population. Global industrial strategies will include the undeclared search for cheap labor and collectives with a lower impact on authorities regarding environmental safety and quality.

Studies show more cases of psychological distress following human-made trauma than collective trauma caused by nature (Norris et al., 2002; Norris, Friedman & Watson, 2002). One possible explanation for this is the tendency to accept some natural disasters as inevitable, but this is not the case with human-made situations (Halpern & Tramontin, 2007). In most human-made collective or national traumas, the sense of betrayal by other human beings causes various psychological symptoms, such as anger, depression and mistrust (Cairns & Wilson, 1989, 1991; Gample, 1988; Solomon, 1995; Schuster et al., 2001) along with a change of world-view and values (Arvay, 2001a; Janoff-Bulman, 1985, 1989, 1992). Although the cruelty of human beings has been recognized since

24

time immemorial, other human qualities, such as social and moral values, often criticize the tendency to be aggressive and cruel. Unfortunately, such criticism is often associated with the nature of the victims and their political status. Such an association leads to complicated situations where the individuals within the victimized collective, as well as the entire collective, experience human cruelty, but this experience receives inadequate recognition from other societies and nations. Thus, the sense of being misunderstood adds to people's sadness, depression and anger, and increases the level of distress. Therefore, it is important for researchers, practitioners, the media and policy makers to examine the impact of other human behaviors when attempting to understand the nature of the collective or national trauma and render the necessary help.

Natural Disasters

Earthquakes, hurricanes, flooding and wildfires are considered natural catastrophic events that might cause collective trauma and have affected human society since its earliest beginnings. However, we can learn about people's reactions to such events only since the recording of history. Many such events are described in the Bible, for example, the flood that destroyed the entire world, except those who remained in Noah's Ark, or the destruction of the city of Sodom. Many Greek myths describe catastrophic events visited upon different gods, which impacted the earth. All these stories have a common conclusion: that disasters attributed to nature or to the power of God are related to the behavior of humans, or, in the case of Greek myths, of the gods, who behave like humans. Thus, God in the Bible, or the most powerful Greek god, brought these calamities on human society as punishment for disobedience. It is in human nature to seek ways of controlling events and to attach meaning to them. Adherence to divine rulings was one way in which societies attempted to prevent such tragedies, and this perception of natural disasters exists in many collectives even today.

Due to scientific advancement, it is possible to minimize the damage of natural disasters and reduce the potential for collective trauma. As an example, let us take the earthquake that struck Kuzey Anadolu Fay Hattı in Turkey, on August, 17, 1999: 100,000 buildings collapsed, most of them dwellings, killing 17,480 people, injuring 43,953, rendering 505 missing and making 600,000 homeless. The severe outcome was a result of the buildings' cheap design and construction that were unsuitable for the area, whose geological structure meant there was a high risk for earthquakes. Thus, although the original cause of the catastrophic event was natural, the victims, both local people and many tourists on vacation in the area, attached the responsibility to the authorities who had issued licenses for these constructions.

It has been found that poor people in poor countries are generally the most vulnerable in natural disasters (Halpern & Tramontin, 2007; Norris et al., 2002). This is due to several reasons:

1   Limited resources may force people on low incomes to find housing in areas prone to natural disasters, such as the Ninth District of New Orleans, where the majority of the population was poor, and where their dwellings were situated very close to the levees. The levees in this neighborhood were neither high enough nor strong enough to withstand the floodwaters following Hurricane Katrina in August 2005. Over 1,800 people died, mainly from poor neighborhoods. Furthermore, very few people of higher socioeconomic status lost their lives and they were in a stronger position to demand insurance compensation for the damage to their property. Some of the national discourse criticized the Federal government for behaving like a Third World country, which in itself is evidence of the common public knowledge that poor collectives are more vulnerable in natural disasters.

2   As previously mentioned, construction in poor countries or areas is of lesser quality than in richer locations. Thus, an earthquake of similar magnitude might cause considerably more deaths, injuries and suffering in poor countries than in those where the possibility of an earthquake was taken into consideration at the planning and construction stage, especially in high-risk areas, such as California or Kuzey Anadolu Fay Hattı (Langston, 1992).

3   Poor countries have less adequate warning systems than wealthier countries (Wijkman & Timberlake, 1998). Even if a warning system does exist, it is often used ineffectively, due to irresponsible considerations, such as underestimating the potential damage. For example, the tsunami that affected Indonesia, Sri Lanka, Thailand and India in 2004 caused so much death and injury due to the lack of an effective warning system.

4   Poor countries and poor people have fewer resources to help the population following a natural disaster. Therefore, emergency aid, such as avoiding dangerous sanitary conditions, providing emergency medical supplies, basic needs and long-term help, such as speedy repair of damage to property, is likely to be more readily available in wealthy countries than in poor countries. Furthermore, even within wealthy countries, people with greater resources will have the financial means to cope with the damage or the power to demand such help from the relevant authorities.

In sum, it can be argued that only part of the collective trauma resulting from a natural disaster is induced by nature (Elliott, 2003). Often, a meaningful part of the collective trauma is created due to the behavior and attitude of governments, states, countries and even the entire world toward the victims. Thus, collective trauma resulting from a natural event might shatter sufferers' belief in others, to the same degree as with human-made trauma.

Durations: One-Time vs. Recurring or Ongoing Traumatic Events

The duration of the traumatic event is another important variable in understanding the nature of collective or national trauma. African American slavery lasted from the beginning of the 17th century until the mid-19th century. Even after this time, African Americans still had to fight for their rights and to gain power in the United States. These people had been uprooted from their homeland in Africa, and had experienced years, and sometimes generations, of suffering and humiliation. To survive, they initially had to change their identity from being free people to being slaves. Instead of being members of an African tribe, they were forced to join a new collective—of slaves. Their suffering, lack of hope, negative self-identity and low self-esteem in regard to white people were passed down the generations. This long-term suffering left its mark on African American people and served as a basis for creating values, beliefs, norms and rituals. The experience of their uprooted ancestors, the suffering and humiliation of their parents, grandparents and great-grandparents had led to depression, desperation and suspicion which was shared by the entire collective but also had impact on the individual level. Although the conditions of the African Americans have changed significantly since the end of the slave trade, bringing greater equality, as well as the financial, social and academic success of many individuals within this community, they still share a traumatic history. Thus, if an African American person has difficulty in trusting others (Grabowski-Kouvatas, 2006; Miles, 2008; Purdie-Vaughns et al., 2008; Terrell et al., 2008; Usher, 2007), it is my belief that this is derived from the collective trauma. Why should they trust others? Can they ignore the pain induced by white people through the years and the failure of the African American adults to protect them from these difficult social and financial circumstances? Why should they not be angry with a society that allowed such things to happen? How are these feelings part of the African American legacy, which is based on collective trauma?

The Holocaust lasted almost six years. The murder of six million Jews of all ages, the intensive torture, humiliation, hunger and fear experienced by the Jews of Europe and North Africa during World War II has left its mark on the national identity of Jews for over sixty years. A strong sense of mistrust, a constant search for security, a deep sense that "no one really cares for us so we must take care of ourselves" and a strong need to produce continuing generations are just a few examples of how these six years impacted Jewish national identity. One similarity between the collective and national traumas of African Americans and Jews is related to the duration of these occurrences. Both lasted for a prolonged period and changes in the collective or national identity within the two groups began to intensify, while the traumatic events were happening. Thus, along with other variables, such as the nature of the pain and the nature of the victims, it is understandable why these traumatic events take place not only as "a memory," but rather as part of the collective or national identity that impacts these groups' daily existence.

It is difficult to differentiate between the impact of a one-time traumatic event, such as the 9/11 terror attack on the World Trade Center in 2001 or the tsunami in South/Central Asia in 2004, and the impact of recurring events such as terrorist attacks in Israel, Ireland and Latin America, as well as recurring natural disasters, for example, in areas at risk for earthquakes, tornadoes, or hurricanes. Besides the suffering, both types of events create a strong sense of uncertainty. Uncertainty is known to be associated with stress levels (Breznith, 1967) and is affected by two elements: its length and its intensity, namely, the probability of the event's recurrence. Living with ongoing uncertainty requires various coping mechanisms that impact the daily life of a collective or a nation. Among these coping processes are suspicions, which increase alertness to warning signs. For example, an unattended bag in the street or in any other public place in most areas of the United States or Europe will probably draw little attention. Most people would just assume that someone has forgotten the bag and may come back to collect it. Some may even bring it to the lost-and-found center. However, an unattended bag in Israel immediately creates panic. People call the police to report the "suspicious object," as it might be a bomb. Police will usually arrive on the scene within a very short time and will evacuate everyone from the area. No one will touch the bag and a specially trained bomb disposal unit will detonate it. The need for constant awareness of objects without a visible owner has been part of daily life in Israel for the last three decades. One might ask how this need impacts the collective. How does it affect the ability to trust others? Although daily life in Israel continues as if there is no danger, where people eat at restaurants, enjoy rich cultural activities and use public transportation, stress lurks beneath the surface, and is dealt with through a defense mechanism of denial. This is a healthy denial, in the sense that it allows people to continue functioning. However, when used in excess, it may raise the question of the price the residents of Israel are paying, as a nation. Since ongoing stress often harms people's physical condition, one might ask whether and how the ongoing stress impacts the health of Israelis. Or how does it affect moral and human rights issues?

28

We can extend the Israeli example to other situations where people live under constant uncertainty. We can claim that although on the surface, the population may seem to have developed resilience to cope with possible danger—whether natural and/or human-made—it is impossible to ignore its outcomes on the deeper level. In sum, time is an additional aspect that must be taken into consideration when understanding collective or national trauma. Although that time can be measured, the quantitative time differences between the various types of traumatic events are not necessarily related to their force of impact, but can affect the quality of the impact.

Constructing a Paradigm for Analyzing and Understanding Collective and/or National Trauma

To sum up, collective or national trauma can be understood in the perspective of three domains: space, time and significant others (see Figure 1.2 and Table 1.1). These domains are often used to analyze phenomena according to the existentialist and phenomenological traditions (Van den Berg, 1972).

The *space* domain includes two types: physical, measurable space and psychological space (Becker, 1992). In regard to physical space, the

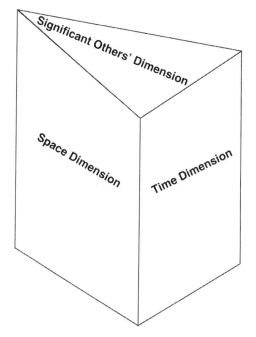

Figure 1.2 Paradigm for analyzing collective and national trauma.

Table 1.1 Guidelines to analysis of collective or national trauma

Space Domain	Time Domain	Significant Other Domain
Physical Space	*Measured/Objective Time*	*The Nature of the Victims*
• Where did the event happen? • How far from central locations (developed and Western countries) did the event occur? • How large is the area in which the event occurred? • Did the traumatic event subsequently receive any "space"? If so, where and how?	• Duration: one-time event versus recurring or ongoing event • When did the traumatic event happen? • The duration of the event: Did the event evoke previous traumatic events in the collective or nation? • Did the traumatic event impact other events within the traumatized collective or nation following its occurance? What were these events and how were they impacted by the traumatic event?	• Gender • Age • Socioeconomic status • Ethnicity/race • Immigrants versus citizens • The victims' place in the broader society: central versus marginalized • Victims' relationships with the broader society: attitudes and prejudices toward the victims • Cultural aspects of the victims' collective or nation that impact the perception of the trauma
Psychological Space	*Subjective Time*	*Source of the Traumatic Event: Natural Disaster Versus Human-Made Disaster*
Nature of Pain		*Natural Disaster*
• Gender • Age • Socioeconomic status • Ethnicity/Race	• How did the victims experience the sense of time during the event?	• What type of disaster was it?

- Immigrants versus citizens
- The victims' place in the broader society: central versus marginalized
- Victims' relationships with the broader society: Attitudes and prejudices toward the victims
- Cultural aspects of the victims', collective or nation that impact the perception of the trauma

- Were they aware of the passage of time? If so, in what way?
- After traumatic events, do the victims live in their present reality, or within the traumatic period?

- Could the damage have been reduced if the correct policy had been used before the event?
- Type of help given after the event: Could the damage have been reduced and for less time if the correct policy had been used and suitable help provided after the event?

Human-Made Disaster

Nature of the Perpetrator

- The place and power of the perpetrator (or those responsible for the disaster) in the broader society: Central versus marginalized
- Perpetrator's relationships with the broader society: Attitude, prejudices towards the perpetrators/those responsible for the disaster
- How the perpetrator/those responsible for the disaster recruited bystanders

following kinds of questions are asked: Where did the traumatic event happen? How far is the location from "central" places in developed or Western countries? How large is the area in which the event occurred? Regarding psychological space, the questions that will be asked are related to the nature of the pain—mainly the type of damage, loss and suffering, and the nature of the cause, either human-made or natural disaster.

The *time* domain, like the space domain, includes two kinds of time: time on the clock, which can be defined objectively and measured, and time experienced subjectively (Becker, 1992). Focus on clock time can raise questions as to when the traumatic event occurred: Was it a singular event, a recurring event, or an ongoing traumatic event? Did additional events, of a different type from the original traumatic event, occur later and resonate with the traumatic event? Issues related to psychological time are often included in the narrative of people who have experienced the traumatic event and might contradict the objective information regarding the duration and order of events.

The *significant other* domain focuses on the nature of the victims and their relation to society—for example, marginalized collectives or nations; poor vs. rich collectives; collectives or nations in developing countries vs. collectives or nations in the developed Western world; beliefs or prejudices regarding the victimized collective, and more. In regard to human-made traumatic events, the nature of the perpetrators and their relation to society needs to be considered. Thus, the same characteristics that were mentioned in analyzing the nature of the victims need to be examined regarding the nature of the perpetrators. In cases of natural traumatic events, it is important to analyze the involvement of governmental authorities in reducing possible damage prior to the event and in providing help immediately after the event, as well as in the long term. Is it possible to give a clear definition of the perpetrator and the victims? In many collective or national traumatic events, it is. For example, the Africans did not cause any pain to the Americans. They held no responsibility for slavery. It is clear that in this situation, African slaves were the victims and Americans were the perpetrators. But who were the victims and who were the perpetrators in the bombing of Dresden in Germany by the British Royal Air Force and the United States Army Air Forces between February 13 and 15 in 1945? This attack remains one of the most controversial acts of the Allies in World War II. Those who supported the Dresden bombing might say that this action was necessary to bring about the surrender of the Nazi regime in Germany, while others would say that no military power in Dresden or anywhere in Germany was about to surrender, and claim that it was merely British revenge for the German Blitz over London. Thus, in analyzing the nature of the victim and the perpetrator, it is unrealistic to expect total objectivity. It is important to be aware of how the set of beliefs constructs the definition of victims and perpetrators in such traumatic, but unclearly defined, events.

In regard to significant others, the nature of the victims and the nature of the perpetrators can provide some explanation of why foreign forces bring to an end some traumatic events more quickly than others, and why some collectives or nations receive acknowledgment of their pain, while others receive none.

The interaction between different aspects within each domain, as well as between the three domains, must be considered when analyzing the traumatic event. Such analysis can present a picture of the "voice of the trauma" within human society. It can explain the magnitude and intensity attached to certain collective or national traumatic events within society's awareness and discourse. To illustrate such an analysis, I will attempt to analyze a collective, national event that had a strong impact on the entire world during the 20th century, which continues into the 21st: the Holocaust.

The Holocaust: Illustration of the Paradigm

Before I begin to analyze the Holocaust as a national, collective trauma, I must acknowledge that I cannot be truly objective about this event, if such objectivism is possible for anyone. I am Jewish, and Israeli, and lost my grandparents, aunts, uncles and cousins, whom I never knew, during the Holocaust. My father, who joined a Jewish unit of the British Army, was caught by the Germans and was held as a prisoner of war for three years, when he suffered threats to his life, hunger, humiliation and ongoing uncertainty. I learned about the Holocaust within the Israeli education system and read many books written by survivors, such as Ka-Tzetnik, Primo Levi, Elie Wiesel and others. As a child, I was surrounded by peers whose parents had survived the Holocaust, which had left its mark on the atmosphere in the family, and which I noticed whenever I visited them: the overprotection, the unexplained concern, particularly surrounding food issues, and more. Thus, it is no simple task to analyze a collective or national trauma, such as the Holocaust, according to a specific paradigm, while it evokes so many emotions. I will follow the Holocaust survivor and author, Ka-Tzetnik, who, during the trial of Adolph Eichmann, said that the concentration camps, such as Auschwitz, were on "another planet," incomprehensible to humans. However, in 1989, Ka-Tzetnik wrote in his book *Shivitti: A Vision*, that the Holocaust was not perpetrated by the Devil, but by human beings "like me and like you" (p. 121). Therefore, if this was a human operation, it can be understood in human terms.

The word Holocaust is of Greek origin, meaning *holos*, "whole" and *kaustos*, "burnt." The Holocaust is the term generally used to describe the genocide of approximately six million European Jews during the Second World War, a program of systematic state-sponsored extermination by Nazi Germany. Although the Germans also exterminated gypsies, homosexuals and people with physical and mental disabilities, the word Holocaust is used mainly to describe the Jewish genocide.

Space Domain of the Holocaust

Physical Space

The Holocaust occurred in nearly all the countries that were occupied by the Germans during World War II, including those that were allies of Germany. The extermination included Jews from countries in Western, Central and Eastern Europe, as well as from North Africa, especially Morocco and Algeria, which were ruled by the French pro-Nazi regime. It is important to note that Europe held a central position in the world at the beginning of the 20th century. This central position prevented the Nazis from concealing the systematic genocide of the Jews.

Several issues regarding space characterized the Holocaust. During the 1930s, before the outbreak of the war, and shortly after the Nazis came to power in Germany, Jews were forbidden to own farms or engage in agriculture. Jewish lawyers and judges were dragged from their offices and courtrooms, and Jewish physicians, professors and teachers were also dismissed from their jobs. Jews were denied entry to public places, such as theaters, restaurants and parks. Jewish people's space was further restricted by the establishment of ghettos, the only areas in which Jews were allowed to be. The ghetto areas were small in relation to the number of Jews living there. For example, while 30% of Warsaw's population was Jewish, the ghetto occupied only 2.4% of the entire area of the city. The lack of food, medical supplies and bad sanitary conditions led to high morbidity and mortality rates. Berenbaum (2005) described the ghetto as an instrument for slow, indirect murder. Jews were forbidden to leave the ghetto, but those with Aryan appearance (that is, blue eyes and blond hair) would sneak outside the ghetto, to the "Judenrein," the *space* that was "clean of Jews," to search for food. Thus, the space outside the ghetto was also a source of life, and for a small number, a way to escape the deportation to concentration camps and almost certain death.

The Germans planned the ghettos as a merely temporary solution. In their attempt to cleanse Europe and the world of Jews, they sent them to the concentration camps which had been constructed for that purpose. Most were situated in German-occupied Poland. Many Jews attempted to hide in order to save themselves, in shelters that were often very small and cramped in relation to the number of people hidden there. In some cases, there was not even room to stand up. The famous diary of Anne Frank, which describes such a place in Amsterdam, imparts the sense of a lack of space and privacy while in hiding. In Geving's (2003) book about the Holocaust, she describes being a young child when the Germans conquered the Ukraine and started sending Jews to their deaths. She ran away and was sheltered by a farmer's family, although concealment of Jews was forbidden. Geving describes how she was hidden in a small space behind the oven, where she could only lie with her knees bent. There was no room to sit up. She spent several months there, until the family found her a better hiding place.

Most Jews could not run away or hide, and were deported to the camps in inhumane conditions, by rail freight cars, in a confined *space* without food and water, for days or weeks. Many died on the journey. The physical conditions in the camp were inhumane. Hundreds of people lived in each barrack, sleeping on narrow wooden bunks shared by nine or ten people. There were no private toilets, only latrines, whose filthy sanitary conditions were the source of much disease. The camp was surrounded by an electric fence, making escape impossible. In the labor camps, the prisoners were literally worked to death. The prisoners had to perform strenuous labor for ten to twelve hours a day, regardless of the weather, and received meager food rations of very poor quality. They were made to dress in prison uniforms that were unsuitable for the weather conditions.

It is important to note that the prisoner's physical space was often a basic condition for survival. A person working in an enclosed space had a better chance of survival than someone working outside in the freezing cold, and kitchen workers had more opportunity to obtain extra food. Prisoners found to be no longer effective were sent to their deaths. Most deportees to the death camps were smothered in the gas chambers upon arrival, unless they were "fortunate" and received a job in the industrial death machine, such as transferring the corpses from the gas chamber to the crematorium, or extracting silver and gold teeth from the bodies (Gutman & Manbar, 1984).

In sum, the Nazi genocide of the Jews was begun by enclosing them in a small, restricted space, either in ghettos or concentration camps. Besides the inhumane physical conditions, the Germans forced Jews from different countries, who spoke different languages, came from different cultures and were accustomed to different behaviors, to share a space in which daily life was directed toward systematic extermination through suffering, humiliation and mass killing. Since the ghettos and concentration camps were enclosed areas, it can be assumed that the local population living "outside" these spaces did not really know what was going on there, thus limiting the voice of the trauma. However, witnesses' accounts after the war revealed that many of these populations did know what was happening, but did not wish to disclose what they knew, or were afraid to do so. Hence, for more than five years, what went on in the camps was just "a whispering" or an "unproven fact" (Arendt, 1976; Horwitz, 1990). Examining the impact of the Holocaust on the Jewish nation might raise the following questions: How did the encounter of these Jews from various countries and different cultures impact the sense of collectiveness after the Holocaust, when the physical aspect was not the only survival issue? Why do Jews, especially in Israel, insist on having a secure place—an independent state—that is specifically a Jewish state? How did the small, restricted space of the ghettos and extermination camps impact the sense of security of the Jewish population in Israel, who are surrounded by countries and populations who do not acknowledge their existence? The answer to these questions is associated with the impact of the physical space, experienced by the Jews during the Holocaust, on their psychological existence as individuals and as collectives both during and after the events. Before analyzing the psychological space, I will focus on the physical space of the Holocaust that still exists today, many decades later.

This physical space exists today in many museums and monuments in Europe, Israel and the United States. Some concentration camps are also preserved as museums to commemorate the victims. Among the most famous are Yad Vashem in Jerusalem, the U.S. Holocaust Memorial Museum in Washington, DC and the Anne Frank House in Amsterdam. In addition, the physical space of the Holocaust is expressed in hundreds of books, including academic studies and narrative fiction, as well as many films, plays, paintings and sculptures that have created a space for the national traumatic event. Furthermore, in the last twenty years, Jews and Jewish youths from all over the world have visited many of the concentration camps, experiencing physical presence in the *space* where the genocide happened. Many relate to this visit as a recovery ritual, and as evidence that the Jewish nation is still alive and strong, despite the Nazis' systematic attempt at extermination.

Psychological Space

The psychological space is strongly related to the nature of the pain. I will start with one of the first damaging effects of the Holocaust—to self-identity. In a relatively short time, hours or days after the Germans conquered territories in Europe, they began to implement their plan to rid the world of Jews. The formal authorities suddenly recognized many people as having only one identity—"Jew." Other identities, such as nationality, profession, socioeconomic status, gender and age, became irrelevant. The difference between individuals, between different groups of Jews and different citizenships were no longer considered. It was as if the Jews were one body and had no value as individuals. Gergen (2000) indicated that one's identity is constructed by the interaction between self and others. The "others" at that time were those who implemented the Nazi policy toward Jews, as well as those who cooperated with them directly and indirectly, overtly and covertly (Arendt, 1976; Horwitz, 1990). The Jews were made to attach a yellow star to their outer clothes, for immediate recognition.

Primo Levi (1986), author and Holocaust survivor, claimed that to shatter the Jews' and other prisoners' desire to resist the deletion of their identity, the Nazis immediately removed basic human elements. People were allocated a number instead of their name and these numbers were tattooed on their forearm. They were dressed in identical rags, and their heads were shaved. All this was accompanied by humiliating comments, screams, kicks and punches. People did not understand why they deserved this kind of treatment and were denied the psychological space needed to figure this out. They were focused solely on finding physical and psychological strength—for survival. In one of Levi's interviews after the Holocaust (Levi, Gordon & Belpoliti, 2001), he described one of the most difficult moments for him in the camp, when a prison guard wiped his hands on his clothes, perceiving him as an object, rather than a human being. No physical hurt was involved, but this was another example of the attempt to destroy his individual identity as a human being. Levi (1986) claimed that people in the camp were focused on survival. In such conditions, this often meant putting human values and morals aside.

Alongside the demolished sense of identity was significant damage to people's sets of beliefs. People changed their conceptions of good and bad, morality and immorality and of parental and family roles from those upon which they had been raised. For example, many parents gave their children to non-Jewish families, to save their children's lives. According to accepted belief systems, this could be considered abandonment. However, in the contemporary reality, leaving the children in a different space was the only way to save them. Both parents and children had to rapidly transform their set of beliefs in order to survive. People often had to steal, tell untruths, or harm others, even when the others were victims like themselves, and with whom they may have had previous relationships. The Holocaust created a different psychological space in which values, norms and human culture shared by most human beings did not exist and new beliefs about moral issues, norms and values had to be developed for the sake of survival.

The change in self-identity and sense of belief pushed many Jews to perceive being Jewish as bad, especially children, who managed to escape and find shelter in churches and monasteries, or on farms. Consequently, many began to practice Christianity and even after the war, some were afraid to acknowledge themselves as part of the Jewish people once again.

The change of psychological space on the individual level was associated with the change that occurred on the collective level. Jews in Europe, who were characterized by a strong sense of community, based on various community institutions concerned with education and welfare as well as strong leadership, were suddenly faced with these institutions' loss of power or complete destruction. Thus, the supportive network to which they were accustomed no longer existed. Many testimonies and studies have been written regarding the role of Jewish institutions under the German occupation during World War II (Friedlander, 2007). The different testimonies reflect the debate regarding the role of these institutions during the Holocaust. Some of the witnesses supported the institutions' activities, claiming that they were trying to function under impossible conditions in an attempt to reduce the Germans' demands. Others perceived them as collaborators, who cared only for their families and close friends. Reading these testimonies shows that whatever the position taken by witnesses concerning the activities of Jewish institutions during the Holocaust, they were, almost without exception, located at one extreme or the other. This is a clear example of how the Jewish collective was torn, divided and damaged, branded with an identity of powerlessness, helplessness and victimization. Another fact that exemplifies this damaged collective self-esteem is the attempt at repair by Jewish youth organizations, through resistance to the Germans in various ghettos. None of them expected to beat the Germans, but the opportunity to die an honorable death through resistance, rather than as helpless victims, empowered their Jewish collective self-esteem (Kermish, 1986; Krakowski, 1984; Zukerman, 1993).

Many other issues filled the victims' psychological space during the Holocaust. The murder of the inconceivable number of six million Jews meant that almost all survivors lost family members: children, parents, spouses, brothers, sisters and extended families. They lost close friends and sometimes the majority of their community members were murdered. The need to cope with these losses added to the tremendous amount of physical and psychological energy necessary for survival. Many victims lost their will to live, while others repressed their feelings in order to be able to cope with the daily torture and humiliation; for some, the hope of being reunited with their loved ones gave them a reason to continue their efforts to survive (Frankel, 1970). For some victims, the ability to survive and to tell the story of the Holocaust and thus memorialize those who were murdered or died was also a meaning for survival. However, it is important to note that in spite of the importance of the psychological power and its contribution to survival, the basic condition for survival was, as mentioned, the physical space. Nevertheless, the psychological space provides information about some part of the survivors' experiences.

Time Domain of the Holocaust

Measured/Objective Time

The Holocaust began with the outbreak of World War II in 1939. However, for Jews living in Germany, it started earlier, as soon as the Nazis came to power. It can be described as an ongoing event, in which the focus of extermination moved from one country to the next, depending on the advancement of the German occupation in Europe and North Africa, and on the cooperation they received in the conquered or allied countries. It depended also on the efficiency of the extermination process in the gas chambers. Even after the Germans began to retreat from occupied countries, most of the extermination camps still under their control continued to operate at even higher "efficiency," or Jews were transferred via death marches to areas still under Nazi occupation. During these death marches, many prisoners died of hunger and exhaustion, or were murdered by the Germans; hence the name. Thus, the extermination continued until almost the last day of the war. I do not think that other people can have any conception of the meaning of over six years under those physical and psychological conditions.

The Holocaust was not the first event in history that was perpetrated against the Jews. Jewish history is rife with traumatic, anti-Semitic events that occurred in the much more distant past. Wistrick (1994) argued that the Holocaust was the last and most extreme manifestation of a long European history of anti-Jewish attitudes and activities. These included the Spanish Inquisition and deportation of Jews from Spain at the end of the 14th and beginning of the 15th centuries, and blaming the Jews for the Great Plague in 14th-century Europe. (This accusation was based on the fact that a relatively small number of Jews died from the disease, as they adhered to the Jewish religious rules of hygiene.) Throughout history, many pogroms were launched against Jews in Europe. The term "pogrom" was originally used to denote extensive spontaneous or premeditated violence against Jews: in 1096 in France and Germany, from 1189 to 1190 in London and York, from 1881 to 1884 in Russia, and more. "Modern" anti-Semitism in Europe, since the mid-19th century, included "scientific" racism, which was incorporated into Nazi ideology used against the Jews. Comparing past traumatic events that were directed toward the Jews, the Holocaust was a unique event due to its systematic plans of genocide, designed and implemented by an official regime as a core part of its political ideology. This turned the number of people murdered and their murderous methods into a "death industry," characterized by specially planned, legitimate cruelty. In addition, this was the first time that not only were

Jewish people murdered, but there was an attempt to destroy everything that had been created by Jews: literature, music, scientific achievements, etc. Although the Jews had experienced collective disasters before the Holocaust, and although these disasters left a mark on their collective history, the Holocaust was an event which could hardly be compared to the past, and most historians relate to it as unique (Hilberg, 1996).

There is a debate as to whether the Holocaust should be seen only as a unique event in Jewish history, or whether it resonates with the long list of Jew-hating events that occurred in Europe before the Holocaust (Bartov, 2000). However, the consensus is that either way, it has had a significant influence on Jewish collective and national identity ever since. This is manifest through formal memorial days in Israel and in Jewish communities all over the world. An overwhelming number of studies have been produced by the many museums, Holocaust research centers and university departments, in addition to the hundreds of books written by survivors, either as private memoirs or as recognized literature, such as Primo Levi, Elie Wiesel, Aharon Appelfeld and more. In the art field, many Holocaust memorial sculptures have been erected in different places around the world, and many movies focus on different aspects of the Holocaust.[1] Many of these activities include therapeutic aspects that help the Jewish nation to heal some of the pain.

It seems that the most significant influence is by the traumatic aspects that modify the Jewish nation, especially in Israel. Today, Israelis carry the Holocaust with them through their daily lives, even if they are not of European origin. However, in the years immediately following World War II, even before the establishment of the State of Israel, when a huge influx of survivors immigrated there, the Holocaust was hardly mentioned. The encounter between the Palestinian Jews under the British Mandate, who were fighting heroically for independence, and the Jewish survivors from Europe, who were perceived as having "gone like sheep to the slaughter," was not an easy one. Since the Eichmann trial in 1961, this perception of Holocaust survivors has undergone a gradual change. Nessman (2005) brought to light many examples of how the Holocaust wounds remain fresh for Israel and form an integral part of Israeli society's national identity. In an interview to the BBC in January 2005, Segev, an Israeli journalist and author of the book *The Seventh Million: The Israelis and the Holocaust* (1994), claimed that the Holocaust is part of daily life in Israel and that it is sometimes difficult to distinguish between the genuine wound that resonates with the complicated political situation between Israel and its Arab neighbors, and when it is being used manipulatively by Israeli politicians. One can agree or disagree with Segev's claim, but for the purpose of this analysis, it is important to emphasize that the experience of the Holocaust has left deep wounds within Israeli society, creating a sense of emergency concerning every issue of Jewish safety and Jewish existence. Dasberg (1987) and Danieli (1982) have described the individual and collective psychological effects of Holocaust trauma upon Israeli society. They assume that a trace of the tragedy will always remain imprinted upon the collective consciousness and unconsciousness of the Jewish people, even if this is not easily discernible through the years. This fits Brave Heart's (2004) view of the impact of historical trauma. It is important to note that many studies and clinical works have addressed the impacts of the Holocaust on the mental health and well-being of second- and third-generation survivors (Sagi-Schwartz et al., 2002, 2003) and have produced different findings regarding these impacts. However, there is no doubt that the experience of the Holocaust has left its mark on the Jewish national identity in general and in Israel in particular. The impact of the Holocaust on Israeli society and on Jewish society around the world can explain some of the volume given to the "voice of the trauma" of the Holocaust.

Subjective Time

When referring to subjective time, it is important to address issues such as whether the duration of the event was perceived as long or short, and whether at that time, the victims were concerned with the past, the present, or the future. This is a complicated issue, as it has not been directly discussed in existing literature or research. Levi (1987) stated that although he described significant events that happened in the concentration camp, the most destructive aspect was the most difficult to describe, namely, the boredom and the monotony. Every day was the same, with the long hours of work, humiliation and hunger. The days seemed so long because there was "nothing." Levi said that when looking at the camp experience, most people remember particularly horrible, particularly positive, or unusual experiences, which colored the recollection and eliminated the memory of the endless, monotonous existence.

Other survivors refer to the place of the future during the Holocaust. Mrs S., a survivor of the concentration camps, applied for therapy fifty-two years after the war. She described as follows: "And there were nights when we would lie on the wooden bunks, exhausted after the working day. We were very hungry and would start to fantasize about the food that we would cook after the liberation. Believe me, there were so many good and varied recipes." This provides evidence of giving a place to the future during the Holocaust; maybe only for a short time and not every day, but the future was a source of hope. The Jewish Partisans' Hymn mentions the future: "You must not say that you now walk the final way, because the darkened heavens hide the blue of day. The time we've longed for will at last draw near . . . and if that day will be a long time in coming, this song will transfer the hope from generation to generation."[2]

41

As regards subjective time, it is important to note that the Holocaust affects many survivors until their dying day. Memories haunt their day-dreams, are the source of nightmares and are evoked on other special occasions, whether happy or sad. Most survivors have succeeded in cop-ing and rebuilding their lives, and have made a significant contribution to society, both in Israel and in the Diaspora. But the wounds of the Holocaust have also left their mark on those who did not develop physical and mental symptoms. These were often kept under control until a crisis arose, echoing the history. Shamai and Megged-Levin (2006) found that some people's wounds surfaced only as they aged and began to look back at their life narrative. They also found that in contrast to deal-ing with other kinds of trauma by working through the traumatic event and including it in an integrative life narrative, the survivors' ability to contain their Holocaust experience in a "closed capsule" results in bet-ter coping with daily life challenges and a reduction in the potential for mental symptoms. I reiterate here that the impact left by the Holocaust resonates in the daily lives of the Jews as a collective and a nation, espe-cially in situations where they sense their existence to be at risk. This has significant impact on national and collective attitudes, behaviors and political decisions.

Significant Other Domain

The Nature of the Victim

The victims of the Holocaust were Jews, regardless of gender, age, socioeconomic status and citizenship. Even Jews who had converted to Christianity, or who were children of converts, were considered Jews and sent for extermination. The ability to plan and implement such genocide was rooted in the long-term prejudices against the Jews and the long his-tory of anti-Semitism in Europe and around the world (Wistrick, 1994). Thus, in spite of Jews' contribution to the different countries in which they lived, hatred based on prejudice existed overtly or covertly. If the formal authorities did not protect them, they lost all political status, becoming merely Jews with a predetermined fate.

The impact of the trauma on the Jewish nation has already been dis-cussed. However, in analyzing the nature of the victims, I will mention how the Germans used Jews' cultural aspects to assist their implemen-tation of the genocide. The first was the Jewish communities' internal organization, which granted power to their leaders and is characteristic of Jewish communities all over the world. This is based on the obliga-tion for public responsibility and commitment set down in Jewish law, as well as on the norms that developed through decades of being a per-secuted minority. The Germans appointed these community leaders to

42

select which Jews would be sent to concentration camps and in spite of attempts to negotiate with the Germans, in order to reduce the number of people and to improve conditions in the ghettos, these Jewish leaders were forced to obey the Germans. Many conflicts and debates about these leaders' impossible role took place after the Holocaust. Being a persecuted, powerless minority for so many years led the Jews to create an adjustment culture. Adjustment is a strong defense mechanism that can be used to minimize difficulties. The Jews adjusted to the difficult situation, believing that it would pass, and trusting that they would not have to encounter the kind of persecution faced by Jews in other countries. Thus, many of the victims remained in denial about what was happening, even when living under horrible, humiliating conditions. Even as the war progressed, they believed the Germans' lies about special relocation areas for Jews, and only when they reached their destination, discovered that they had actually been sent to the death camps.

Another cultural aspect of the victims is the Jewish custom of "telling from generation to generation," which can partially explain the hundreds of books and studies produced about the Holocaust (in addition to the uniqueness of the event, as already addressed earlier in the chapter, as well as the therapeutic value of "telling"). Every year at Passover, the Jews follow a special family ritual of telling the younger generations the Biblical story of the exodus from Egypt and of the redemption from slavery into a free nation. This ritual has existed for thousands of years. Many Jewish holidays are associated with Jewish historical events and are transferred down the generations via rituals and stories. A second cultural explanation for the abundance of Holocaust literature is the prominent position of scholarship in Jewish tradition, which has expanded its focus from religious studies to non-religious subjects, including the intensive study of the Holocaust. Third is the central place of the written word in Jewish tradition, starting with the Bible and the Talmud, and influencing other types of writings. These cultural aspects can explain part of the "voice of the trauma" given to the Holocaust.

Source of the Traumatic Event: Human-made Trauma

The Nature of the Perpetrator

Different opinions exist regarding the identity of the perpetrators. Some readers will criticize my reference to the "Germans" in this analysis, rather than "Nazis" or even "Nazi Germany." I made the decision to use the word "German" because the Nazi regime was elected democratically to come to power in Germany, and if we are to learn from history, it is important to remember that even a democracy, which is considered the most progressive type of political system, can create a fascist dictatorship.

However, based on studies and testimonies of survivors, the Germans could not have implemented their ideology without the cooperation of bystanders (Bartov, 2000; Horwitz, 1990). According to Bartov (2000), the genocide could not have happened in a vacuum. He quotes Mao Tse-tung, who claimed that in order to carry out their assignments, guerrilla fighters must feel like fish in the sea. Bartov takes this claim and makes a general analogy to the Nazi genocide. He points out that the perpetrators must feel that they are operating within an environment that is either supportive of or indifferent to their actions, or that is so terrified that no one dares to act against the genocide. The environment is the one element with the power to increase the volume of the voice of the trauma. Regarding the Holocaust, it was clear that relatively few people helped the victims and took risks to hide them. A large percentage of the population was either too afraid to help, due to the authorities' constant threat that those found hiding Jews would be punished, or they were indifferent. However, a significantly large number of people supported the Nazis and helped them round up Jews, by referring them to the Nazi authorities or reporting families who tried to help the Jews. In addition, it is important to mention that even the Allied countries did not help the victims. The Swiss, for example, in their attempt to maintain neutrality, closed their borders to Jewish refugees. A group of Jews who managed to escape from Germany in 1938 in a boat named the *St. Louis* tried to enter to the United States, but were turned away. These Jews were accepted into some Western European countries and were murdered later when the German occupation reached these locations. Hitler used these examples to support his claim that no one wanted the Jews and that, by their rejection, these countries were indirectly encouraging his acts of genocide. Refugees who tried to escape to Palestine, then under the British Mandate, were refused entry and sent to refugee camps, where they lived under difficult physical and psychological conditions, but at least they were alive. Thus, it is impossible to ignore the role of the bystanders in any collective or national trauma and their responsibility at least to inform the world of what is happening there.

This illustration, which was complicated by the complexity of the analyzed national trauma of the Holocaust, presents a way to understand the impact of a collective and national trauma, by answering the basic questions regarding the trauma: 1) the nature of the pain; 2) the nature of the victims and their position and role within the larger society; 3) natural versus human-made trauma and the nature of the perpetrator in cases of human-made trauma; and 4) duration of the trauma: one-time, ongoing, or recurring events. The answers to these questions were organized on the dimension paradigm: space, time and significant others. The analysis of a collective or national trauma, or at least part of it, is the fundamental act that is necessary to provide help in both the short- and the long-term.

I have chosen to analyze the Holocaust in this book, due to my personal interest and involvement. It is possible that some readers will emphasize different aspects of this paradigm, which will shed light on other elements of the Holocaust. As mentioned above, an illustrative analysis of a collective trauma cannot be totally objective. However, if different analyses construct completely different pictures, a careful examination of these analyses will be necessary, including the way the known facts were used. Yet the paradigm still remains the basis for understanding the trauma.

Notes

1 This is only an illustration for the purpose of analyzing collective and national trauma, and I do not profess to mention the phenomenal number of books, museums, movies and studies that focus on the Holocaust.

2 The last sentence was not translated into English, but is a free translation from Hebrew by the author of this book. The song was originally written in Yiddish by Hirsch Glick in 1943, while he was still in the Vilna ghetto. Glick joined the Jewish Partisans and was killed in 1944.

2

SYSTEMIC IMPACT OF COLLECTIVE AND NATIONAL TRAUMA

In the first chapter, I focused on the definition and analysis of "collective and national trauma." In the present chapter, I discuss the effect of collective and national trauma on culture, society, community, families and individuals. I refer to this as "systemic impact," of which the main feature is the difficulty to differentiate completely between the types of effect on four systems: culture, nations and society, communities, and families and individuals. This is because of the connections and interactions between the systems before, during and after the traumatic event. When a very large number of individuals and families are impacted by a traumatic event, their communities might be affected; and the suffering resulting from traumatic stress among many communities within a collective and/or nation might impact the collective and the nation, and vice versa. According to cybernetics models, information transmitted from one system to another operates as a feedback loop, which determines not only the direct impact of the traumatic event on one or more of the four systems, but also the "impact of the impact" of one system on the others (Weiner, 1948).

Before describing the systemic impact of collective and national trauma on the different systems, it is important to note that traumatic events are often defined as such based on their impact (consequences). Some events are potentially traumatic, but the ability of relevant systems to deal with them effectively or the systems' resilience minimizes their painful impact and they are perceived, rather than traumatic events, as "potential traumatic events."

Also important to mention is the complication involved in assessing the systemic impact of collective trauma: Should the assessment of the impact be based on the perception of individuals within a specific system? Or should it be based on the functioning of the entire system as seen by outsiders? Who are these outsiders? Which elements should be assessed to determine the impact of the traumatic event? As there are no clear answers to these questions, special caution is called for when exploring the impact of collective trauma. Questions such as the following are crucial to understanding its systemic impact: From what professional perspective was the subject studied? How was the information gathered and analyzed?

Systemic Impact of Collective and National Trauma

Let us inquire further into the term "systemic impact," starting with a short illustration. At the beginning of the 1980s, Dr S. emigrated from Yugoslavia to a Western country, where he developed his career as a mental health professional. He was outside Yugoslavia when the Communist regime collapsed and during the years that followed this political change. Therefore, neither he nor his family members were involved in the wars between Serbia and Croatia, or Bosnia and Kosovo. However, when refugees from Bosnia, Croatia and Kosovo began to seek asylum in the Western country where he was living, and met with Dr S., mainly in a professional capacity, they were very suspicious when they heard his typical Serbian last name. Furthermore, Dr S. himself began to feel guilty regarding Serbia's behavior, as he and his family and friends did not support the policy and behavior of President Milošević of Serbia. They were ashamed to have the same nationality as the Serbian soldiers, who carried out such brutality. Dr S. and his friends experienced the war as trauma, even though they were neither witnesses nor direct victims of the Serbian soldiers' cruelty, and in the words of Dr S.: "Since the war, there is a stain on my identity." Thus, in spite of being far from the war zone, he and his friends suffered indirect harm because of their blemished identity as Serbs.

One main characteristic of systemic impact is related to the issue of belonging. By belonging to a specific system (family, community, tribe, or nation), events that happen, or actions performed by part of the system, impact the entire system. Individuals from the perceived perpetrator system find themselves labeled as perpetrators, even if they were not involved in these actions. Similarly, individuals from the victimized collective tend to be perceived as victims, even if they have not been directly victimized. Thus, the impact of collective/national trauma includes subsystems within the collective or nation as affected by the traumatic experience. As a result, even if individuals or groups within a collective do not feel directly linked to the traumatic experience, they might be pushed into it by others, who identify them as part of the collective based on the specific narrative attached to it.

Another aspect of the systemic impact is that of time. Let us continue with the example described above. As time passed, Dr S. and some of his Serbian friends tried to understand the rationales behind these wars. While severely criticizing the behavior of the Serbian regime and its soldiers, they started to mention the fact that parts of Kosovo and Bosnia were populated by Serbians and that, with their new-found independence, these states gave no thought to the status of the large minority of Serbians living there. Furthermore, they claimed that historically, the majority of the population in Kosovo used to be Serbian and it was only toward the end of the 19th century, due to the discrimination of Christians in the Ottoman Empire, that many Albanians, who had converted to Islam, moved to this area and became the majority (Banac, 1984; Veremis, 1008). Dr S. and friends did not share these thoughts with any non-Serbians, for fear of being considered as supportive of the Serbians' brutal actions, and they kept their thoughts to themselves in conversations regarding the war. The keeping of any secret requires much energy. As time passed, this limited their spontaneity and openness in conversations and relationships with people from other nations in the former Yugoslavia area, as well as with colleagues and friends around the world.

Although I am not Serbian, Dr S. and his friends came to share their secret with me because, as a Jew, I was able to identify with this continuous perception of being good or bad through the passage of time. I told them about a conversation I had with a Jewish secretary at work, in Israel, during the war between Croatia and Serbia. This woman was born and raised in Croatia and during World War II, she ran away to Serbia after hearing that the Serbians were secretly helping the Jews, whereas many people in Croatia supported the Nazi persecution. She was hidden by a Serbian family, but unfortunately, was caught and sent to Auschwitz. Luckily, she survived the Holocaust and immigrated to Israel, where she had been living ever since. Before leaving for Israel, she had searched for the family who had helped her during the war, but had not been able to find them. She learned from neighbors that the family had been severely punished after they were caught hiding her, as were many other families who were caught helping Jews, and that they had since disappeared. When she heard the news about the Serbo-Croatian war, she expressed strong satisfaction with the Serbian victory. When I queried her satisfaction with a war, she responded angrily that, during World War II, the Serbians supported and helped the Jews. She stated repeatedly that many Serbian families were severely punished as a result, whereas the Croatians helped the Nazis. Although she had left Serbia more than four decades previously, and the reality there had changed since then, the Serbians, for her, would remain forever good. Through my story, Dr S. and his friends learned about the attempts of many Serbians to help the Jews during the war. Unfortunately, they dared not even mention this as part of their collective identity, as others might perceive it as accounting for the Serbians' behavior after Yugoslavia was torn apart to form several different states. They also felt a sense of loss since the division of Yugoslavia; one of them said: "we used to be friends, to sing the same songs, listen to the same music, from all the different nations in Yugoslavia; our identity was

Yugoslavian; being Serbian was secondary." Nonetheless, they dared not express this sense of loss to other former Yugoslavians for fear of being accused of the desire for control over the other nations.

The story of Dr S. and his Serbian friends can be analyzed in various ways, including through the focus of time. Due to the traumatic experiences resulting from the division of former Yugoslavia, they had to ignore or keep secret their past identity; otherwise, they would be considered as supporters of the brutal acts perpetrated by Milošević's regime. Thus, their only overt identity was of the "bad and brutal Serbian." They had to avoid mentioning any past positive acts of their nation or collective, which was part of their covert identity, so as not to be aligned with the perpetrators. An additional aspect is the focus on space. The story was told to me by Dr S. in a Western country, whereas the event had taken place in former Yugoslavia. I knew about what was happening in the area through the media and through Israeli volunteers who had worked with Bosnian children in a refugee camp. I had additional information from the woman living in Israel who had survived the Holocaust in Serbia. These different places that were directly and indirectly included in the story, as well as the different points in time, which added to its construction, can illustrate the concept of "systemic impact of trauma." The systemic impact of trauma depends also on the "voice of the trauma," a concept discussed in the previous chapter. Landau (2007) illustrated the impact of the 9/11 terrorist attack on the World Trade Center, looking at the individual (biological and psychosocial system), at families, communities, states and the entire world. She referred to damages that occurred within the different systems; and the links between the different systems that magnified or reduced these damages. Although Landau (2007) referred to a specific case of national trauma and analyzed it from the intervention and resilience perspective, it can still shed light on the impact of various cases of collective and national trauma and on the way it might affect different systems based also on the link between them.

Reverting to the story told by Dr S., it is possible to assume that people from Croatia, Bosnia, or Slovenia, who felt they were powerless minorities when they were united as one state under Yugoslavia, would tell a different story. Some have stories about how their collective identity was erased under the Communist regime that rejected national identities. For many of these individuals and groups, the opportunity to create their own state after the demise of the Communist regime meant the possibility of regaining the rights of their national identity. However, the price they had to pay was in massive civilian casualties (in some cases, intentional genocide), including physical and psychological torture, loss of property and humiliation. Many individuals, families and communities have been dealing with the traumatic outcomes of the attempt to experience and practice their national identity. Therefore, it is possible to understand how their collective and national trauma includes elements of rage and hatred toward the Serbians. The different views of various communities, collectives and ethnic or national groups often complicated the provision of a clear picture of the impact of the trauma. Thus, the systemic impact includes also the issue of perspective: From which perspective is the assessment being performed? It can be performed from different ethnic/national/community groups; it can be performed from different professional perspectives, looking at different points in time, and more. For example, some historians might use the time perspective to analyze collective trauma in the different countries of former Yugoslavia. They might refer to it as "just" another war in the Balkans, which continued the history of wars started by various Balkan nations against the Ottoman Empire at the beginning of the 20th century, and before, during and after both World Wars. According to many historians, the reasons for all these wars centered on the sense of ethnicity and nationalism, extending to economic and social issues (Vermis & Kofos, 1998). This is a completely different perspective than that which might be used by mental health professionals when referring to the same event. Mental health professionals would focus on the pain, and the physical and emotional damages that the event caused to different individuals, families, communities and other groups that were directly and indirectly exposed to it. However, holding a systemic view leads us to appreciate the analysis from various perspectives, as adding to the understanding of the collective and/or national traumatic events. Therefore, from the historical or time perspective, we can go back to the issue of belonging, as described in Dr S.'s story, and come out with the following questions: How do these ongoing wars impact the culture of the societies and nations in the Balkans, or is there something in the culture of the Balkan societies and nations that encourages these wars? The first part of the question can be generalized to other situations of collective trauma: How do traumatic events impact the culture of those who experience it; and how does the culture impact the collective response to the traumatic events? The second part of the question can be generalized to various situations of human-made potential traumatic events. These questions can lead us to address the impact of collective and national trauma on cultures as an additional step to understanding the characteristics of systemic impact.

Impact of Collective and National Trauma on Cultures and Societies

In contrast to the massive body of knowledge regarding the impact of trauma on individuals, we are very much in the initial stages of understanding how cultural variables intervene in the types of response to potential traumatic events. Even less evidence exists regarding the impact of a collective trauma on cultures; and most of the existing studies focus on the rituals created by different cultures to cope with such events (DeVries, 1995). This lacuna might be rooted in the characteristics of the term "culture." Culture is often used in a general sense, referring to the culture of a society or a nation, the culture of an organization, a community, or a family. Thus, a discussion of the systemic impact of collective and national trauma on various human systems might easily include the same or similar terms used to describe the impact of trauma on culture in general. In this book, the impact of collective trauma on culture refers to a relatively large group of people who share the same system of knowledge, including behaviors, beliefs, values and symbols, which have been passed down the generations by communication and imitation. Thus, ethnic groups from different nations might belong to the same, specific culture, as might populations of several different countries, who share the same beliefs and values, such as Western culture, Eastern culture, modern versus traditional culture, Muslim culture, Christian culture, and so on. In relation to the impact of collective trauma, it is often difficult to make a complete distinction between the cultural and social systems, as well as to differentiate between social and national systems. Therefore, in this section, I will focus on the impact of collective trauma on society through a cultural perspective, and in the next section, I will center on the impact of collective trauma on nations through social perspectives.

Due to the limited knowledge, it is important to ask, initially, whether a collective or national trauma can have *any* impact on a culture. If the answer to this question is positive, other relevant questions can be added, such as, how does it impact a culture? Can we define or describe resilient versus vulnerable cultures? Or what are the variables within the culture that create resiliency or vulnerability? To deal with these questions, first let me clarify my definition of culture in the context of this discussion. Culture refers to a set of shared human beliefs, knowledge, attitudes, values, meanings and activities used by a specific group, which are transmitted from one generation to the next through human capacities for social learning and symbolic thinking.

In general, it is possible to claim that collective or national traumas create a challenge to cultures as they add some new or repetitive knowledge and experiences. The important question is whether and how this knowledge and these experiences change or maintain the shared set of beliefs, attitudes, values and meanings of those who are part of this culture. In his theoretical article regarding the characteristics of cultural trauma, Sztompka (2000) claimed that one of its basic consequences is "cultural disorientation," which occurs when the regular and known context of individual and social life loses its stability and coherence. Activities, beliefs and expectations that were known to people in a certain group or nation become suddenly diversified and even polarized.

However, we still do not have systematic, reliable knowledge regarding the impact of collective and national trauma on cultures. Therefore, a possible way to discuss this issue is through induction, making an initial assumption based on several examples.

The first example refers to what has been described by Legters (1988) as the "cultural genocide" of the American Indians. This included white men's actions against the natives, which destroyed the integrity and continuing viability of their existence, as well as their existence according to cultural values and norms. White men performed certain acts to control the Indians, including concomitant displacement, destruction of resources necessary to the Indians' survival, disruption of kinship and familial relations basic to their social structure and treatment based on modes of definition that obliterate a group's identity. The basic element of the cultural genocide was the attitude toward the Indians, which could be summarized by their being called "savages." As "savages," American Indian families were assumed to be incapable of raising their children. Therefore, the children were sent to boarding schools where they received the constant message that their culture was inferior to the white men's culture. Besides losing their families and role models, the American Indian children were beaten for speaking their native languages, thus losing a basic part of their cultural symbols (Noriega, 1992; Unger, 1977). The children internalized the notion that their original culture was "wild" and "bad," and that, on reaching adulthood, they would not be able to raise their children according to traditional Indian culture. It is possible that many of them even lost the knowledge of their own culture.

Following their displacement, many American Indians moved into urban areas, mainly because of economic difficulties. Life in urban areas prevented them from practicing their traditional Indian culture and required their assimilation into the "white" culture (DeBruyn, 1978). It can be assumed that those who stayed on the Indian reservations had somewhat better conditions for practicing their culture. This notwithstanding, having been torn from their land and having mingled with other communities, their existence in a larger context, where their culture of origin was perceived as "wild" and inferior, limited the maintenance and development of the Indian culture.

The basic differences between the white man's culture and the Indian culture were described by Luther Standing Bear (1933/1978), an American Indian. According to the Indian culture, "the great open plains, the beautiful rolling hills, and winding streams" (p. 13) were not considered "wild," but tame: "Earth was bountiful and we were surrounded with the blessings of the Great Mystery" (p.13). Thus, whereas according to the white culture, ownership of land is a significant value, for the American Indian, "land, plants, and animals are considered sacred relatives, far beyond a concept of property" (Brave Heart & De Bruyn, 1998, p. 62).

Based on cultural differences and as a result of the white men's attitude to the natives, the original Indian culture was severely damaged. The natural process of generational transmission of a culture was disrupted. The language, symbols, religious and other rituals were not practiced as a daily routine. One way of looking at this is as if the original Indian culture was destroyed by the white men, as well as by other traumatic events experienced by the Indians, leading to collective trauma. However, Indians today are still familiar with various elements of their traditional culture and different attempts are being made to retain them, even if they are not practiced as in the past. In their deeply moving work with the Lakota people, Brave Heart and De Bruyn (1995, 1998; Brave Heart, 1998) illustrated how they used Indian cultural rituals to work on the unresolved grief of the cultural genocide; however, generally speaking, the original Indian culture, as an entity, was dismantled.

The second example refers to the impact of World War II on the development of the welfare state. It was initiated in the 16th century, with the Poor Law in Britain, followed by slow development in the 17th, 18th and 19th centuries, facing many different attempts to criticize policy and to urge the state to take some responsibility for poor populations. However, the welfare state's heyday was after World War II. In his classic book, *Essays on the Welfare State*, Titmus (1958) claimed that some of the dynamics of war forced governments to be more involved in the daily lives of their citizens, if only to recruit the population for the war effort. The experiences to which people in Britain were exposed during World War II were somewhat different from previous wars. This was a war that required the efforts of all citizens and not only of specific combatant groups. The length of the war and the price paid by the population, in the form of death, injury, hunger, loss of property and various kinds of psychological symptoms, compelled the authorities to address "civilian morale." One way of doing this was by what Falls (1941) referred to as "demostrategy," which was based on a realistic assumption that the British population, civilians and combatants alike, could win the war only if convinced that their state had something better to offer than the enemy, not only during but also after the war. Various significant voices called for social justice, for more equitable distribution of income and wealth, and for drastic changes in the economic and social life (Titmus, 1958). Thus, it is not surprising that in the middle of the war, in November 1942, the Beveridge Report on Social Insurance and Allied Services was issued. This report symbolized the British aspiration for a better society, and its principles would go beyond social security. It included a system of family allowances to prevent poverty in large families in which the head of the family was working, it made comprehensive health and rehabilitation services available to the entire population, and made the government responsible for maintaining a high and stable level of employment (Sleeman, 1973). These directions for change echo cultural changes, including changes in beliefs, knowledge, attitude and values regarding the perception of human rights and changes in social and state responsibilities. All these changes created a different culture that was named the "welfare state." This culture spread to different Western European countries and was considered to be a humanistic way of life compared to the inhuman conditions that allowed the rise of Nazi ideology.

It is important to note that a somewhat similar direction of policy, which resembled some elements of the welfare state, was taken during the Great Depression in the United States—the New Deal policy, which continued to be part of U.S. policy even after the end of the economic crisis. According to Sztompka's (2000) conception, it is possible to assume that the impact of World War II was one of the main reasons that allowed the continuation of welfare state policy within different countries, especially in Western Europe, where the capitalist culture prevailed. These changes were not accepted by all. For many, who believed in the concept of laissez-faire, this new culture was traumatic because it violated their belief values and financial behavior, which emphasized minimal activity and involvement of state authorities in social and economic processes. As the welfare state demanded wide and pervasive government activities, which often limited absolute free market processes (Sleeman, 1973), it was perceived as a violation of freedom as defined by the laissez-faire values and capitalistic culture.

Throughout human history, we can find many cultures or parts of cultures that were destroyed following traumatic events such as wars and occupation by other tribes or nations, as illustrated by the story of the Native Americans. Nevertheless, collective or national trauma can modify a culture as part of the process of coping with the trauma, as was the case in the development of the welfare states after World War II. Another way of analyzing the impact of collective and national trauma on a culture is through the way in which the traumatic events are perceived.

Whereas some cultures perceive traumatic events as fate, others perceive them as collective punishment, usually sent by God; and other cultures look for logical and/or illogical causes. These different cultural perceptions may lead to different effects on the cultural structure. In some cultures, they may lead to some changes in values, meanings and beliefs, whereas in others, the existing set of beliefs and meanings are strengthened, when used to explain the traumatic events. It is important to note, however, that collective and national trauma scarcely changes or destroys the core beliefs of religions, which are often a significant part of human culture. Meanings or rituals might be added or modified, and some structure of the religious institutions might be modified, but the basic principles of the religion are usually powerful enough to resist traumatic events. It is possible even to claim that many human-made disasters that caused collective and national trauma throughout human history happened on account of religious commands. It is well-known that societies, communities, families and individuals experiencing collective or national traumatic events often turn to religion for comfort (McFarlane & van der Kolk, 1996). This human tendency to cope with traumatic events directed various mental health professionals to include religion, or what they refer to as "spiritual aspects," when working with traumatized systems and individuals (Shah, 2010; Kamya, 2009; Walsh, 2009).

In sum, it is possible to argue that collective and national trauma might impact culture. The impact can be described as a continuum ranging between a low level of impact, which can be a minimal change created by adding or modifying rituals, to a higher level of change, such as changing the collective set of beliefs or meaning. For example, the Holocaust undermined the sense of security of Jews in general, which later extended to the State of Israel (see Chapter 1). An even more extreme example is the destruction of most of the significant elements of a culture, such as in the case of the Native Americans. However, due to the limited research on the topic, clear determination of a resilient versus non-resilient culture is impossible. Does a resilient culture mean a culture that is preserved without changes? Can a resilient culture change according to the "new reality," even if this means relinquishing basic beliefs, norms and values? Or is it something in between? There are types of traumas in which the collective ability to hold to a strong set of beliefs helps to protect the culture, whereas in other situations, the ability to be flexible and tolerant is crucial for its protection. When considering all these questions, it would seem that even if further data on these issues were available, they might be subject to a tautological analysis based on the researchers' cultural background. Thus, when studying the resiliency of culture, it is first important to define its meaning, and how the cultural context impacts this definition. Despite the lack of knowledge regarding the definition of resilient culture, we do have evidence that human systems use aspects of culture as a source of comfort, such as religious beliefs, meanings, rituals, and types of human relations in situations of collective trauma.

Impact of Collective and National Trauma on Societies Within Nations

In this section, the impact of collective trauma will be analyzed through the lens of societies within specific nations. By "societies within nations," I refer to people living in a particular country with shared customs, laws and organizations. In general, collective and national traumas play a significant role in accelerating or inhibiting the rate and direction of enduring social change (Pastor, 2004). For example, Read (1993) claimed that the explosion of the nuclear reactor in Chernobyl, Ukraine in April 1986 and the way the Soviet government dealt with it was a significant element that played a catalytic role in the political changes that led to the collapse of the Soviet Union five years later. Read (1993) based his assumptions on interviews with the engineers and operators who conducted the fateful test on the night of April 25 and with the director of the power station. In addition, he visited some top-secret institutes to look for protocols and interviewed various staff members, such as engineers and physicians, as well as different people from Obninsk, which was declared a closed city after the event.

An example of a natural disaster mentioned by Pastor (2004) was an earthquake in Mexico City in 1985. The ruling political party of Mexico failed to manage the consequences of the disaster, leading to the first change in the Mexican political regime for more than eighty years.

The unexpected changes that result from a collective or national trauma are characterized by uncertainty and confusion of individuals and social systems. This uncertainty and confusion may limit the ability of the society's existing institutions to function as they were accustomed, because the consequences of traumatic events often require quick solutions based on initiative, which are not provided by formal institutions of a society on a daily basis, and might be even more difficult to achieve under stressful conditions. In addition, the quality of the solution provided by the formal institutions might determine the impact of the traumatic event on society, and therefore might be largely responsible for whether society would perceive the event as traumatic or whether it would remain as only potentially so. I will illustrate this with the natural disaster known worldwide as Hurricane Katrina, which occurred in August 2005 in the city of New Orleans.

Hurricane Katrina caused severe damage along the Louisiana coast and was a deadly catastrophe for the city of New Orleans. The damage included multiple deaths and injuries, severe loss of property, including basic human needs such as housing, food, clothing, workplaces and more. The damage extended beyond the direct victims and the direct loss, however. The consequences of Hurricane Katrina harmed the U.S. population's civic trust in the ability of various government institutions to help them in times of disaster. The ripples of this phenomenon spread beyond the United States, as people began to ask whether less developed countries would be able to protect their citizens in a similar situation. In Chapter 1, I referred to the place given to a traumatic event in global cognition as the "voice of the trauma." The damage created by Hurricane Katrina due to the incompetence of the local, state and federal government institutes had created a loud voice. The reason for this is rooted in the question it raised regarding the values under which social institutions operated, especially regarding the way they perceived the responsibility for those who elected them directly and indirectly. It also shed light on society's limited ability to trust its leaders and some social institutions (Miller & Rivera, 2008). Additional harm was connected to society's perception of scientific development of knowledge: Why couldn't all the scientists, engineers and professionals in a world-famous institution dealing with such a disaster, the Federal Emergency Management Agency (FEMA), predict the intensity of the hurricane and the ability of the existing levees to protect against the flooding? Some accounts attributed this failure to the incompetence of President Bush's administration (Dyson, 2006; Parker et al., 2009). Along with Pastor's (2004) claim regarding the place of collective and national traumas in creating social change, one might ask whether the failure of the Bush administration to deal with Hurricane Katrina's consequences was maybe one of the main reasons why Americans sought completely different types of leaders and elected Obama and the Democrats in 2009. In keeping with this line of thinking, it is possible that the harm to the American civic trust created a sense of uncertainty, which, in different societies with much fewer resources, might have developed into anomie, the sense of social incompetence, social friction, severe distrust and crisis of identity (Sztompka, 2000).

As to the long-term impact of Hurricane Katrina on American society as well as on the entire world population, it seems that the "voice of the trauma" became much less intense. Since August 2005, the global population has experienced other national disasters. However, when looking at academic publications and journalistic material, the experience of Katrina appears vivid (Picou, 2009). Thus, it is possible to assume that not only societies of journalists, researchers and practitioners of the helping professions still experience the consequences of Hurricane Katrina, but the memory of the event is still located in the back of the minds of many people in the US and other places around the world. It is revived not only when discussing issues related to natural disasters, but also when touching on issues such as discrimination of populations, racism, poverty and social exclusion. Four years after Katrina, the American Family Therapy Academy arranged its annual meeting in New Orleans. This academic meeting included a tour of the damaged area, where we discovered several facts. First, four years after the storm, some damaged neighborhoods were still empty of their residents. The reason for this was that only a very low percentage of the neighborhood's population could afford to rebuild their houses. Second, one area of public housing that had not been damaged in the storm was surrounded by a fence and the residents could not return to their homes. The local authorities declared their plan to build public housing throughout the city, rather than in specific areas, but no one knew whether or when this plan would be implemented. Meanwhile, the residents had to look for other arrangements. Was this the government's way of ridding themselves of people with low socioeconomic status? Third, one of the hospitals in the city that served people mainly from poor neighborhoods was hardly damaged (only the first floor and part of the second). Four years after the storm, the hospital was not yet in operation and instead of repairing the relatively small amount of damage, the authorities intended to close the hospital. On the day of our visit, hospital staff members were demonstrating against this decision. In addition to their distress caused by the hurricane, they had lost their place of work. Fourth, people from the community painfully described how the strong sense of community and neighborhood, which characterized mainly the lower and lower-middle class in the city, had been severely damaged because many of the people had to look for other places to live. This damaged the natural social support that was part of the daily life in these neighborhoods among different age groups. Although some might refer to this as the impact of national trauma on the community and not on the entire society, various books, documentaries and articles in journals that appeared in the United States described this as a community wound as well as a social wound.

The intensity of the impact of collective and national trauma is often associated with the pre-event functioning of the society. Norris and colleagues (2008) pointed to several variables that might predict that a community will function well, and this may be generalized to wider systems, such as a nation or a society. Among these variables are first, economic resources, referring to the financial state of the specific society, and second, resource equity, referring to the level of diversity in resources among different groups in the society. Large differences between groups in a specific society might cause a sense of unfairness, which increases the sense of social vulnerability and reduces the sense of belonging to the entire society and the willingness to contribute. A third variable is social capital, referring to the ability of a society to challenge individuals and groups to invest for the sake of the society through formal and informal activities (Norris et al., 2008). It is assumed that pre-event functioning is associated with the level of resistance to the traumatic event, which will be expressed by adaptive functioning to the situation before the traumatic event. It is also assumed that the society's ability to quickly mobilize required resources can shorten the period of transient dysfunction and lead to resiliency, which will allow the society to function through the learned experience of the traumatic event. Along with the painful consequences of the event, this might create a sense of social strength. The ability to rehabilitate the damage of the traumatic event is correlated with its intensity. In addition, the society's ability to develop ways to memorialize the loss caused by the event and taking responsibility when appropriate also play a role in curing the impact of the traumatic event.

Thus far, I have illustrated two types of impacts of traumatic events on societies and nations: The first referred to the way the Soviet government dealt with the nuclear accident at Chernobyl as a catalyst for the political change that led to the Soviet Union's collapse (Read, 1993). The second referred to Hurricane Katrina, which preceded the change from a Republican regime in the United States to a Democratic regime led by President Barack Obama. At this point, I will bring two examples of when political changes created national and collective trauma that lasted for many years. One, in Northern Ireland, was resolved by political change, and the other is still impacting two nations: Palestine and Israel.[1]

The conflict between Catholics and Protestants in Northern Ireland goes back to the 17th century, when England subdued Ireland and began the colonization policy of Plantations, sending English and Scottish Protestants to settle in the northern part of the country. The Irish perceived this as a deliberate attempt to bring about demographic change by replacing the Catholic majority with a Protestant population. They also perceived it as a way to separate the northern area from the rest of Ireland. This was followed by almost three centuries of fighting, surrounding cultural, national, political and economic issues. In 1949, Ireland was declared a republic, and the intensity of the armed conflict abated. However, six counties in Northern Ireland, inhabited by many Protestant settlers, remained part of the United Kingdom. At the end of the 1960s, the intense armed conflict erupted again and lasted for twenty years—a period known as "the Troubles." This period ended on April 10, 1998, when The Good Friday Agreement was signed between the main political parties representing the Catholics and Protestants. This peace agreement created a political change, in which the Catholics received a share of the political power in Northern Ireland, and the Republic of Ireland was given a voice in Northern Irish affairs. In return, Catholics were to relinquish the goal of a united Ireland and remain part of the United Kingdom.

During the Troubles, the Irish Republican Army (IRA) and paramilitary Protestant groups carried out many terror acts, in which approximately 3,700 people were killed, over 40,000 were injured and thousands were affected directly and indirectly (Fay, Morrissey & Smyth, 1999). The impact of this period goes beyond the individual victims, however. It affected the families of the casualties, while economic conditions deteriorated and people were in constant fear of being injured in the ongoing violence. The differences between Catholics and Protestants living in the same community were emphasized by the violence. In Belfast, for example, a fence separated the Catholic and Protestant neighborhoods, preventing joint instrumental and social activities. Economic, educational and cultural possibilities were thus limited, undermining the sense of belonging to the same community. The conflict appeared to accentuate the different Irish and British national identities, as well as the different religious Catholic and Protestant identities, while diminishing other aspects of identity that could be a basis for connecting populations living on the same piece of land.

The national conflict can be described as a spiral that impacted all subsystems in Northern Ireland society. It has damaged the national identity of the two groups in the area, which impacted individuals belonging to these two groups, who tried to repair their damaged collective identity by turning to armed conflict. The many terror attacks in turn caused losses to other individuals and families, increasing hate and suspicion between the groups. This in turn caused tension and conflicts within communities in the area, which increased the sense of national and religious differences, which intensified the damage to the national identity, and so on. The severe impact and damages caused by the longstanding conflict continued to be felt in 2015, over 15 years after the armed conflict ended. A lot of work is needed on societal, community, family and individual levels to overcome the traumatic outcomes.[2]

The second example of national conflict is between Israel and the Palestinians. This conflict began toward the end of the 19th century, when Zionist Jews began immigrating to their historical homeland of Palestine, at that time under the rule of the Ottoman Empire. At the beginning of the 20th century, when the area was under the British Mandate, there were several periods in which the conflict between the Palestinian Arabs and the Jewish Yishuv intensified.[3] In November 1947, the Arabs in Palestine and the large Arab countries rejected the United Nations Partition Plan to divide the area into two independent Arab and Jewish states, leaving Jerusalem under international supervision. After Israel was declared an independent state on May 15, 1948, a combined invasion of the new Jewish state by Egypt, Jordan, Iraq, Syria and Lebanon, in support of the Palestinian Arabs, turned the conflict into a war—named the War of Independence by the Israelis and the 1948 War by the Palestinian Arabs. Many of the Palestinian Arabs either fled or were expelled, resulting in the depopulation and subsequent destruction of Palestinian Arab towns and villages. Many of these people settled in the Arab countries surrounding Israel, mainly Jordan, Lebanon and the Egyptian-occupied Gaza Strip, and since then have been regarded as refugees. The Palestinians call Israel's Independence Day the "Nakba Day," which means the Day of the Catastrophe. They perceive the Nakba as a collective trauma, for which they blame Israel. This blame has fostered hatred, which, according to some Israeli politicians and groups, has increased the sense of a Palestinian national identity.

After the Six Day War fought by Israel in 1967, against Jordan, Egypt, and Syria, the Israeli–Palestinian conflict intensified. This was largely because Israel had taken control of East Jerusalem, Judea and Samaria (which Jordan had named the West Bank), the Sinai Peninsula and the Gaza Strip. Since 1967, the Palestinians have strengthened their demand for independence. Attempts to solve this ongoing conflict have not yet succeeded. The mutual sense of threat, the Palestinians' motivation to fight for an independent state and Israel's motivation to fight for security, has frequently escalated to armed conflict, and has resulted in extensive loss of human life and damage to human health, as well as increased hatred and demonization of the other by people on both sides. This hatred is transmitted to the next generation, which perpetuates the situation. Thus, the ongoing conflict impacts all areas of life in both societies, creating continued fear and tension around the existence of both nations.

Impact of Collective and National Trauma on Community

The definition of "community" refers to several different elements. Cree (2000) points to three basic elements. The first two are community as referring to a specific physical space, such as a neighborhood, village, town, or city; and community as a social network referring to interactions between people living in the same location. These two elements describe what is often defined as geographical community (Mitchell, 1985). The third element is community as a relational system, which refers to the joint sense of identity among individuals who do not necessarily live in the same location or even have any private relationships or acquaintanceship. This element describes a functional community, which refers to a specific group of people who share a common identity, problem, goal, or interest. Cooperation between the individuals belonging to the specific community can result in new ways of dealing with challenges faced by the group (Wegner, 2000). Among the functional communities is the lesbian, gay, bisexual and transgender (LGBT) community, and communities based on religion, ethnicity, or race, or on specific health situations. Some collective trauma might target a specific community, such as the mass shooting in Tel Aviv in 2009, by a gunman who entered a club frequented by the LGBT community; other examples include various activities of the Ku Klux Klan, which targeted mainly the African American community predominantly in the southern United States. Unfortunately, history is full of such events, in which minority communities were the target of violence, resulting in a traumatic response by the targeted community, even those who were not under direct exposure. In addition, rage originating in a specific group can cause some individuals to perform violence against the majority, such as 9/11 in 2001. These terror attacks symbolized the rage of some fundamental Muslim organizations toward Western society as represented by the United States. As well as resulting in traumatic reactions within the targeted majority community, traumatic reactions were manifest also in the mainstream Muslim community, who directly and indirectly received the blame.

Yet it is important to note that most of the knowledge regarding the impact of collective or national trauma centered on geographical communities (Patton & Johnston, 2001; Summerfield & Toser, 1991; Tobin, 2000). In addition, the focus is mainly on issues of recovery and interventions that are offered to individuals and groups within the community. In general, different studies show that collective and national trauma weakens community (Adger, 2000; Kimhi & Shamai, 2004; Patton & Johnston, 2001; Norris et al., 2008; Sonn & Fisher, 1998; Turner, Wheaton & Lloyd, 1995). Norris and colleagues (2008), who referred to the impact of terror and war on community, asserted that war and terror reduced the community's ability to function as a unit and caused individuals to perceive their community as significantly less strong and functional. These changes in the community as a unit added to the large number of individuals within the community, who developed stress symptoms that affected social relationships and well-being, and therefore, the community as a unit. Although Norris and colleagues (2008) referred to situations of war and terror, these outcomes were found also in studies of the impact of other types of disasters. Bleich, Gelkopf and Solomon (2003) claimed that long-term exposure to war and terror may result in developing an avoidance style, which reduces creativity, productivity, financial activity and morale. It also damages the community's ability to renew the resources that were lost due to the traumatic events.

An additional impact of collective and/or national trauma occurs in the social processes that develop immediately after the traumatic event. These processes show a significant increase in community cohesiveness, often characterized by homogeneity and monolithic thinking that does not allow for differences or conflicts. Sometimes, these social processes prevent the community from being open to outside help. Although these social processes serve the community in the short term, they reduce the community's ability for long-term re-establishment of resources and functioning (Lahad & Ben Nesher, 2005). Paradoxically, in situations of significant threat, communities tend to perceive themselves as a resource for their members; yet, at the same time, preserving the sense of community efficacy is more difficult (Norris & Stevens, 2007).

Many of the studies that were quoted describe the impact of collective or national trauma as potentially weakening community resilience (Kimhi & Shamai, 2004; Landau, 2007; Norris & Stevens, 2007; Norris et al., 2008). This claim raises the following questions: What is community resilience, and how is this resilience damaged by collective and national trauma?

Community resilience is described differently in various studies and is defined rather loosely (Kulig, 2000; Sonn & Fisher, 1998). In general, the descriptions take three different directions: a) the resistance direction, which refers to the ability of a community to absorb perturbation (Halling et al., 1995); b) the recovery direction, which focuses on the speed and ability to recover from the stressors (Adger, 2000; Breton, 2001; Patton & Johnston, 2001); and c) the creativity direction, which addresses the ability of a social system to maintain a constant process of creating and recreating, so that the community not only responds to adversity, but in so doing, reaches a higher level of functioning (Kulig, 2000; Kulig & Hanson, 1996). Some studies, like those of Norris and colleagues (Norris & Stevens, 2007; Norris et al., 2008), take into account all three directions without necessarily integrating between them. The differences among studies are even greater regarding the elements that comprise community resilience. Adger (2000) referred to community resilience in terms of resource dependency, that is, the quantity and quality of resources on which a community relies and the extent to which these can be modified. Adger's analysis focused also on the relationship between the sole community system and its ecology, as a resource that defines the community's resilience. Breton (2001) claimed that resilience is dependent upon a stock of human and social capital, consisting of people, networks, or local voluntary associations, through which members of the community can be mobilized for action, and an adequate service infrastructure. In contrast to Adger (2000) and Breton (2001), Clauss-Ehlers and Lopez-Levi (2002) referred to community resilience as culture-dependent. In their study of Latino and Mexican youth living in the United States, they identified three factors as being crucial to community resilience: the obligation to nuclear and extended family members, the authority of the elder community members, and the character of relationships, which are valued for their own merit and not as a means to some other end.

Norris and colleagues (Norris & Stevens, 2007; Norris et al., 2008, 2002; Norris, Friedman & Watson, 2002), who studied communities that had experienced traumatic events such as exposure to mass violence, and natural and/or human-made disasters, discovered four variables that construct community resilience, which are necessary in the community's regular daily functioning, but are crucial in disaster situations. Norris and colleagues' work can be a basis for developing systemic interventions with populations that experienced traumatic events and thus requires special attention.

The first element indicated was economic development (Norris & Stevens, 2007; Norris et al., 2008, 2002; Norris, Friedman & Watson, 2002). This element was mentioned also when describing the impact of collective trauma on the entire society. The economic situation often relates to basic human needs and therefore, is strongly connected with the economic status of the society in which the community is located. It is possible to assume and expect that a community located in a rich and developed society will receive greater and more rapid help than a community located in a poor and undeveloped society. The element of economic development includes the level of diversity of financial and economic resources and equity of resource distribution. The basis of community resilience depends on the level of physical capital, accessible housing and employment opportunities. As was noted in Chapter 1, in describing differences between the damages of natural disaster in poor, undeveloped countries or communities, compared to wealthier and developed countries and communities, a negative correlation was found between socioeconomic level and severity of consequences. This means that populations with a lower socioeconomic level have less instrumental, psychological and social ability to resist disaster than populations with a higher socioeconomic level. They suffer from greater physical and psychological damage and lower resources of healing than in populations with a higher socioeconomic level (Halpern & Tramontin, 2007; Norris et al., 2002; Norris, Friedman & Watson, 2002). Based on these studies, it is possible to assume that wealthier communities that have better economic resources will have better community resilience, and therefore, will be able to resist traumatic events as well as undergoing more successful healing than poor communities. In Chapter 1, I addressed "the voice of the trauma," a term that can be used here also, indicating that wealthier communities have more resources to create a louder voice that provokes acknowledgment of the needs of the population resulting from the traumatic event. Such an acknowledgment might affect the quantity and quality of financial and other instrumental support that will be provided to the population within the community, as well as to the community as a unit.

In addition, it is important to focus on the sense of equity of resource distribution among the community population, especially after the traumatic event. Kaniasty and Norris (1995), who studied the mobilization of social support following Hurricane Hugo in 1989, which struck some Caribbean islands and parts of the United States, mentioned two rules of resource distribution. The first and preferred rule is the rule of relative needs, which allocates the most support to the most needy residents or neighborhoods in the community. The second rule that is, unfortunately, implemented very often, is the rule of relative advantage, which enables more resources for those in the community with power and therefore with better access to them. As was found in further studies, these rules of resource distribution following collective or national traumas characterize distribution not only within but also across communities. Thus, powerful communities often receive more resources than non-powerful communities that are often in greater need. It is obvious that unequal resource distribution might increase the sense of deprivation of community members and as a result, reduce the social capital and community competence, which are the additional variables that construct community resilience (Norris et al., 2008).

Let me illustrate this by quoting Mr Henry Elkasslasy, the chairperson of Natan—the Israeli Network for International Disaster Relief—about his experiences following collective and/or national traumatic events around the world:

> in most places, you found just a chaos. One characteristic of this chaos is that groups and people who feel more powerful try to get more food, tents, blankets, clothes, medical supplies and other things that we bring with us as basic needs for the population. Sometimes, they will try to use their power against us. For example in . . . we came and tried to let the staff out of the airplane and suddenly found ourselves surrounded by armed soldiers. They threatened to kill us if we wouldn't give them some of the aid. I had experienced this before and knew that they were planning to sell it on the black market to people who could afford it, who would then sell it to people who really needed it for a higher price. In most cases, the aid delegations did not wish to confront them and would give them some of the aid, but we are a small organization, and our founder said that people had donated money to those who are in need and not to those who are in power. So I told my people not to take out the aid and told the armed leaders that we would go back into the airplane without helping their country. I pointed out to them that this would get into the media and they could kill me, if they want, but the plane is ready to take off . . . they put down their guns and we started working together . . . but it is important to understand that in most places, those who have the power get more aid, and equity is hardly taken into account, although it is so important.

Mr Elkasslasy, whose humanitarian set of beliefs includes the value of equity, emphasized in the interview how it might determine the amount and type of help that populations might receive. It is important to remember that outcomes of traumatic events might leave populations lacking in basic needs. According to Maslow, when these basic needs are not supplied, people cannot deal with other human needs, such as equity, which is part of the human moral code. The strength of the community might impact the way people and groups within the community are able to maintain some values, in spite of the difficult conditions. One might ask whether communities in which equity was not part of the values and daily life before the traumatic event might develop it under the conditions that it created. This question has complicated answers, but the simplest answer is no. When people are hungry, and have lost their homes and/or their family members, and have suffered physical and psychological injury, it is unrealistic to expect them to form a different set of values referring to higher human needs, as described by Maslow (1962, 1970). However, as was mentioned earlier in this chapter, collective traumas sometimes evoke social change, including in values and in moral code.

Social capital was another element mentioned by Norris and colleagues (2008), as constructing community resilience. Social capital refers to the network of community organizations and the links between them. Communities that are characterized by such networks can use existing organizations for the emergent goals of the community, both during and after traumatic events. The number of citizens participating in such organizations, the citizens' trust in their formal leaders along with flexibility to allow grass-roots leaders without perceiving them as a threat to the existing structure is part of what can be considered as social capital (Bohem, Enosh & Shamai, 2010).

It should be noted that communities in a crisis sometimes lose confidence in the existing organizations in the community and in community leaders, particularly when the leaders have no clear solution to the problems created by the crisis. As a result, they tend to replace them with new leaders in formal and/or informal ways (Robinson, 1994; Wachtendorf, 1999; Osborn, Hunt & Jauch, 2002; Turkel, 2002; Webb, 2002; Helsloot & Ruitenberg, 2004). When such a process does not tear the community apart, but increases the trust in the leaders, it adds to the community's social capital.

The leadership variable was found to be an important element in the perception of community resilience by the citizens of these communities (Ink, 2006; Lisitza & Peres, 2008; Kimhi & Shamai, 2004). Trust in the leaders' ability to deal with the crisis and to be attuned to the citizens was related to the sense of security of residents within communities and was expressed by lower levels of distress and higher levels of well-being after experiencing an episode with collective trauma potential (Kimhi & Shamai, 2004).

An additional variable that impacted the communities' level of social capital was the citizens' sense of having enough formal and informal resources from which to receive social support. Social support, whether actual or perceived, is especially important under stressful situations such as collective trauma (Kaniasty & Norris, 1995, 2004; Shamai & Kimhi, 2007). However, some complexities are involved in assessing this variable. As was previously mentioned, one impact of collective trauma is the weakening of resources. However, people living under collective threat might sometimes report higher social support than those living in quiet locations, because they look for this support. This can be illustrated by an unpublished finding of Shamai and Kimhi, who conducted a research report regarding the reactions of the Israeli population living close to the Lebanese border as a result of Israel's withdrawal from

Lebanon in 2000 (Kimhi & Shamai, 2004, 2006; Shamai & Kimhi 2006, 2007; Shamai, Kimhi & Enosh, 2007). The study showed that teenagers in northern Israel, who had experienced traumatic events, reported higher levels of social support than the comparative group from central Israel, who had not been directly exposed to the event. Thus, it might be assumed that social support can impact the resiliency of community in such a way that there is a positive correlation between perceived social support in the community and perceived community resilience. Yet, at the same time, collective traumatic events are correlated with social support, as the tendency to look for social support is greater in traumatic situations.

It is clear that the way social support is constructed within the concept of community resilience needs further analysis. Meanwhile, it is possible to assume that the way to describe social support within the community is according to a curvilinear line, meaning that under peaceful conditions, people will report less social support in the community, mainly because it is much less needed. Under moderate community stress, due to some traumatic events, people will report greater social support, which might be based on their having sought and found it. Under higher community stress, due to collective trauma, people might report lower levels of social support. This might be the result of searching for it without positive outcomes due to the low level of social support in the community before the traumatic event or due to the impact of the event that impoverished the community. When referring to social support, it is important to consider the issue of time. Some communities will show very high levels of community cohesiveness after the traumatic event, and hence, members of the community might report a high level of social support. But if the cohesiveness prevents the community from being open to outside help in the long term, it can cause an impoverishment of resources, including the ability to obtain social support.

Social capital refers also to the sense of belonging and commitment to a community. Perkins and Long (2002) defines it as a "sense of community," including trust and belonging to other members in the community and in cases of geographical communities, also emotional connection to the place. These connections to the members and the place are often expressed by a sense of commitment to the community, which is expressed by willingness to contribute, especially in situations of crisis.

The role of social capital in the construction and perception of community resilience is clearly illustrated in Shamai's study (2012) that explored the resonance throughout the lives of people aged 64 to 75, who were children and young teenagers during the attack on their community during Israel's War of Independence in 1948. The findings showed that the strong connections between the adult members of the community, their commitment to the community—Kibbutz Mishmar HaEmek—and the strong belief in the community's ideology and values, based on socialism and Zionism, as well as the connection to the place (place attachment), were transmitted to the children in the socialization process and experienced by the children as a psychological buffer against the traumatic event. In turn, the perception of the community as having strong social capital impacted the ongoing attitude toward the community. This resulted in the preservation and increase of the community's social capital as part of the community resilience.

The third element mentioned by Norris and colleagues (2007) as constructing community resilience is the existence of reliable information resources and open communication within the community. Whether a traumatic event is human-made or takes the form of a natural disaster, it breaks the daily routine, leaving the population with uncertainty that increases anxiety and anger, while reducing coping capability. Communities that can provide accurate and trusted information immediately after or even before the traumatic event (if it can be foreseen) increase the population's ability to cope with the outcome of the event and to trust the community leaders. Previous trust of information resources as well as having a variety of communication resources enable the community to function during emergencies. The ability to provide accurate information during emergencies increases the level of trust in the given information and in the leaders that provide it (Halpern & Tramontin, 2007). Some of the impact of traumatic events might cause damage to potential communication resources. For example, damage to electricity supplies prevents the use of media such as radio, television, telephones, or the Internet, or lack of certain knowledge prevents the ability to provide accurate information. Leaders sometimes believe that their role is to reduce panic, and therefore provide incorrect information, undermining public trust, especially at a time when trust is so important.

It is important to note the ongoing debate regarding the type and amount of information that should be given. Some people claim that, nowadays, the media tends to overwhelm the public with information, increasing anxiety and even secondary traumatization. Some people compare the present situation unfavorably with the past, saying that less communication is necessary to allow people to function in emergencies, claiming that the most important thing is the sense of trust in the information provided (Allport & Postman, 1947). This leads us to the question: What kind of information should be provided before, during and/or after a traumatic event? This will be discussed later in the book, but at this point, it is important to take into account that information and communication might be damaged as a result of traumatic events, but are important for providing a sense of security to members in the communities who are exposed to the trauma directly and indirectly, as well as to those who can provide help to these communities.

Another variable that colored the communication is the meaning people attached to the traumatic experience and the way it is transmitted among the community members—in other words, the community narrative. Kimhi and Shamai (2004) claimed that one important variable that impacts the community's ability to deal with traumatic events is the creation of a resilient community narrative, which positively impacts the members' perception of their community resilience. In their study, which focused on the population living next to the Lebanon border in northern Israel, they quoted Azaryauo (1997), who described this population's cultural and human capital aspects. Azaryauo claimed that the population in the area has managed to cope, to grow and develop in spite of the war and threat of terror that has lasted for almost eighty years. Kimhi and Shamai (2004) explained this partly by the community culture that has developed in the shadow of war and terror attacks, including heroic narratives and a sense of pride in being a resident of this part of the country. Shamai's work (2012) regarding the impact of the attack on Kibbutz Mishmar HaEmek in 1948, mentioned above, shows how the narrative of the community before the attack, which was characterized by perceiving the community as strong and unique, helped the children to cope with the traumatic event. In addition, the narrative of the community's resistance and the ability to protect itself, including rituals that were formed in memorializing the heroism of the community in fighting for its survival, were used for further coping processes after the traumatic event.

An additional illustration of the impact of community was the narrative created following Hurricane Katrina in New Orleans. This is a complicated narrative that can be described in relation to two chapters. The first chapter focused on the history of the city and the second, which seems more relevant in recent years since the hurricane, focused on the period during and after the event. This part of the narrative is characterized by anger and criticism of the policy makers. People of the community mentioned that police officers paid more attention to lawbreakers than to rescue activities, whereas many of these "lawbreakers" were merely people attempting to reach their homes to collect their possessions or protect their property (Tierney, Bevc & Kuligowski, 2006). In their presentation regarding the impact of Katrina on New Orleans, the staff of the School of Social Work at Tulane University described the pain of the city's demographic change. According to their stories, many residents, especially lower-class African Americans, were unable to return to the city, either because they could not afford to repair their houses, or because public housing was closed in spite of not being damaged. Another part of this chapter in the narrative focused on the long period of time that the city took to rehabilitate. During this time, some of them doubted whether the city would ever return to normal life. One woman from the staff described the first sense of hope being the return to operation of the streetcars, which symbolized the special transportation in the city of New Orleans. Mentioning the streetcars connected the two chapters of the narrative. When describing the impact on the community, they turned to the past, that is, the first chapter of the community narrative, and mentioned the unique history of the city's African American population compared to other places in the United States, mainly their release from slavery. They talked about the special relationships that were formed among African Americans in the neighborhood, which served as a strong resource of social support. It seems that the sense of community strength and uniqueness was somewhat damaged by the experience of Katrina, especially due to the population's sense of abandonment by the federal, state and city authorities. One might wonder which will be the dominant chapter of the New Orleans city narrative. It is possible to assume that the first chapter of the narrative impacted the city members' resiliency while coping with the traumatic event. However, the painful experience of Hurricane Katrina partially impoverished the sense of resiliency and changing the narrative's dominant focus requires special attention. The way to rehabilitate the community's narrative will be described in the second part of this book.

As events of collectives or national traumas have impacts on community narratives, in their measurement of community resilience, Kimhi and Shamai (2004) included an item that explored the appraisal of the community's ability to deal with future events that have traumatic potential compared to past capability of coping with the stress. This item can provide information regarding the changes in the community's narrative and the impact of these changes on community resilience.

The last element of community resilience that was mentioned by Norris and colleagues (2007) is community competence. Community competence, like the other elements mentioned, might be a buffer against collective trauma but might also be impacted by it. Community competence refers to the ability of community leaders, organizations and members to create collective efforts in resisting and coping with traumatic events. Such a collective work means developing and using problem-solving and decision-making skills that will empower the entire community, as well as groups within the community, to cope with the challenges created by traumatic events, rather than developing conflicts or helplessness that prevent the community from dealing with these challenges. This means also special skills for assessing deficits in the community resources and capability to request and use specific outside help.

Impact of Collective and National Trauma on Families and Individuals

A human-made or natural disaster can cause much damage to families and individuals, including death of family members, physical and/

or mental injury of one or more members, loss of property and income resources, confusion of roles, sudden changes in family homeostasis, displacement and more. The traumatic event might include the direct exposure of all family members, in the cases of living in a war zone or experiencing natural disasters, or it may involve indirect exposure, where only part of the family is directly exposed and others are indirectly exposed to the traumatic event. These cases include families in which one or more members took part in a war while the others were living in a secure place; families whose members were directly exposed to a terror attack while the others were elsewhere, or family members who were exposed to a natural disaster, while others were not in the area. Nevertheless, even if not directly exposed to the traumatic event, their relationships with those who were directly exposed to and hurt by the event can still lead to severe outcomes (Ben-Arzi, Solomon & Dekel, 2000; Dekel & Solomon, 2006; Figley, 1988, 1995a, 1995b; McCann & Pearlman, 1990; Mikulincer, Florian & Solomon, 1995; Shamai, Itay-Askenazie & Mol, 2006; Solomon et al., 1992; Turnbull & McFarlane, 1996; Waysman et al., 1993).

Figley (1995a, 1995b) studied and worked with families in which one member, usually the husband and father, had returned from the Vietnam War with posttraumatic stress disorder (PTSD). He pointed to a phenomenon, experienced in many families, which he named "secondary traumatization." Secondary traumatization refers to indirect exposure to trauma through a first-hand narrative of a traumatic event. The vivid recounting of traumatic memories to the other family members, who care for their suffering member and are emotionally and cognitively involved with his or her pain, might result in a set of symptoms and reactions similar to those of PTSD, such as re-experiencing, avoidance, anxiety and hyperarousal. Secondary traumatization is also referred to as compassion fatigue (Figley, 1995a, 1995b) and vicarious traumatization (Pearlman & Saakvitne, 1995). It is important to note that secondary traumatization does not affect only the spouse and/or parents of the suffering person (Ben-Arzi, Solomon & Dekel, 2000; Dekel & Solomon, 2006; Figley, 1995a, 1995b; Shamai, Itay-Askenazie & Mol, 2006), but might be transmitted to the second generation, as was found, for example, among some offspring of Holocaust survivors (Danieli, 1982).

It is interesting to note that in spite of the fact that many studies pointed to the important role of the family as the closest resource for support in situations of collective trauma (Catherall, 1999; Halpern & Tramontin, 2007; Landau & Saul, 2004; Walsh, 2007), relatively little research has focused on the impact of the consequences of collective trauma on family and couple dynamics. However, some of these studies, mainly those of Hill (1949, 1958) and McCubbin, Hamilton and Patterson (1983), created a theoretical base for assessing and evaluating the impact of stressors on a family as a unit. Their models might also be useful in conceptualizing possible impact of collective traumas on families.

Theoretical Models Conceptualize the Impact of Family Stress

The pioneering studies regarding family stress in general examined families in situations of collective and national trauma. Hill (1949, 1958) studied the impact on the family of the recruitment of American men during World War II and the impact of reunification after the war. Based on these studies, he developed the ABC-X model, which allows assessment of the level and intensity of family stress resulting from specific types of stressors. The "A" stands for the provocative event or for the level of disturbance of the family's steady state. The "B" stands for the resources (instrumental, psychological and social) of the family that might be used to buffer the stress. The "C" stands for the meaning and appraisal of the stressor. The interaction between these three variables determines X, which describes the amount of impairment caused to the family by the stressor—in other words, the family's ability to resist the stressor.

Based on the ABC-X model, McCubbin, Hamilton and Patterson (1983) presented the Double ABC-X model, which, besides the ABC variables, takes into consideration an additional variable that describes how families managed past stressors. The conceptualization of the Double ABC-X model was based on studies focusing on the impact of the U.S. war in Vietnam on families in which one member had served in Vietnam. The Double ABC-X was further developed by Nelson Goff and colleagues (2007), who focused mainly on the impact on couple relationships and satisfaction among deployed soldiers suffering from traumatic symptoms, and named it the CATS model (couple adaptation to traumatic stress). The model referred to a systemic interaction between each partner's individual level of functioning, predisposing factors and resources, and couple functioning as determining a couple's adaptation to the stress.

It is beyond the scope of this book to focus on individuals separately from the systems in which they live. However, it is important to note that although the research literature regarding the impact of stress and collective trauma on systems is relatively limited, hundreds of studies have focused on its impact on individuals, including studies that focused on the ability of individuals to resist and cope with the stressor (Bonanno, 2008; Bonanno & Mancini, 2008). Some studies perceived the ability to resist the stress as personal traits (Antonovsky, 1991; Kobasa, 1982; Lazarus & Folkman, 1984) and examined various personal constructs. Others focused more on situational variables, such as the Conservation of Resource Theory, which stresses the loss and gain of resources as predictors of individuals' ability to resist the stress (Hobfoll, 1998, 2001).

Whereas in previous years, most of the studies focused on the outcomes of exposure to collective trauma, emphasizing mainly PTSD, in the last decade, most of the studies examined resiliency, as it was found that only a relatively low percentage of the population tend to develop PTSD. The majority succeed in coping with the trauma in spite of the pain and harm it creates (Bonanno, 2004; Halpern & Tramontin, 2007). In addition, people might experience personal growth resulting from the traumatic experience, such as increased self-esteem based on the ability to cope with the painful situation, investing time and energy in developing meaning in life, which is often expressed by special activities within the family, community, or even society. Tedeschi and Calhoun (1995) referred to these changes as posttraumatic growth (PTG). However, it should be noted that even if people do not develop PTSD, the experience of collective trauma is painful, associated with depression, anxiety, anger, vulnerability, changes in world-view and more. These reactions may appear in various behavioral responses, such as social withdrawal or the opposite—either over-controlling the others or dependency. Due to the central place of PTSD, resilience and PTG in family and individual responses to collective and national trauma, there is further discussion of these concepts later in this chapter.

In the sections below, I will focus on possible specific outcomes of collective and national trauma and their impact on the families and their members. Among these outcomes will be the death of a family member, physical and/or mental injury, forced relocation, loss of property and sharpening of trans-generational messages.

Death of Family Members Resulting From Collective and/or National Trauma

Death that occurs as a result of collective or national trauma is considered as a traumatic death, often called traumatic loss, as it cannot be foreseen in the same way as a death that occurs due to sickness or aging (Walsh & McGoldrick, 2004). Traumatic loss of one or more family members in situations of collective trauma raises many difficulties that hardly exist in other situations of traumatic loss. The first type of difficulties relate to instrumental issues, such as the number of people the family lost. What was their role in the family? Were they parents? If the parents died, who will take care of dependents, such as children or older members of the family? Although these types of difficulties might be typical to many kinds of traumatic loss, in situations of collective trauma, where mass losses occur, finding solutions to these difficulties is far more complicated. Natural support systems, such as extended families, might deal with similar difficulties, whereas formal systems, such as community institutions, might be damaged or overwhelmed by the large number of cases.

The second type of difficulties combine instrumental and emotional issues, such as, how can the families mourn while having to take care of survival? Or how can we bury the dead if the body is missing? In many cultures, the mourning process includes ceremonies in which the family receive social support from the extended family, neighbors, friends and sometimes also from community institutions, such as religious congregations and leaders. In situations of collective trauma, these supporting systems often do not exist, as they too experience losses while fighting for survival. Raphael (1986) claimed that the absence of suitable grieving conditions and the need to survive might push the remaining members to function and to detach from their painful emotions. This coping mechanism might be helpful at the beginning, but the pain does not just disappear and might surface unexpectedly in different ways and at different times. It might sometimes be expressed by feelings of sadness and depression, which are appropriate to situations of loss. However, in some cases, the mourning will be colored by guilt or shame (Aarts & Op den Velde, 1996; Levi, 1986; Krystal, 1968), especially in cases where people feel that they did not do enough to rescue their family members, or feel guilty that they survived whereas others did not. Besides the personal feelings of guilt and shame, some family members might blame others for not doing enough to rescue the others. These dynamics usually have a destructive impact on family relationships. Due to the sadness, depression, shame and guilt, some families may avoid discussion or even mentioning the dead person's name or how they died. Such avoiding behavior often creates secrets within the family, which results in generalizing the avoidance to various communicative areas needed for the family's physical and emotional functioning. It can also cause deterioration in coping abilities and can create emotional distance between family members (Imber-Black, 1993, 1998).

The third type of difficulties is emotional and might be characterized by the phenomenon of ambiguous loss, guilt, shame and depression, which impact the family narrative that is transmitted to future generations. In situations of collective trauma, such as war, terror, or natural disasters, a missing body means no concrete proof that the family member really died. In spite of the rational understanding that the person was killed, a doubt always exists as to whether it really happened. Boss (1999, 2007) defined this phenomenon as ambiguous loss, and it was described in the first chapter of this book, when discussing the nature of the pain as one of the characteristics of collective and national trauma. The ambiguous loss does not allow the family to continue the mourning process as it raises feelings of guilt: Why are we mourning when we are not absolutely sure about the death? Have we invested enough in finding out whether the victim is still alive? Maybe we were dealing with our own survival instead of looking for our missing relative? In addition, the narrative regarding the missing/dead relatives becomes part of the family narrative and remains an unsolved issue that includes the painful feelings attached, with which the family lives for generations.

The fourth type of difficulties characterizes human-made traumatic events, such as wars, genocide, or other forms of political violence, and relates to the way the person died. Were they humiliated and/or tortured before they died? How much did they suffer before they were killed or murdered? These kinds of questions often lead to endless thoughts that lead to unsolved mourning, which might be accompanied by the sense of guilt and shame.

All these difficulties, specific to traumatic loss resulting from collective trauma, are added to other difficulties arising from the natural death of a family member and from a situation of sudden death when family members had not been able to say goodbye to the dying person. In some cases, their last interaction with the person might have been negative (Charles, 2010).

Physical or Mental Injury Resulting From Collective and/or National Trauma

Various studies have described the impact of physical injury on couple and family relationships. The studies point to differences between types of injuries, such as the duration of recovery, permanent versus temporary injury, the severity of the injury and its effect on the family and couple relationships. The injured person often needs care from other family members, which places some burden on the caregiver. Dekel and Monson (2010) indicated that caregiver burden is one of the main factors that explain the impact of physical and/or mental injury on couple relationships. Therefore, it can be assumed that this has an impact on the entire family. The concept of caregiver burden originally emerged in the literature on caregivers of individuals with chronic physical or mental illness (Chakrabarti & Kulhara, 1999; Cuijpers & Stam, 2000; Gilbar & Ben Zur, 2002). It is defined as the extent to which caregivers perceive their emotional or physical health, social life, or financial status to be affected by their care for a relative with impairment (Zarit, Todd & Zarit, 1986). In addition, conflicts between different caregiver roles, as well as between the caregiver and the injured person, also play a significant role in the intensity of caregiver burden (Gilad & Lavee, 2010; Marks, 1998; Shamai, Itay-Askenazie & Mol, 2006).

In situations of collective trauma, additional issues arise, which might impact the family and/or the couple. First, in many cases of collective trauma, accurate diagnosis and immediate medical help is not available. This can be because of the multitude of people in need of emergency assistance, the inability to communicate with medical centers that have medical staff, equipment and medicines needed for appropriate help, and the planned prevention of help to increase injuries, illness and death among the victims' collective, in planned cases of genocide and war. Thus, light injuries may become more complicated and severe, requiring more intense help from the caregiver. Second, in situations of collective trauma, several family members can be injured and the caregiver role might be left, for example, to children, who must deal with tasks inappropriate to their age—although it is sometimes fascinating to see children's resiliency and initiative in such situations. In some cases, the caregiver will be torn between several family members, who are all in need of the limited available care. Third, many situations of collective trauma are characterized by what has been defined as "shared trauma" (Dekel & Baum, 2010; Kretsch et al., 1997; Ron & Shamai, 2011; Shamai, 1998, 2001, 2002, 2005; Shamai & Ron, 2009). "Shared trauma" is defined as a situation in which both the caregivers (spouse, parent, therapist) share the same reality as the people receiving their care. Therefore, it is possible to assume that personal resources that are needed in the care-giving process might weaken due to the caregiver's personal experience. As a result, the help of a spouse or other family member might be limited and might not fit the requirements of the injured person. This may be expressed by anger toward the injured person, the caregiver may feel a sense of guilt and shame; this might even reduce the caregiver's self-esteem, which may add to their burden. All these might reflect a family process of coping and functioning in situations that require intensive coping activities and a high level of functioning.

Posttraumatic Stress Disorder as the Most Prevalent Mental Injury Resulting From Collective Trauma

Although this book focuses on systems and systemic interventions in situations of collective and natural trauma, the posttraumatic stress disorder experienced by individuals cannot be overlooked, as it is considered to be one of the most extreme reactions to trauma (Halpern & Tramontin, 2007; Keane, Marshall & Taft, 2006; van der Kolk & McFarlane, 1996). Whereas many of the acute reactions to collective trauma are transient, some reactions might endure and prevent natural recovery, among them PTSD symptoms. PTSD was acknowledged as an official mental health diagnosis only in the third edition of the *Diagnostic and Statistical Manual of Mental Health Disorder* (*DSM*, 1980), long after it was acknowledged and treated by mental health practitioners. *DSM* (1994) points to several groups of symptoms that comprised PTSD, including hyperarousal (hyper-vigilance, difficulties in concentration, sleep disturbances and exaggerated startle responses), re-experiencing (flashbacks, intrusive thoughts, nightmares regarding the traumatic event, psychological reactivity when exposed to some cues that resemble or symbolize the traumatic event) and avoidance (investing in efforts that avoid memorizing the traumatic event, inability to recall parts of the event, feelings of detachment and restricted range of affect). In addition, a PTSD diagnosis includes functional impairment (at work, adaptation in interpersonal and social relations). These symptoms must be associated with events that involved actual death or injury or threat to the bodily integrity of the self or others (*DSM*, 2013). Concerning recovery time, symptoms that persist for more than one month and less than three months are defined as acute PTSD; symptoms that last for longer than three months are defined as chronic PTSD. In cases where symptoms are manifest later, the diagnosis is of delayed PTSD (*DSM*, 1994). As was found in recent years, PTSD often correlates with anxiety, anger, shame, depression and substance abuse (Breslau et al., 2000; Budden, 2009; Halpern & Tramontin, 2007; Resick & Miller, 2009; Shin & Handwerger, 2009). The International Statistical Classification of Diseases and Related Health Problems (ICD-10) developed by the World Health Organization (WHO, 2007) indicated the possibility that chronic PTSD may lead to constant changes in personality.

As PTSD is a relatively new diagnostic category, debates in the field are still ongoing regarding the phenomenon. Among the debated issues are:

1 The place of culture: Is PTSD universal or is it typical only of Western cultures? If it is universal, can cultural differences be detected in the expression of the symptoms? Although many studies claim that the impact of trauma is basically similar and causes changes in memory, emotions, behavior, relationships and structure of self (Wilson, 2004; Yeomans & Forman, 2008), there is a strong claim that it is expressed differently depending on cultural context (Wilson, 2006). Some studies reported that whereas symptoms of re-experiencing are similar in various cultures, the hyperarousal and avoidance symptoms are culturally dependent (Afana et al., 2010; Marsella, 2010). Other studies claimed that the attempt to diagnose people from non-Western cultures according to the *DSM* criteria is a constraint imposed by Western culture in situations where it is inappropriate (Friedman & Marsella, 1996; Yeomans & Forman, 2008, Wilson, 2006). This debate should be taken into consideration while implementing interventions with systems and individuals in various cultures. Mental health professionals have a duty to learn the specific codes according to which emotions and meanings of behavior are expressed, to make an accurate diagnosis and provide appropriate intervention.

2 Normal versus distinct response: Is PTSD a normal response to different levels of stressful events that can be described on a low–high continuum (Brewin, 2003) or is it a distinct phenomenon in responding to extreme levels of stress?

3   Prevalence of PTSD: Various epidemiological data show that only
     a small percentage of people who are exposed to potential trau-
     matic events in their lives develop PTSD (Breslau, 2009; Keane,
     Marshall & Taft, 2006). Although the percentage was found to
     be low in most of these studies, the precise percentage was differ-
     ent in each. Among these studies are those of Shore, Tatum and
     Vollmet (1986), who reported 3.6% of PTSD. Kessler and col-
     leagues (1995, 2005) reported 7–7.8%, and Norris and colleagues
     (2002) reported 18–21%. However, Norris and colleagues (2002)
     and Norris, Friedman and Watson (2002) included other types of
     severe responses in this description, in addition to PTSD. Bonanno
     and Mancini (2008), in their article regarding resilience, claimed
     that typically, PTSD is observed only by 5–10% of individuals
     exposed to the traumatic event. As was found by Keane, Marshall
     and Taft (2006), the percentage of people suffering from PTSD in
     developing countries was higher than in the developed countries;
     for example, a comparative study between four developing coun-
     tries found 37.4% suffering from PTSD among the population in
     Algeria, 28.4% in Cambodia, 15.8% in Ethiopia, and 17.8% in the
     Palestinian Authority (de Jong et al., 2001). I agree with van der
     Kolk and McFarlane (1996) that it is difficult to come up with a def-
     inite percentage regarding the prevalence of PTSD, due to the fact
     that it is often measured by different instruments, in different types
     of potential traumatic events, within the different levels of exposure
     and, I will also add, different levels of losses of resources and dif-
     ferent types of cultures where traumatic experiences are expressed
     differently than in the Western culture.

Nevertheless, several components might be predictors of higher risk for
the development of PTSD. I would like to focus on some demographic
variables, such as age. Children are at greater risk than adults of developing psychological reactions to traumatic events. The elderly population
is considered vulnerable because of potential physical limitations due
to the aging process. However, regarding the psychological conditions,
they often have better resources based on life experience (Phifer, 1990;
Aarts & Op Den Velde, 1996). Gender, painful family history, lack of
social support and low socioeconomic status are among the variables
that might be predictors of developing PTSD. However, it should be
noted that these variables might carry different weight among different
types of cultures, different events and different levels of exposure. In spite
of the fact that most studies show that a relatively low percentage of the
population tend to develop PTSD, most studies of the impact of collective
trauma focused around this subject.

Impact of PTSD on Families

Although PTSD is a diagnosis given to an individual, it is important to inquire into its impact on people who live with or near the injured person and with whom they are emotionally and instrumentally connected. Unfortunately, only a few studies have described the impact of PTSD on the entire family (Dekel & Monson, 2010; Taft et al., 2011). In a qualitative study that explored the impact of injury in national terror attacks on couples in Israel (Shamai, Itay-Askenazie & Mol, 2006), it was found that many spouses of injured persons described the major difficulty to be as the result of the traumatic stress symptoms and not necessarily from the physical injury. Many of the spouses expressed this as: "living with a different person" or "I don't know him/her." These findings were similar to those of other studies in Israel regarding the impact of PTSD on marital and family life among families in which the husband/father had been a prisoner of war or exposed to dangerous and painful situations in wars or during their military service (Ben-Arzi, Solomon & Dekel, 2000; Dekel & Solomon, 2006). The study findings are in keeping with other studies performed in the United States with families of veterans of the Vietnam War (Hogancamp & Figley, 1988). Hogancamp and Figley (1988) named their study "War: Bringing battle home," describing, in four words, the reality of families living with a person suffering from PTSD. This reality includes the person's feeling of being misunderstood by family members who have not been exposed to the horrible situation that caused the traumatic stress. Often, people do not want to share the horrible experience, as they are afraid of being misunderstood, do not wish to cause pain to their family members, or are afraid that talking about it will evoke the traumatic memories. The silence might turn into nervousness and anger that is targeted toward those to whom they are closest. It should be noted that the role of culture should be taken into account when reviewing the impact of potential traumatic events, as in some cultures, the emotional issues are considered to be private and are not discussed even in intimate systems. In addition, in many cultures, men's expression of pain or weakness is unacceptable, even in the couple system. Thus, repressing emotion does not necessarily mean that the individual, spousal and family systems were not affected by the traumatic event to which only some of the family members were exposed.

In situations of national disaster, where the entire family is exposed to the traumatic event, more than one person might be at risk for developing PTSD. Taking into account the loss of additional resources, which are typical to situations of national disasters, it is possible to assume that coping might require great strength, which might be beyond the family's limits.

Besides many similarities of physical and mental injuries resulting from collective and national traumas, specific types of trauma can have unique aspects. Mental or physical injuries resulting from national disaster might be attributed mainly to fate, while injuries resulting from war, genocide, or national terror might involve feelings of rage and anger toward the persecutors; disappointment with those who were expected to defend the members of the family (national or local institutions as well as other family members, such as parents); sense of humiliation and helplessness especially by family members who were tortured or raped, as well as by those who perceived their role as protectors of the hurt family members. In sum, physical and mental injury of a family member impacts the entire family on both physical and mental levels. In situations of collective trauma, the natural and institutional support systems might be unavailable to supply the family's needs. Thus, high level of family resiliency is required to resist, cope with and adjust to the situation created by the traumatic event.

Forced Relocation

One painful impact of collective and national trauma is forced relocation. The International Association for the Study of Forced Migration (IASFM) uses this term to refer to the movement of refugees and internally displaced people (by conflicts) as well as to people displaced by natural or environmental disasters, famine, or development projects (www.forcedmigration.org).

Conflict-induced displacement involves individuals and families who are forced to leave their homes because the state regime is unable or unwilling to protect them. All these people and families are victims of armed conflicts including civil wars resulting in violence and persecution based on nationality, race, religion and political or social group. A large proportion of this group attempts to escape across borders to other countries in search of refuge. Some seek asylum under international law, but the majority remain anonymous, fearing rejection and forced return to the country from which they escaped (Bhui et al., 2006; Fazel, Wheeler & Danesh, 2005; George, 2010). The IASFM reported that since the end of the Cold War, there has been significant escalation in the number of armed conflicts, many of them internal, between different ethnic and/or religious groups, such as in former Yugoslavia and Darfur. The United Nations High Commissioner for Refugees (UNHCR) is responsible for this group of people and is involved in approving their asylum requests.

Disaster-induced displacement involves people and families who are displaced due to natural disasters, such as floods, volcanoes, earthquakes and human-made disasters (industrial accidents, radioactivity). In most cases, they remain within their country's borders. However, they have had to leave their homes, and often lose all or most of their property, including their natural support systems. Besides the governments of the countries that are supposed to help these populations, several international organizations provide assistance, among them the International Federation of the Red Cross and Red Crescent Societies, as well as many international and local non-governmental organizations (NGOs).

The third group of forced migration involves people and families who must leave their homes due to policies of project implementation, designed to enhance development, such as roads, dams, ports and national "vanity projects." Although these acts are not considered to be collective or national traumas, their results could be considered as a collective trauma for the many communities and groups who experience forced displacement. The displacement is often carried out without adequate compensation, forcing the population to resettle in areas that do not allow them to continue their regular private and social life. For many groups and communities, this displacement is considered a collective as well as personal trauma.

The impacts of forced relocation, either in the same or a different country, often result in families being torn apart. In cases of armed conflict, when families try to escape, they often must separate. Sometimes, the escape conditions are beyond the physical abilities of the young or elderly members of the family, and the dangers, and uncertainty causes families to encourage some of their members to escape, while the rest remain in the dangerous conditions. Even if the escape is successful, contact with the family is often limited, for technical reasons or because it might put the family in the danger zone at high risk. This leads to an uncertain and anxiety-ridden reality for both the family who remains behind and for those who escaped. In many other situations, failure to escape can cause death of family members, leading to a high probability of developing ambiguous loss symptoms (Boss, 1999, 2007).

Mr L., a tour guide in Vietnam, told the following story that can illustrate the narrative of many families of refugees:[4]

My family ran away from China when the Communist regime took over. Like other Chinese, we came to South Vietnam and rebuilt our life here. My family had a successful business and my brother was recruited to the South Vietnam Army. He became an officer and expressed his beliefs in the right of South Vietnam to remain a free country and not to be under the Communist regime. When the Communists took over, he was arrested and was sent to re-educational camp, which was, in fact, a prison where the inmates were forced to do hard labor. He got sick and died after six months. My parents were afraid that this would not be the end of the Communists' revenge against our family and decided to try and escape from the country. As I had a romantic connection with a Vietnamese woman, which was not approved by my parents, I decided to stay. My family escaped in a small boat like many who escaped from Vietnam at that time. My two sisters drowned during the trip. So my parents arrived in England with my youngest brother. Well, my parents still think that my sisters managed to swim ashore and survive and I hope that one of them will knock on my door, some time, or that I'll get a message from my mother that at least one of them is alive. So, from being a family with five children, they now have one, and their other child—me—living far away without open channels of communication. They do not have as much property as they used to have . . . My father was an excellent businessman, so he did really well and after a few years, they gained the economic status they were used to. But socially, they felt isolated, they missed their dead children and at that time, they missed me. They were afraid to communicate with me in case I might get hurt. They would not send me direct letters, but sent them through a friend who left China and came to England and who had never been a Vietnamese citizen. In spite of the economic success, my father became depressed. His physical health deteriorated and he died of a severe heart attack nine years later . . . when things changed here and we were allowed to visit Western countries, my mother invited me. All these years, I tried to repress my feelings toward my parents and family, but the minute I saw her, I was overwhelmed. Men do not cry in our society, but I felt like crying. She had become so old and sad. I was happy to have the chance to meet her and finally to get her approval of my marriage. She told me about the feelings of loneliness and missing my dad and my brother and sisters. She repeated many times that she still waited for my sisters to appear and that the family "died" after the Communists took over . . . Unfortunately, after so many years of separation, my youngest brother and I did not develop an open and warm relationship. He informed me when my mother died, and helped me financially, as he is doing very well in business. We call each other no more than twice a year and share information regarding our families, but it is not a family anymore, each one of us sees things so differently, we have lost the old ties . . . my mother was right, in spite of the fact that we are both doing fine and have built our own families, the family has died . . . .

As can be seen from this story, even families who successfully escape to another country often experience losses; and in addition to the mourning and to other traumatic events they had experienced in the process of the escape, they need to invest energy in their adjustment. In many cases, their adjustment takes place in an unwelcoming social context, which might include fear among the locals that the group of refugees will increase in size and use the hosting country's resources and change its culture. For many of the families, it means starting their life again from scratch. Superficially, this might be likened to the immigration process, but there are some significant differences that should be indicated. In planned immigration, families or family members choose to take this action. Even though in many cases the decision to immigrate is based on difficult economic conditions and immigration seems to be the best option to improve the situation, it is still performed out of freedom of choice. This is contrary to families and individuals who escape from their home as a result of life-threatening events. Furthermore, in the process of escaping, people are often exposed to traumatic events that added to the already-traumatic experiences that led to this escape. These might include robbery, rape, torture and more. These events are fertile ground for the development of traumatic symptoms in individuals and families, with which the families must cope, in addition to the complicated adjustment to their new location and society.

A well-known phenomenon experienced by many survivors is the sense of guilt for surviving while other members of the family did not (Danieli, 1982; Mallimson, 2006; Mendelssohn, 2008). The sense of guilt sometimes includes self-blame for not being able to save their relatives. These feelings accumulate with their other painful experiences and add to the difficulties in the adjustment process. In many cases, the sense of guilt and the self-blame are kept secret from the remaining family members or from the survivor's new family. As was mentioned before, keeping a secret is a complex task and impacts the well-being of a family (Berger & Paul, 2008; Imber-Black, 1998). It can be a secret known only to some family members or even to just one member, but the way in which the secret is "told" (or, most of the time, acted out) creates tension in the family. Thus, it often poses a dilemma for family members as to whether they can ask about the hidden material, whether they need to worry or take care of the person carrying the unknown feelings, which might provoke unexplainable anxiety and could turn into anger. In many cases, the secret remains closed and the behavior of the person who is keeping the secret is attributed to their "past experiences" of the traumatic event. In many other cases, the secret might be told when the person is dying and needs to free themselves from the sense of guilt and self-blame. In Israel, for example, many Holocaust survivors could not share these feelings with their children, but did so with their grandchildren. In both cases, the impact of the overt or covert secret regarding the sense of guilt and self-blame remain as part of the family's history, which passes from one generation to the next, either as a behavior or as a family narrative.

An interesting example regarding the impact of guilt on self and family is described in Mark Kurzem's book *The Mascot: Unraveling the Mystery of My Jewish Father's Nazi Boyhood* (2008), in which he tells his father's story. After sixty-three years of oppressive silence that created an atmosphere of tension in his family, Mr Kurzem, who was in his seventies, came to his son, who at that time was a doctoral student of history in England and asked him to help explore his roots. Mr Kurzem had immigrated to Australia after World War II, together with a group of Latvian Nazi supporters, who had run away from Latvia, as they were afraid of being tried by the Soviets for implementing and/or supporting crimes against the Latvian population. For this group, as well as for Mr Kurzem, it was a forced relocation. As a boy, he had escaped into the forest, where he had hidden and had witnessed the murder of his mother, brother, sister and many other Jews from his hometown. The traumatic experience had been mostly repressed and cognitively forgotten. He had been found by Latvian soldiers, who were in the service of the Germans, who raised him, believing him to be a Russian child and knowing nothing of his Jewish roots. He became their mascot. Although Mr Kurzem had forgotten his past on the cognitive level, it was still present in his subconscious mind. Thus, the feelings of guilt and self-blame were manifested through tension and restlessness, which he could never put into context. The tension, restlessness and unclear past impacted his relationships with his family, who knew that certain issues should never be questioned and discussed. It took Mr Kurzem over half a century to tell his unclear story finally to his son, who helped him to find the meaning of the covert memory. However, the way the secret was enacted through the years left permanent marks on the entire family. Unlocking the secret after many years was in itself a painful process for them all, and Mr Kurzem was accused by some Jewish organizations as cooperating with the Nazis. They were unable to accept that repressing the past was a psychological defense mechanism (dissociation and amnesia) that helped the young child to deal with the traumatic experience. In addition, Mr Kurzem and his family had to deal with the old-new identity regarding their Jewish roots, which posed additional challenges.

Intergenerational Impact of the Trauma

The intergenerational impact of collective trauma has been studied intensively in the last decade (Brave-Heart, 2004; Danieli, 1998; Dekel & Goldblatt, 2008; Joubran-Saba, 2014; Song, Tol & de Jong, 2014). A large number of studies focused on families of Holocaust survivors (Danieli, 1982; Sagi-Schwartz et al., 2002, 2003). Despite the different findings regarding intergenerational impacts, there is no doubt that such painful experiences have left their mark. They might or might not have impacted the second generation's level of functioning and mental health, but they have affected the family narrative according to which individuals construct their self, the surrounding society, and the meaning ascribed to it (Somers, 1994; Riessman, 2001).

Joubran-Saba (2014) studied the intergenerational submission of the experience of the Palestinian refugees who remained within the borders of the State of Israel in 1948, when many Palestinians living in Palestine under the British Mandate either fled or were evicted from their homes during the Nakba. One of her main findings was that in spite of differences between the families in coping strategies, all the families emphasized the importance of perpetuating the displacement story. This involved various rituals, such as visiting the location of the old village, maintaining contact with other families from there, or keeping the keys of their old homes, which they pass on from one generation to the next. This finding also showed that whereas the first generation was preoccupied with the need to adjust and survive in the new situation, the second generation began to create rituals to memorialize the loss of the family home and the third generation turned the pain, which most of them had not directly experienced, into political activities. Based on Joubran-Saba's (2014) findings, it seems that the pain of the first generation turned into anger and hatred toward Israel and the Jews, but this anger is being expressed through democratic means, such as demonstrations, the use of the media, active political roles, and more. From a systemic point of view, it is possible to assume that the wider political context surrounding the family system has evoked anger rather than depression, as in other cases of collective trauma, such as that of the Native Americans or the Holocaust, where the surviving generation that directly experienced the traumatic event showed mainly symptoms of depression (Brave-Heart & De Bruyn, 1998; Brave Heart, 2004).

An additional example of the intergenerational impact of collective trauma refers to a phenomenon which has spread in areas of armed conflict, where children were forced to take part in the conflict as child soldiers. Song, Tol and de Jong (2014) found that when these children grow up and raise children of their own they transmit the trauma to the next generation through education, teaching their offspring that the world is an unsafe place. Therefore, the children need to be very cautious regarding what they do and say. To ensure the transmission of these educational messages, the parents often use violence to discipline the children. In addition, the parents' traumatic symptoms interact with the parental anxiety involved in raising children, and are transmitted to the next generation as the meaning of both childhood and parenthood. Helping parents and children overcome the intergenerational transmission of the trauma requires a high level of resilience, support and containment of a larger system, such as the extended family or the community.

Even though families do not wish to transmit the parts of the traumatic event that related to humiliation, anxiety and depression, they are often unwillingly transmitted to the next generation through world-view, sets of beliefs and uncontrolled behaviors. Many families insist on preserving parts of the traumatic event as part of the family history and narrative. This is described by Botros, a participant in the study by Joubran-Saba (2014): "I have taken my children to the place where the village was located. They have to know that we are from there; that we had land and property and that today we are refugees . . . we have not managed to retrieve what belonged to us, but we can at least preserve the memory and our family's story." Intergenerational transmission occurs in every family and has been indicated by family theoreticians, such as Bengston (2001), Boszormenyi-Nagy (1987) and Bowen (1978). Nevertheless, traumatic experiences usually leave deeper scars on the individual narrative, carrying the greater potential of unconscious or even conscious transmission of the trauma to future generations.

In spite of the painful impact of collective trauma on families and individuals, various studies pointed to the ability of most families and individuals to cope with the difficulties. This phenomenon can be described as individual and family resilience (Bonanno, 2004, 2008; Ungar, 2010, 2011; Walsh, 1998).

Family and Individual Resiliency in the Face of Collective Trauma

In recent years, there has been a tendency to emphasize the place and role of resilience following trauma, as many studies found that people tend to be more resilient than professionals tended to think.

The tendency to look at people from their strength and health perspectives is known as the "salutogenic" approach, a term coined by Antonovsky (1979, 1987). The term "salutogenic" is made up of two words: the Latin word *salus*, which means health, and the Greek word *genesis*, which means origin. Antonovsky constructed his studies in a different direction than the traditional medical model. Instead of focusing on the question of what causes sickness, he asked how people manage stress and stay well (Antonovsky, 1987). This direction of research evolved from some earlier studies, in which he found that some people had faced impossibly stressful events, such as in concentration camps during the Holocaust, and yet were not impaired by this and could cope, adapt and overcome. Antonovsky (1979, 1987) suggested that the impact of stress factor (pathogenic, neutral, or salutary) depends on the generalized resisting resources (GRR). Any resource that is effective in reducing or avoiding stress is considered as part of the GRR; among these resources are social support, ego strength and instrumental resources

(Antonovsky, 1979). Antonovsky claimed also that positive use of GRR accumulates and will increase the individual's self-esteem, which in itself might be a significant coping tool. In 1987, he proposed the concept of Sense of Coherence (SOC), which he described as an individual orientation based on three components:

1   Comprehensibility—belief that things that happen throughout life are predictable and explicable.
2   Manageability—the belief that one has the internal or external resources to manage various demands and stress situations that occur throughout life.
3   Meaningfulness—belief that there are reasons and purposes for investing energy and dealing with good and bad events that happened throughout life.

According to Antonovsky, meaningfulness is the most significant component in coping with stress. If a person believes that there is no reason to confront challenges, they will have no desire to make the effort to comprehend and manage events. Many studies that were performed in different cultures used the concept in measuring impact of stress, either as mediator or as moderator between the stressful event and its consequences (for example, Ron & Shamai, 2001; Shamai, Itay-Askenazie & Mol, 2006). Antonovsky and colleagues (Antonovsky & Sourani, 1988; Sagy & Antonovsky, 1992) expanded the SOC concept from individual to Family Sense of Coherence (FSC), using the same components that comprised the original SOC and found it to be an adequate concept to describe family resilience in confronting different stressors in life. Shamai and colleagues (2015) used the term in measuring the impact of life on marital quality in ongoing war situations. As was found in the study, the sense of coherence served both as mediator and moderator between the stressful event and its impacts. Thus, couple SOC was a buffer against the stressful event of the ongoing war and was positively correlated with marital quality, meaning that a high level of couple SOC was used to resist the impact of ongoing war on marital quality.

Walsh (1996) investigated the concept of family resilience, and asserted that it is the ability to endure the consequences of crisis and adversity and to cope with them. Simon, Murphy and Smith (2005) added that, based on this ability, the family emerges from the stressful situation feeling strengthened, more resourceful, and more confident than in its prior state. Several qualities characterized resilient families, including commitment to the family system and family members, which means having the sense of togetherness, having clear roles and responsibilities and at the same time, being flexible to changing roles and responsibilities based on the initial impact of the traumatic events. Another characteristic was communication—talking things through with each other; this requires family members to be mutually open and honest and to be willing to listen to other members' views regarding the issue under discussion, supporting each other within the family and looking for external resources of adequate support. Problem-solving skills were important also, based on communication abilities for clear definition of problems and goals and searching for ways of reaching these goals.

In general, the concept of resilience refers to processes that either associate with or lead to adaptive outcomes in the face of stress and trauma. The concept is used in the literature to describe several dimensions: outcome and process. When used in the outcome dimension, it often refers to "recovery," meaning adaptation to the new situation or returning to pre-event functioning (Lepore & Revenson, 2006). Some researchers claim that there is a difference between recovery and resilience, for example, Bonanno (2004), who said that resilience means either absence of negative impact or quick recovery. Bonanno (2004) defined resilience as the ability to maintain relatively stable and healthy levels of psychological and physical functioning. Another distinction between resilience and recovery is that in recovery, people often experience some low and inconsistent levels of symptoms even after "full recovery," whereas resilient people might experience some inconsistent short-term worries, such as several weeks of sporadic preoccupation. Generally, however, they exhibit healthy functioning over time, as well as the capacity for generative experience; factors that enhance the development of positive outcomes. Other researchers, such as Lepore and Revenson (2006), claim that returning to normal functioning after a traumatic experience, even if the process is slow, expresses resiliency compared to people who do not recover. When resilience is used to describe the process dimension, it often refers to resistance, meaning the ability of individuals or systems to maintain normal functioning during and after the potential traumatic event (Bonanno, 2004; Lepore & Revenson, 2006). It is important to note that normal functioning during potential traumatic events does not necessarily mean similarity to previous functioning, but the ability to create different and appropriate functioning in the face of the stressful condition, as well as the ability to resume the pre-event functioning at the termination of the stressful event. It does not mean that the experience of the stressful event is "deleted," but that the experience has not diminished the ability for functioning and adjustment.

As this book's objective is to suggest systemic interventions in situations of collective and national trauma, thus focusing on interventions and not only on research, it is important to note that conceptualizing resilience as the ability to resist stressors is somewhat controversial. Whereas some researchers tend to perceive resistance as functional and as a sign of the ability to cope well with traumatic events (Bonanno,

2004; Lepore & Revenson, 2006; Wortman & Silver, 1989), many mental health professionals perceive it as pathological denial that may cause them to limit themselves in daily functioning and relationships. Although there is no evidence to suggest that maintaining normal functioning following trauma will lead to a delayed reaction at a later date, mental health professionals tend to recommend therapy in the immediate aftermath of the event. Furthermore, some of the interventions offered after traumatic events include techniques that re-engage the clients with the traumatic events in order to "work through" the event. We found this to be unhelpful for many people and even caused deterioration (Everly & Mitchell, 2000; Lilienfeld, 2007). In contrast, maintaining regular functioning, or if that is not possible, creating a routine that is somehow similar to the pre-event functioning, without necessarily focusing on the traumatic experience, might be the best and most helpful way to deal with the traumatic experience. Let me illustrate this by two examples taken from my own experience as an Israeli.

The first example occurred in a special workshop at the Jewish History Museum in New York. The workshop began with a post-Holocaust movie produced in Poland in 1946. The movie describes the life of Jewish children who survived the horrors of the war while they were staying in an orphanage. Also in the film were two adults, famous comedy actors in the pre-war Jewish community in Poland and later in Israel. The movie describes normal children, who played and laughed and fought, just like any other group of children around the world. The children asked the two actors to perform for them and when the actors talked with the director of the orphanage, she told them to address the issue of the Holocaust in the performance, explaining that if it is not talked about during the day, it appears as nightmares. After showing the movie, a panel was held, including psychoanalysts and one man, who had taken part in the movie as a child and who, at the time of the workshop, was a famous professor at an Israeli university. The psychoanalyst focused on the orphanage director's psychological understanding of traumatic effects presented in the movie and on one particular scene, which showed three children sharing their horrific experiences of the Holocaust at night, and casting a doubt on the authenticity of all the other parts that showed the children's normal functioning. The professor, who had participated in the movie, presented a completely different point of view. He focused on the joyful activities in the orphanage, claiming that he was not focusing on the past as a child and teenager. When he immigrated to Israel (which was then still under the British Mandate) a couple of years after the movie was made, he joined a Zionist-socialist youth organization and his activities there became the central meaning in his life. He explained that focusing on the present and future was natural to him, as was the case for many of his Holocaust-survivor friends.

In the discussion, most of the people supported the psychoanalytic point of view, which denied the children's ability to return to normal life after experiencing the horror of the Holocaust. Being familiar with activities for surviving children who came to Israel after the Holocaust, I expressed my point of view, claiming that the parts of the movie describing the "normal children's activities" indeed characterized most of the children and adolescents who survived the Holocaust and arrived in Israel. The scene describing the children discussing their horrific experience of the Holocaust was uncharacteristic behavior for most of them. In response to my claim, one psychoanalyst suggested that I was referring only to strong people like the Israeli professor on the panel, and that most of the survivors were psychologically damaged. However, as most studies of Holocaust survivors and second-generation survivors have found, based on clinical samples, this was not representative of the entire survivor population. In general, most Holocaust survivors adapted and adjusted to life's demands after the war. They built families, developed careers and many of them served in various high positions in different places. This does not mean that they were not affected by the horror of the Holocaust, but in spite of the painful experience, they returned to normal life shortly after the traumatic event. Some survivors spoke about their experiences, and others did not, yet the majority did not suffer from delayed traumatic symptoms. Knowing many survivors on a personal and clinical level, I agree with the conceptualization of Bonanno (2004) and Lepore and Revenson (2006) that most individuals can maintain or go back to normal functioning during and/or immediately after a potential traumatic event. In other words, most people have enough resilience to create some routine of functioning even in completely abnormal and uncertain situations. This is what Walsh (1998), in her conceptualization of resilience, refers to as the ability to be flexible without breaking down and the ability to bounce back.

Another illustration describes a natural disaster that happened in Israel in December 2010. An extensive wildfire on the Carmel mountain range spread rapidly through the forest covering the mountain ridge, burning many houses in several communities and requiring evacuation of many of the area's residents. As a social worker, I was working with one of the evacuated communities and saw how people organized their lives after losing their homes and possessions, including irreplaceable objects of sentimental value such as family photographs and family heirlooms. Most of the people were very active immediately after being informed of the loss and began to make arrangements for reorganizing their lives. They were busy with the insurance companies, and with government ministries that were supposed to provide compensation, looking for apartments to rent and other daily life necessities, such as clothes, furniture and school materials. In a study of the impact of the fire on the population six months after the event, it was found that most people were not suffering from PTSD or other stress symptoms (depression, anxiety and somatization) and most reported a high level of resilience. Some people reported experiencing some symptoms of traumatic stress, in the first and second months after the fire, such as nightmares related to the fire, but these disappeared after several weeks. Some people indicated that their traumatic experience was expressed mainly by anger and sometimes by a sense of desperation, as a result of the negotiation with the government authorities regarding the compensation. Yet, they described intensive daily functioning, which, besides their regular activities, included investing additional efforts in rebuilding their homes. A very special interview was conducted with people living in an artist's village, where many houses had been burned. One artist, who lost her home and studio, immediately rented somewhere small in the village and received a place where she could continue her work. In spite of her anger toward the village and state authorities, she returned to her art work, and looking at her colorful and optimistic pictures, one cannot even imagine her loss. I am sure that these two illustrations are not unique outcomes and characterize the reactions of most individuals and systems that face collective trauma (Bonanno & Mancini, 2008). The memory and/or experience of the traumatic event remain, but at the same time, individuals and systems have the ability to resist and resume normal functioning shortly after. Nevertheless, it is important to point out that instrumental rehabilitation, after the loss of possessions or property as a result of the event, can be a lengthy process. Resiliency means also the ability to function throughout the rehabilitation period.

Posttraumatic Growth as a Consequence of the Struggle With Traumatic Events

An additional concept related to the impact of collective trauma, which at times, might be confused with resilience, is posttraumatic growth (PTG). As was described previously in this chapter, PTG refers to the idea that individual and/or systemic crisis can lead to personal or systemic growth (Berger, 2015; Calhoun & Tedeschi, 2006; Saakvitne, Tennen & Affleck, 1998). The concept has been recognized for many years by researchers and clinicians dealing with crisis interventions (Caplan, 1974; Parad, 1966, 1990), but in the last two decades, it has received special systematic attention. First, it was given the name of posttraumatic growth, and second, a measurement tool was developed enabling the study of PTG using quantitative means (Tedeschi & Calhoun, 1996). In addition, a growing number of qualitative studies are exploring the way in which PTG is constructed and experienced by individuals (Berger, 2015; Paul et al., 2010; Manne et al., 2004; Weiss, 2004). It is interesting to look at the type of association between the level of distress, which may or may not include PTSD and PTG. Although we might expect to find a negative association between level of PTG and distress and a positive association between PTG and well-being, studies have indicated some mixed results. Some studies support these types of associations (Calhoun & Tedeschi, 1998; Carver & Antoni, 2004; Frazier, Conlon & Glaser, 2001; Sears, Stanton & Danoff-Burg, 2003; Tedeschi & Calhoun, 2004; Tennen & Affleck, 1998). According to these studies, people who report high levels of PTG will report high levels of general well-being and low levels of distress, and vice versa.

Several other studies, however, indicated a negative association between PTG and general well-being, and a positive association with level of distress (including PTSD and/or other pathological symptoms) (Cadell, Regehr & Hemsworth, 2003; Solomon & Dekel, 2007; Tomich & Helgeson, 2004). Thus, people who indicate a high level of PTG indicate a high level of distress or PTSD, and a low level of general well-being. This type of result supports different researchers, who claim that PTSD and PTG emerge as two separate yet related processes, and therefore, they are not mutually exclusive and cannot be conceptualized as two opposing ends of the same continuum (Berger, 2015; Solomon & Dekel, 2007). Thus, a person or a system can experience high levels of distress and of PTG simultaneously. In my home country of Israel, this phenomenon is known not only to professionals but also to laypeople. In addition to reporting distress symptoms following a traumatic event, individuals also report some positive changes in their lives as a result of the trauma. Among these are feelings of strength of which they were not aware prior to the event, and changes in world-view, which brought them closer to family members and friends. Some start to be creative through various means, such as art, writing, or movie making. Others contribute to society and become involved in political or social organizations. One interesting systemic expression of growth was the creation of the Israeli and Palestinian Bereaved Families Circle, which aims to work jointly toward ending the ongoing Israeli–Palestinian conflict—which is the reason for the death of their children. Thus, the sadness, depression and other symptoms accompanying a traumatic loss have not interfered with the need to do something that is perceived as a contribution to society. One common characteristic of all these examples is the concrete action taken by people with trauma, as evidence of growth. The role of the concrete action as a type of beneficial outcome of PTG was found by Hobfoll and colleagues (2007). They attempted to clarify the role of PTG as a beneficial process of wellness based on their study regarding the impact of exposure to ongoing terror attacks in Israeli society. Their findings show that reporting higher levels of PTG was associated with reports of higher levels of PTSD symptoms. However, when the PTG was accompanied by actions and was not merely a cognitive maneuver, it was associated with positive adaptation.

Another set of studies that attempted to explain the mixed results claimed that the associations between PTG and stress are more complicated; and a possible reason for the inconsistency of the results is that these associations are not linear but curvilinear (Kleim & Ehlers, 2009; Lechner et al., 2006; Solomon & Dekel, 2007). Thus, people who suffer no distress or PTSD symptoms, and who, therefore, do not perceive the event as traumatic or as a crisis, have no reason to grow as a result. Another group of people who were strongly impacted by a potential traumatic event and who suffer from PTSD and other distress symptoms might be centered on the suffering and report a low level or even the absence of PTG. A third group of people who reported a moderate level of impact of the potential traumatic event, with some inconsistent symptoms of PTSD, reported a high level of PTG, because along with the distress, they had the energy to grow.

Where do all these findings take us? First, even though the concept of growth is mentioned by different religions in different cultures and seems to be a solid phenomenon related to positive adjustment after trauma or crisis, it is important to be cautious when observing it. The inconsistent findings regarding its beneficial consequences require careful assessment of both the pathological and strength aspects, including the aspect of growth. This refers also to contextual variables, such as culture (Berger, 2015; Joyce & Berger, 2007). Second, it is important to note that most studies on PTG were performed with individuals and not with systems, even though much of the growth occurs in the surrounding systems (families, friends, community and society at large, such as the state or nation). Thus, we still cannot answer the question of whether systemic growth exists. How is this type of growth expressed? What are its associations with the systems' distress characteristics? And how can it be systemically operationalized? As this book aims to focus on systemic interventions, it is important to note that understanding the nature of systemic PTG is an additional challenge in developing theoretical and practical knowledge regarding optional directions of intervention following collective and/or national trauma.

Constructing a Paradigm for Analyzing and Understanding the Impact of Collective or National Trauma

The focus of this chapter has been the conceptualization of the impact of collective and/or national trauma as a systemic impact. This means that it not only affects each one of the specific social systems (culture, society, community, family and individuals), but also affects the interaction between the systems. These, in turn, create an additional impact on each one of the systems, therefore adding to the quality of the interaction, and so on. Thus, the quality and intensity of the systemic impact is not static and changes according to the situation in each separate system and its ongoing interaction with all the other systems (see Figure 2.1).

The quality and intensity of the impact is constructed within each system by the three main elements: Damages and negative consequences, resilience and growth. As was discussed in this chapter, the three elements are not mutually exclusive and they interact: The resilience might determine the level of the perceived damage and the ability to cope with it. However, the intensity and quality of the damage might impoverish the resources that construct the resilience. Growth might evolve from the sense of loss and might help in adjusting to the reality created by the traumatic event, while not necessarily omitting the damages and negative consequences of the trauma. Figure 2.1 illustrates the interaction between the damages and negative impact of the traumatic event and resiliency, and a higher level of resiliency might omit or reduce the negative

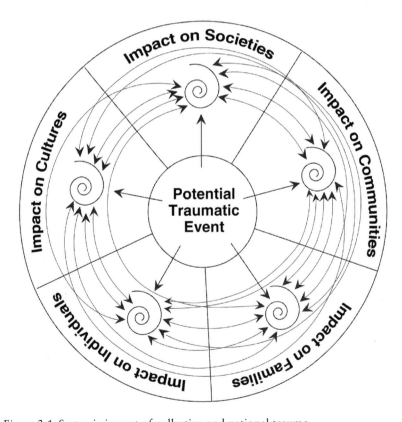

Figure 2.1 Systemic impact of collective and national trauma.

consequences or allow quick adaptation of the system and vice versa. However, as was said previously, the interaction between the damages and negative impact and resilience in each one of the systems exists within the interaction of these forces between the systems.

To sum up, the systemic impact can be described as a "set of hurricane storms" that start at a specific point, which is the location of the potential traumatic event. This has an immediate effect on all systems and the effect creates additional hurricanes (see Figure 2.1). As you can see in Figure 2.1, the systemic impact of a collective and national trauma creates a maze that connects between the various systems in complex ways, challenging the boundaries between these systems. Conceptualizing the impact of the collective and national trauma as a systemic impact calls for interventions, which are guided by systemic assumption, followed by systemic assessment and implementations of the interventions that take into account theoretical and practical knowledge that was developed on the basis of systemic approaches.

Notes

1 Both these national and societal conflicts have long and complicated histories. It is beyond the scope of this book to describe them in detail, but I will provide a general description focusing on their impact on the social and national systems.
2 For example, see the work of WAVE Trauma Center: www.wavetraumacentre. org.uk.
3 The Yishuv was the Jewish community in Palestine under the British Mandate, before Israel became an independent state.
4 To maintain anonymity, this story combines the narratives of three different people, whom I met in Vietnam in 2010. Only one of them was a tour guide.

3

THE ROLE OF MENTAL HEALTH PROFESSIONALS AND SOCIAL WORKERS IN SITUATIONS OF COLLECTIVE AND NATIONAL TRAUMA

One of the most important issues regarding interventions in situations of collective and national trauma is the type of help required to address the basic instrumental and psychosocial needs of the suffering population. An additional issue is the type of professional helpers who are suitable for this task. This chapter addresses the role of mental health professionals and social workers as part of the helping forces in these situations.

In most cases of collective and national trauma, social workers come under the category of mental health helpers. The guidelines on mental health and psychosocial support in emergency settings, developed by the Inter-Agency Standing Committee (IASC) (2007), refer to mental health as a term used mainly by professionals with health-related backgrounds (psychiatrists, clinical and physical psychologists, nurses, clinical and/or psychiatric social workers, etc.) whereas supporting psychosocial well-being is used mainly by social workers and other aid agencies outside the health sector. However, the type of help defined as mental health and supporting psychosocial well-being is often the same or overlapping. A clear definition of each area is based on the specific social context, such as the aid organization or the country in which the traumatic event occurred. Yet, the unique situation of collective and national trauma requires a creative perspective on help, which goes beyond the daily professional interventions provided by helpers from different professional backgrounds.

Mental health professional and social workers have become an integral part of the helping process mainly in the last two decades. This fact leaves us with very simple but crucial questions: Why is the recognition of the importance of mental health and psychosocial support relatively new? And what are the specific roles and characteristics developed in mental and psychosocial health that allow their significant position in the help given to victims of collective trauma?

Recognizing Mental Health Help and Psychosocial Support in Situations of Collective and National Trauma

Regarding the first question, there are several reasons for the relatively recent recognition of the relevance of mental health in the helping forces in situations of collective trauma. The first refers to the recent acknowledgment that trauma can result in psychological damage. It was only in 1980, in the third edition of the *Diagnostic Statistical Manual of Mental Health Disorders (DSM)*, that one of the prevalent mental health impacts of trauma, posttraumatic stress disorder (PTSD), was defined as a clinical diagnosis. Since then, in many cases of collective trauma, mental health interventions have centered on people suffering from PTSD. However, as mentioned earlier, the role of mental health professionals in situations of national and collective trauma is far wider in scope than the focus on psychological symptoms.

Another reason for the late recognition of the need for mental health help centers is that, in many cases, the primary needs of victims of collective trauma are not psychological, but basic physical needs such as food, water, shelter and health care, including prevention of diseases resulting from mass death events and bad sanitary conditions. Mental health help, which is generally concerned with psychological and psychiatric problems, is not usually associated with this type of assistance. Nonetheless, it is important to note that incorporating instrumental help in psychosocial help is an inherent part of the ideology, goals, theories and practice of social work. It is, therefore, natural for social workers to be an integral part of the helping forces and to modify mental health and psychosocial support in a way that takes instrumental help into consideration. This unique function poses a challenge to social workers to define and describe their special and significant roles among the helping forces. Such a description can shed light on the specific help that social workers can provide both under and outside the umbrella of mental health.

A third reason for the relatively new acknowledgment of the importance of social workers and mental health professionals as an integral part of the help forces is the relatively limited and less important place given by society to psychosocial well-being compared to physical needs. Even if the role of mental health in situations of collective and national trauma goes beyond helping those with psychological symptoms, it was mainly the knowledge regarding the psychological impact of trauma, especially the knowledge developed about PTSD, which highlighted the need for psychosocial interventions. PTSD is associated with anxiety, depression, violence and substance abuse (Berenz et al., 2012; Breslau et al., 2000; Budden, 2009; Halpern & Tramontin, 2007; Myers & Wee, 2002;

Resick & Miller, 2009; Shin & Handwerger, 2009). As the presence of these phenomena reduces the probability of spontaneous recovery (Bonanno & Mancini, 2012) and multiplies the damages of the traumatic event, this increased awareness of the important role of mental health aid is relevant and significant for recovery from effects of collective trauma. In addition, knowledge developed regarding typical consequences of collective trauma, such as grief, the grieving process (Neimeyer, 2001) and ambiguous loss (Boss 1999, 2007) broaden the acknowledgment of the need for mental health interventions. However, this significant knowledge still refers to the psychological dimension, which has been perceived as less important than instrumental help.

The change toward the importance of psychological well-being in the shadow of collective traumatic events began when Western cultures, in particular, recognized and acknowledged the important role of psychosocial welfare to the entire well-being of individuals and collectives. It was not only recognition by society, but the understanding of mental health professionals that their types of interventions in situations of collective and national trauma involved elements that are not used regularly in the mental health service. These types of interventions that integrate instrumental and psychosocial aspects of help are an inherent part of social work practice, and focus on the systemic and ecological context as guidelines for intervention. Thus, types of interventions given in situations of collective and national trauma overlap with aid provided usually by social workers.

Specific Roles of Social Workers and Mental Health Professionals

Before describing the social workers' and mental health professionals' roles, I will describe the "not-knowing position" (Anderson & Goolishian, 1992), which I believe to be the preferred stance from which these professionals should approach their role. Accepting the not-knowing position means constant learning from the harmed population about the type of help and the meaning they give to the loss (Neimeyer, 2001). For example, although social workers and mental health professionals have a basis of theoretical and practical knowledge of interventions for situations of collective and national trauma, this knowledge is continuously tested, and needs to be adapted to the specific cultural context, while taking into account the type and intensity of the damage.

Holding the not-knowing position is associated with the strength perspective, which emphasizes people's ability to cope with and adjust to various stressful situations. Thus, one piece of evidence-based knowledge that needed to be in the minds of social workers and mental health professionals is that in spite of the harm and pain, most people are resilient and can either resist the potential damage of traumatic events or cope with them effectively (Bonanno, 2004, 2008; Bonanno & Mancini, 2008, 2012). This implies that the harmed population should be included in all stages of the helping process: in assessing their needs, and planning and implementing both crisis and long-term interventions. This contradicts the paternalistic tendency of certain helping professionals, and therefore needs to be part of the training process of those who intend to work with populations who have experienced collective and national trauma.

In the social work codes of ethics (NASW code of ethics, 2008), there is a clear description of the attitude toward clients, which includes recognition of their dignity and worth. It also states the continuous need for social workers to develop their professional competence by expanding their practical knowledge. Integrating these two aspects of the codes still leaves us with the question regarding the knowing versus not-knowing positions in working with people who experienced collective traumas. The position of knowing *can* respect the victims' dignity and worth. Being in the knowing position requires a basic knowledge of the potential impact of traumatic events on individuals, families and communities, as well as knowledge regarding cultural differences in responses to traumatic events. Based on this knowledge, the helpers are experts, whose professional and personal values brought them to the scene. However, being in the not-knowing position requires an ongoing dialogue between the social workers or mental health professionals and people who directly or indirectly experienced the traumatic event. This dialogue is characterized by equal division of power, meaning that the role of both partners is to exchange knowledge while accepting the superiority of the knowledge presented by the people from the hurt community or society, because they are most familiar with their culture, community and society's characteristics.

I would like the reader to be aware of my use of language in this last paragraph, where I avoid using the word "victim." Instead, I refer to "people from the hurt community or society" or "people who experienced collective trauma." I do not believe the use of the word "victim" to be inaccurate, but the term is often associated with mercy or compassion, which may impact the relationships between the social workers or mental health professionals and the people who are hurt. This would make these relationships hierarchical, pushing the mental health professionals or social workers to their regular position as experts. An expert position might increase the professional tendency to focus on the traumatic outcomes, which often reduces the strength and resiliency of the people who experienced the traumatic event.

Let me illustrate the tendency to be over-compassionate with an example from my home country. For over a hundred years, Israel has experienced an enormous amount of death. Despite the respectful attitude toward bereaved families, there is a tendency to behave in a way that I define as "empathy in the service of avoidance." Expressions of criticism by bereaved persons, through either words or actions, might be attributed to the pain of their loss. The renowned Israeli author, David Grossman, lost his son in the Second Lebanon War in 2006. In one of his speeches, he criticized the Israeli government for its management of the war and for its lack of activity in advancing the peace process. Aware that government ministers and supporters may interpret his criticism as part of his mourning process rather than dealing with its content, he said that, while sadness fills his heart, his brain and ability to think have not been damaged by the loss of his son. Although more than five years have passed since this speech was made in November 2006, during the official memorial ceremony for the assassinated Prime Minister of Israel, Yitzhak Rabin, these words continue to resonate within me. They serve as a guiding light in my research and practice with people who experienced collective trauma. These people are not only the focus of the assessment and the emergent intervention, but it is they who can direct social workers and mental health professionals to the best methods and tactics. (For example, which questions should be asked, based on the cultural context, to assess the level of damage and resilience resources? Where should one look for leaders or possible leaders?). Only the hurt population can evaluate whether the assessment is appropriate to their situations and needs. Rather than the term "empowerment," which is often used by practitioners in the area of mental health and social work in situations of collective and national trauma, I prefer the term "inclusion," which does not imply hierarchical relationships.

The role of social workers and mental health professionals can be characterized by the following areas: 1) protecting human rights; 2) reestablishing social support within the community; 3) restructuring routine; and 4) providing mental health/psychosocial services.

Protecting Human Rights

As the basic aid needed in many situations of collective trauma is instrumental (food, water, shelters, physical health, etc.), it does not come under the role definition of social workers and mental health professionals. However, it is not totally beyond their responsibility (de Jong, 2002), as their role does include assessment of how to distribute resources to meet the basic needs. Such assessment should include detailed information regarding the way the instrumental help is divided among the needy population, and to ensure that the distribution method does not exclude some vulnerable groups. In assessing human rights, it is also important to find out whether clear information exists regarding the times and places of distribution and whether vulnerable populations have access to this information. Social workers and mental health professionals must function as coordinators between the different organizations that supply the basic necessities and contact the relevant institutions if such help is not provided, or in the case of a shortage. In addition, their role is to be involved in establishing a fair distribution system based on equal amounts for the entire population or according to specific needs, such as age group, health condition, level of damage, etc. As often happens in situations of collective trauma (described in the previous chapter by Mr Henry Elkasslasy's report), aid does not reach the people for whom it is intended, when powerful groups, which are often armed, forcibly take control of the material aid (food, clothing, shelters, etc.) and sell it on the black market. In other cases, powerful groups commandeer the distribution process and provide aid only to small and exclusive groups. In creating such a system, it is important to provide guidance for the organizers. When sharing his experiences in providing emergent help in many places of collective trauma, Mr Elkasslasy stated as follows:

> first, people have to eat and to know that they are going to have food . . . when they are hungry, they tend to be violent and this is understandable. They might kill for food . . . but if they are not hungry, then you can start working with them to develop other services that their people need.

Outcomes of collective trauma may create chaos within the hurt society, which may cause different kinds of violent behavior toward vulnerable populations. Rape, child exploitation, robbery and killing of minority groups are all prevalent phenomena when the structure of society is destroyed. The combination of anger and despair experienced by the hurt society along with the destruction or overwhelming of social institutions responsible for law and order is fertile ground for the development of violent behavior. The role of mental health and social workers is first to identify such violation of human rights for safety, then to expose it to the public and guide local organizations to act against it by challenging the leaders to take as much legal action as possible against violent groups and create special services that provide help for their victims. Although both types of actions are needed, most of the mental health help is provided through services for the victims of violence. It is possible that mental health professionals and social workers have more experience in treating people who were exposed to traumatic events than in convincing legal authorities to act specifically to protect all groups in the hurt community or society. Furthermore, in some places, the violent groups may be in close contact with the authorities, or may threaten those responsible for taking legal action against the violent groups. However, in spite of these difficulties, challenging the legal authorities to protect the entire population against violence of specific groups who take advantage of the crisis remains a central role for social workers and mental health professionals.

A special dilemma that may confront social workers and mental health professionals is in offering help to populations in non-democratic countries. Some of these countries refuse outside assistance, especially from Western and other democratic countries, but when the situation becomes unbearable and severe outside criticism creates some threat to the regime, they may accept limited help from various organizations. It is rare to find social workers and mental health professionals among these restricted helping forces. However, if they are present, they have to take into account that great caution is required when encouraging people to share their experiences, feelings and thoughts—a tool used frequently in mental health and psychosocial help. In these locations, people cooperating with the non-democratic regime might inform on people who appear to be criticizing the government or cooperating with foreigners. It is almost impossible to guide helping professionals in how to initiate conversations with the hurt population, but caution is necessary when asking open questions, as well as awareness of signals that the conversation should end. Such caution is needed also when helping people who escaped from areas of persecution, but left families behind, who might be identified and punished. However, when the helping intervention ends and the helping delegations return, it is still the social workers' role to act as social agents and to report to various human rights organizations regarding the limitations of freedom and other rights denied to the population.

Reestablishing Social Support Within the Community

The second role of social workers and mental health professionals is the reestablishment of community support. Substantial evidence shows that social support is a significant buffer to stress (Kaniasty, 2012; Morgan, 2002). Therefore, it is important to identify natural resources of social support in the damaged population. In most cases, it is the community's leaders who can help to create various support systems for people and groups in the community. In some cultures, they will be people in religious roles; in others, they might be people who previously held public roles in education, politics, health, etc. When identifying these leaders, the social workers and mental health professionals need to assist these people to recreate the natural support system that used to exist in the community. Along with this role, both social workers and mental health professionals need to avoid any tendency to take over the role of the natural leaders of any system. Leaders might have been killed, separated from the community, or be physically and/or mentally incapable of assuming the leadership role. Such a situation might tempt helpers to offer their own leadership skills, which is definitely not their role. Instead, they must look for people in the community who can take over the challenge of leadership during the emergent time. Bohem, Enosh and Shamai (2010) found that communities in situations of crisis seek grass-roots leaders, not necessarily officials who work according to a formal definition of their role. People in emergent situations look for leaders who are responsive to the changing needs, are close to the people as a whole and have open communication channels with them. It may sometimes appear as if all the leaders of the community have vanished, but in such emergent situations, it is not unusual to discover people who were not in any leadership circle before the traumatic event, but who have the charisma and appropriate characteristics that enable them to rise to the challenge of leadership in such painful situations. Such people may need the support of the social workers and mental health professionals in setting the leadership in motion and expanding their activities.

In the process of identifying and searching for the community leaders, it is important to take human rights into consideration. Understanding leadership issues of power and responsibility is yet another task of the helping systems. This includes information regarding the following questions: Who are in power in the system? Was power received legitimately or through the use of immoral tactics? Are they using their power to benefit the entire system or only small, exclusive groups? Foucault (1980) claimed that power is an essential characteristic of every relationship and every social system. Thus, the existence of power within a system is inherent, and is not necessary good or bad; it is the way that the power is used that defines it as good, bad, moral, or immoral. The people in power in each system can modify the system's activities, such as the ways of transferring information and social support, which might include or exclude certain populations. It can be concluded that the natural leaders within any system or subsystem can be the best source of social support if their leadership is characterized by fairness and respect toward the people as a whole.

It is assumed that the different types of traumatic events have different impacts on the natural social support resources. A community that stays together is most likely to identify the natural institutions providing social support, such as religious and educational institutions, formal and grass-roots leaders, and other types of community organizations. In addition, discussions with the local people can direct helping professionals to informal resources of community support, and family and friends are often a meaningful and significant source of support to individuals. Along with identifying the systems' resources of social support, there is an emergent need to find out whether these resources may still be available after the event, and whether they need additional help that can be given by social workers and mental health professionals. Sometimes, the natural resources of social support were destroyed, for example, in cases of evacuation or when many community members were killed and the entire community structure was destroyed. In such situations, it is important to establish formal and informal institutions that are familiar with the culture of the population and can provide social support. Several factors need to be taken into account when establishing resources for social support or when supporting existing resources:

Meeting the Special Needs of Vulnerable Populations

Vulnerable populations, such as children, older adults, the sick and people with low socioeconomic status need special attention regarding characteristics of social support. In cases where families have been separated or when parents have been killed, children, older adults and sick people must have a caring system. When possible, social workers and mental health professionals must support the reunion of families. In other cases, an alternative caring system is needed, based on familiar faces or at least, on people familiar with the culture of the previous support system. Effective social support gives the sense of being loved and a sense of belonging. According to Maslow (1954) and Towle (1945), these follow the basic instrumental needs. Although providing basic physical needs is not among the roles of mental health helpers, providing the conditions that create the sense of love and belonging is an essential part of mental health and psychosocial help.

Social Support as a Systemic Process

Social support is a systemic process (Kaniasty, 2012). Therefore, when assessing the level and types of social support within a specific system, it is necessary to focus on the structure of the systems, which includes assessing the boundaries between the specific system (such as family, community, etc.) and larger systems (state, nation, etc.), or systems and subsystems (parents–children, leaders–population). Rigid boundaries prevent information and communication from entering the system, whereas fused boundaries might risk the structure or even the existence of the system. Potentially traumatic events may lead systems to one of the extremes; some systems close their borders and refuse to receive help and social support. The reasons for closing borders depend mainly on formal and informal political decisions. Some systems perceive the need for outside support as a sign of weakness. Others, mainly totalitarian systems, fear exposure to the outside world and jeopardize those in power. Several examples can illustrate this: The first focuses on a large system: the state of Myanmar. Cyclone Nargis hit Myanmar on May 2, 2008, causing catastrophic destruction including over 100,000 fatalities, thousands of missing persons, total eradication of towns and villages, including many rice fields, which were the main food supply for the Myanmar population. The military rulers of Myanmar were afraid to expose the population to the outside world and for a relatively long time, prevented most of the help that was provided by different nations and various organizations from reaching its target. Furthermore, they closed the affected area to the media and did not allow anyone from this area out to report the enormous amount of damage and the unproductive rescue activities.

The second illustration focuses on a kibbutz, a collective community in Israel, located in the Carmel Mountains. In December 2010, a large wildfire spread rapidly over a very wide area. The population on the Carmel was evacuated and approximately 30% of the kibbutz houses were destroyed. A small group of people who remained in the area saved it from total destruction. The evacuated population was hosted in a local hotel and began to organize a daily routine. They were open to instrumental contributions (clothes, games, cosmetics, etc.). However, when social workers and educational psychologists from the regional municipality tried to contact the leaders to find out whether further assistance was required, the leaders either avoided contact or rejected the help. An informal discussion with one of the leaders clarified the reasons for this rejection. First, it was very important to the leaders that the community would be perceived as strong; receiving outside help, especially from mental health professionals, was a sign of weakness. Second, some of the leaders were afraid that previous conflict within the community would surface and increase in intensity in the present crisis. The social workers praised the effective functioning of the community that had been forced to evacuate, and expressed their strong appreciation of the group of people who stayed in their homes, continued to fight the fire and saved approximately 70% of the kibbutz buildings. In addition, they mentioned this community's special place in the history of the State of Israel, as the first shelter for Jews who escaped from Europe during the Holocaust and attempted illegal entry into Palestine under the British Mandate. The number of Jews allowed to enter the country was limited, even if this meant returning them to Europe. This attitude reduced the leaders' anxiety and they agreed to accept outside help. They shared some of their concerns regarding further help in social issues, including the creation of a support system for old and sick people, creating a daily routine for the education system in a strange place, and preparing the population for the return home. The social workers' and educational psychologists' ability to appreciate the strong aspects of the system and, confirming their capability to deal with the crisis, opened the door to cooperation with the professional help. The social workers and psychologists stayed with the evacuated community, and without pushing themselves, talked to the people and the leaders while creating an equal discourse that led to joint work in the process of managing and coping with the crisis. The basic trust between the community members and leaders allowed the development of long-term intervention that helped them to deal with the losses, to work toward rehabilitation and to grow from the crisis. In the second illustration, receiving social support was culturally constructed as weak, which is in keeping with Israeli culture and especially with the culture of collective and cooperative communities in Israel (kibbutzim and moshavim). It is beyond the scope of this book to explain the origins of this culture, but the social workers' and psychologists' attempts to learn about the community's culture from its people, their acknowledgment of and respect for its resiliency and the ability to provide sensitive cultural help allowed the system to open its boundaries to accept the aid. These two illustrations focused on large-scale systems—nation and community—but the connection between types of boundaries (rigid, clear, or fused) impacts the ability to receive and provide social support in systems of all types and sizes. The type of social support and the way it is perceived is culturally constructed and depends on the location and context of the system.

Restructuring Routine

Structuring the daily routine is essential to preserving well-being and preventing severe traumatic consequences. Although most of the literature describing the role of social workers and mental health professionals does not directly specify this task, it is implicitly mentioned in the descriptions of risk factors in situations of collective trauma and when discussing well-being in general. Yet, many protocols of crisis interventions in situations of collective trauma include tasks that aim to create routine. The role of routine as an empowering coping tool could be explained by various approaches and theories that deal with health and stress. Based on Melanie Klein (1946), it is possible to assume that the routine might represent the "whole object," which was not destroyed by the external and internal consequences of the traumatic event. Another explanation of the impact of the routine is based on the Conservation of Resources Theory (COR, Hobfoll, 2001). The ability to create routine is proof of preservation of resources, despite the stressful situation, therefore preventing escalation of stress. Thus, the creation of a partial routine, although different from usual, can reduce some of the chaos resulting from war. In some events, the daily routine seems to continue without many interruptions, for example, during the many terror attacks on civilians in Israel between 2001 and 2005. The population was shocked, and many people called their family members, relatives, or friends if they expected them to be in the area of attack, and many people tended to spend far more time than usual watching the media. However, the education, transportation and communication systems continued to function, and people still went to work. People discussed the horror of the attacks. Teachers discussed it with their students. Adults and children who were close to the event or to victims were able to receive mental support via the health systems or various non-profit organizations, but the daily routine continued. This was the case in most parts of the United States and even in various parts of New York City after 9/11. However, one may wonder whether it is possible to restructure a routine in situations of traumatic events in which a large number of people are killed, are evacuated from their homes, and/or lose their entire property due to war (Bosnia during the closing decades of the 20th century, Darfur during the first decades of the 21st) or natural disaster (Hurricane Katrina, the 2010 earthquake in Haiti, or the 2011 earthquake/tsunami in Japan). It is my belief that in many situations of traumatic events, the return to the pre-event routine is impossible, but it is possible to help people to create a temporary routine. This might not be similar to their original routine, but gives structure to their time and some meaning to their lives.

It is important to note that most of the restructuring activities focus on children—not necessarily because children are considered a more vulnerable population than adults—but because they are more responsive to such activities, and in many cases, receive their parents' approval. Based on specific studies of the impact of war on children (Garbarino & Kostelny, 1996; Garbarino, Kostelny & Dubrow, 1991; Osofsky, 1997; Shamai & Kimhi, 2006), organizing a routine also conveys to the children that the adults, even if partially damaged, are still dependable figures and able to offer support. In addition, some routine activities, such as playing, painting, etc., might help the children to reenact or work through some of the traumatic experiences. Some examples of restructuring routines for children follow.

The first was in Palestine in April 1948, a month before the British Mandate ended and Israel became an independent Jewish state. Kibbutz Mishmar HaEmek was under heavy cannon fire by the Arab Liberation Army. After two days, the British imposed a truce to evacuate the wounded and the children from the kibbutz. The children of Mishmar HaEmek, as in other kibbutz communities in Israel, were raised in what was called "collective education." According to this ideology, child-rearing responsibility was transferred from the parents to the community as a whole, and the children were cared for by a specially trained caregiver, or nanny (*metapelet*) and teachers. Each age group lived in a communal building called a "children's house," which was operated by a *metapelet* and a teacher. Both these figures were defined as educators, and were dominant in the children's daily life. Every afternoon, the children spent four to five hours at their parents' homes, but slept in the children's houses at night (Shamai, 2012). Therefore, the children were evacuated with their entire age group and their educators to other communities in the area, mainly to other kibbutzim. On arrival in the hosting communities, the educators immediately created a routine for the children: they studied during school hours, organized social activities, as they were used to doing at home and received age-appropriate information regarding the battle at the kibbutz. Although the fighting ended after ten days, the children stayed in the host communities for another three months until the children's houses were renovated following the severe damage. During this time, their parents visited them only once a week. Sixty-one years later, when I interviewed people who were children during the attack, I discovered that, in spite of their longing for their parents and their home, none of them had developed either PTSD or other traumatic symptoms. All of them mentioned the belief among the adults in the community that establishing a routine was the best way to deal with the event. In addition, some of them added that knowledge about consequences of traumatic events was scarce among the educators at that time, but they had the natural intuition to take simple but helpful action (Shamai, 2012).

It is possible to minimize the first illustration on the grounds that it provides an example of a special collective community that exists only in Israel and its organization enabled the creation of routine under war and evacuation. Thus, the second example is brought from a refugee camp, populated mostly by people from Kosovo, during the war between Kosovo and Yugoslavia (at that time, mainly Serbia) in 1999. The camp was operated mainly by helping forces sent by NATO member states and some groups from other countries, including Israel. The Israeli group included young adults, aged 22–30, who had experience as young guides in various youth organizations in Israel. They were responsible for organizing educational activities for children and adolescents. These activities were not like those of the regular school or kindergarten, but created some structure in the disordered and uncertain situation. The activities included two sessions each day: in the morning, mainly arts and crafts, and in the afternoon, centered on drama and dance, focusing on the children's experiences. Thus, many of the plays produced and acted by the children and helpers ended with the appearance of the NATO forces, who saved them. Through the art activities, the children had the opportunity to work through their painful experiences. Whenever possible, the organizers tried to arrange the different activities according to the children's age groups, and to include the adolescents in their organization. Although the parents were informed of the time and place of the children's and adolescents' activities, the organizers would walk around the camp about an hour before they were due to start, to remind the parents and invite the children to participate. These repeated invitations were based on observations by the helpers that most of the parents were depressed, desperate, or even bored, resulting in passivity. Thus, they did not always pay attention to time, to specific activities in the camp, and to their children's needs, beyond the basic necessities of food and clothing. Instead of blaming these parents, the helpers drew their attention to the activities being arranged. Most of the parents, especially of young children, joined in with the activities, which enabled the mental health professionals present to do some work with the parents.

The third example focuses on creating routine for adults. After the tsunami that hit Sri Lanka in 2004, helpers arrived from Natan—the Israeli Network for International Humanitarian Aid. The following is an excerpt from Mr Henry Elkasslasy's description:

> We brought food supplies and built a kitchen, as thousands of people had lost their homes and had nowhere to cook . . . then there were many chefs and waiters who used to work in the hotels in the area and we suggested that they come and pre-pare the food with us . . . As the concept of volunteering is unknown in this part of the world, we first explained to them that we were also volunteers and were receiving no payment for our work, and that they would be doing this for their own people and for themselves. They agreed, and instead of doing nothing all day and dwelling on the pain and the loss, they had something to keep them busy. After the earthquake in Haiti in 2010, we helped to build a school, a public school in St. Mary . . . there was no public education in Haiti; most schools were private . . . and we invited teachers from the community to teach and run the school.

These three examples show that restructuring the routine after a collec-tive traumatic event is possible, even if it is not the regular routine but is adapted to the situation, the conditions and the needs. Although people without mental health training can restructure routine activities, the presence at the scene of social workers and mental health professionals can lead to positive by-products, mainly by offering mental health and psychosocial intervention for those affected by the trauma.

Providing Mental Health/Psychosocial Services

The fourth role of social workers and mental health professionals has dual focus, which includes assessing the psychosocial state and level of mental health of the harmed population while providing crisis interven-tion. The assessment is the basis for designing interventions, but in the short term, most of the interventions are not fully planned and are often based on the helpers' intuition and experience. These kinds of unplanned and intuitive interventions are one of the main characteristics of the helping process in situations of collective trauma. These interventions are somewhat similar to the model of crisis interventions (Caplan, 1964) that is adjusted to specific situations according to the cultural context, the type of traumatic event and characteristics of mental health and psychosocial damages.

As mentioned earlier, assessment is not a separate phase of the helping process; it is performed in parallel to the actual acts of helping and can be defined as a circle in which crisis intervention and assessment are mutually enriching. Thus, mental health and social work helpers have to assess the following areas:

1   The people's experiences of the event, which includes their perception of the damages created, perceived causes of the event and short- and long-term consequences.
2   Signs of psychological distress, such as withdrawal, disorientation, emotional arousal, aggressiveness, sleep problems, excessive use of alcohol and drugs as well as other indicators of distress that are typical to the local culture. In assessing the level of psychological distress, it is important to take into consideration the normal reactions to loss, based on the local cultural norms.
3   Ways of coping, which include religious and political belief systems, receiving and providing social support, narratives regarding adversity (how populations dealt with stressful situations in the past).

During assessment, it is important to start crisis intervention, which includes the following actions:

1   Reaching out to people in distress through community leaders and volunteers.
2   Direct meetings with the population, where they could share their pain and be heard and supported. Immediate unofficial guidance for parents or relatives regarding children and adolescents. Guidance of local leaders in providing support and referring people in need to emergent mental health services.
3   Establishment of services that provide emergent mental health help to individuals, families and groups that include local professionals or volunteers and informing the population about the exact location of the service, and the type of difficulties that may be entitled to help in the service.

In the last decade, crisis intervention following a collective traumatic event was named "Psychological First Aid" or "Early Psychological Intervention." However, I prefer to use the term "crisis intervention," as all these early interventions include areas that go beyond the psychological domain. This is illustrated by the following example: On March 5, 2003, a suicide bomber boarded a bus in the city of Haifa and detonated an explosive belt. The terrorist chose the hour at which many high school students use this bus line on their way home from school. Seventeen people were killed—mostly teenagers aged 14–17. Shortly after first aid forces reopened the scene of the explosion, hundreds of teenagers and adults arrived to light candles, place flowers and letters and just sat there, crying. Social workers joined the teenagers and asked about their relationships with the victims, about their feelings, about their plans for attending the funerals, etc. For an entire week, the teenagers continued to visit and spend time at the scene, paralleling the *shiva* week in Jewish tradition, the official first stage of the grieving process, when the bereaved sit at home and receive visitors. Social workers remained there during this week. They listened to them, provided support and encouraged them to visit the victims' families. In addition, especially in the schools whose students had lost their lives, teachers received guidance from educational psychologists as to how to introduce discussions about loss and mourning in the classroom and how to refer students, who needed further help, to the educational psychologists.

Regarding the families of the victims, a clear protocol exists based on previous terror events in Israel in general and in Haifa in particular (Ron & Shamai, 2011; Shamai & Ron, 2009) and was implemented in this case. First, social workers assisted families to search for missing loved ones in the three main hospitals in the city. In each hospital, social workers formed an information center regarding the injured people. This process often took some hours, as this specific type of terror attack caused severe damage to the bodies, resulting in identification difficulties. In addition, many of the injured were unconscious and were rushed to the operating theaters immediately, without means of identification. Meanwhile, the social workers talked to the families in an attempt to collect as many details as possible to identify the injured or the dead. If a person was not found in any of the hospitals, the family was asked to go to the morgue. A team of social workers was sent to the morgue immediately after the first aid helpers publicized the fatalities, to prepare to receive the desperately anxious families. In addition, two social workers accompanied each family whose loved one had not been found in one of the hospitals. Due to the type of the terror event, identifying the bodies was a complicated process and many families were asked to bring additional information, such as tooth X-rays, which could be of assistance. Throughout this process, the social workers supported the families by being with them at this chaotic time. Some families, unable to accept the terrible reality, still believed that a miracle would happen and that their loved one would not be found in the morgue, but would somehow be discovered in the hospital or at the home of a friend. After the body was identified, social workers helped the family with the funeral arrangements, including any special requirements, such as babysitting for young children who would not be participating. They guided parents in how to break the news of the death to younger children in the family. In some cases, the social workers provided brief intervention for the bereaved families, and in other cases, referred children from these families to educational psychologists. Brief intervention was provided by social workers or health psychologists for injured people during the period of hospitalization.

Specific characteristics, a detailed guide and examples of crisis intervention will be described in the following chapter, which will address various types of systemic intervention for the short- and long-term. The long-term role of the mental health professional focuses on rehabilitation and dealing with posttraumatic stress of both systems and individuals. Another role of mental health professionals and social workers is to support mental health services that existed before the traumatic event or that were established as part of the early intervention. As illustrated above, some locations have mental health and social work services available, with professionals trained to function in situations of collective trauma. In these cases, it is important to support those helpers who provide the intensive assistance (this will be discussed in detail in Chapter 5). In situations where mental health services were not developed or were severely damaged, the role of the external mental health helper is to train people in the community and provide ongoing guidance and supervision for the local professional people in their long-term intervention with the harmed population.

In sum, the role of the mental health and psychosocial helpers can be described as a ladder, on which the first step is protecting human rights in general, particularly regarding accessibility to instrumental help. This is followed by identifying local community leaders, reestablishing social support within the community, restructuring the routine based on the type and severity of the damage, and providing psychosocial first aid (crisis interventions). Once the needs of the population are assessed, the mental health and psychosocial services can be established and strengthened to provide emergent and long-term help.

Part II

MENTAL HEALTH AND PSYCHOSOCIAL SYSTEMIC INTERVENTIONS IN SITUATIONS OF COLLECTIVE AND NATIONAL TRAUMA

4

SYSTEMIC INTERVENTION IN SITUATIONS OF COLLECTIVE AND NATIONAL TRAUMA

Systemic Intervention: The Basic Principle

As systemic intervention relates to interactions, feedback and context, the response of micro or macro systems (couples, families, groups, communities, nations or societies) to potential collective/national traumatic events is understood according to the following data:

1   the context in which the specific response was constructed;
2   how the response interacts with the contextual norms and values;
3   how the system interacts with larger relevant systems in the context (for example, interactions between the community and the governing authorities or between families and volunteer organizations).

Systemic thinking, in general, includes concepts from various theories and approaches, including General System Theory (von Bertalanffy, 1968), Cybernetics (Weiner, 1948), Constructivism (Kelly, 1955) and Social Constructionism (Gergen, 1994). An integration of the different concepts can be a useful guide to understanding human behavior both in regular and stressful situations, and can be the basis on which interventions can be formed.

General system theory (von Bertalanffy, 1968) provides basic concepts and assumptions that have shaped, and continue to shape, systemic thinking. For several decades, General System Theory assumptions have been shaping family and community interventions for populations living with ongoing stress, such as poverty or illness (McDaniel, Hepworth & Doherty, 1992; Minuchin et al., 1967; Rolland, 1994; Sharlin & Shamai, 2000; Shamai, 1998). Thus, these assumptions might also impact understanding, assessment and interventions in situations of collective and national trauma. It is important to indicate that many psychosocial and mental health interventions in situations of collective and national trauma might appear, on the surface, to be systemic interventions because their targets are mainly systems, such as communities and societies

(Brave Heart, 1998; Halpern & Tramontin, 2007; Saul, 2013; Zinner & Williams, 1999). However, the principles behind these interventions, which include assumptions regarding the impact of the traumatic event, the assessment, and the entire sets of intervention goals, are not based on the assumption and principle of system theory. Most of these interventions are based on research that focuses on the results of collective trauma and mainly on practical experiences, but lack a theoretical framework. One may ask why the theoretical framework is important when help is urgently needed. Is it not only the need of those who analyze and research collective trauma but also the need of the helping forces? I think that a theoretical framework can modify the assessment process, the goal and the evaluation of the intervention, even if the techniques used are similar to systemic and other types of interventions. As an example, let us take an intervention within the school system after a traumatic event to reduce its impact and identify children at risk of developing traumatic stress symptoms. If such intervention is conducted based on studies and practical experience of interventions in situations of collective trauma, the basic target population will be the children, who, in many studies, have been found to be a high-risk population (Apfel & Simon, 1996; Halpern & Tramontin, 2007; Osofsky, 1997). The person implementing the interventions with the children will be either someone from within the school system, such as the school psychologist, counselor, or educator. However, if the intervention is implemented within the systemic framework, the first question that will be asked is regarding the target population: Is it only the children, or the children together with their immediate support system, such as parents and families? How will these immediate systems be involved in the process? What is the place of the school as a system in providing support or other types of help to the children? Who are the figures in the school who need to be part of providing such help? These types of questions originate in systemic thinking and require a different direction of assessment than interventions based solely on trauma theories, even if parts of or even the entire intervention may be similar.

Some of the system theory assumptions that are most relevant to interventions in potential collective traumatic situations are discussed below.

A system is more than the sum of its parts because it includes the interactions between each individual part and all the other parts.

These interactions have an impact on each individual part as well as on the entire structure and processes of the system. The type of interaction between the parts of the systems can explain why a certain response to the traumatic event is experienced as a difficulty or a problem. Responses of people within the system and in the surrounding systems to an individual, group, community, or nation can often define behaviors and thoughts as "right" or "wrong," "normal" or "not normal." These definitions are not objective and depend on the relationships within and between the systems, and on other systems. This is true also when suggesting any kind of interventions for part or all of the system. The types of interaction between parts of the system may determine whether the suggestion will be accepted and followed. Therefore, when working with either micro or macro systems, it is important to look at each part separately as well as at the interactions between them. Working according to this principle has significant meaning for mental health interventions in situations of collective trauma, and I will illustrate this by describing some of the debates among mental health professionals in Israel.

As a result of the ongoing war situation and terror attacks, higher rates of PTSD than previously are being reported in Israel among people living close to the line of fire. Analysis of this information from the point of view of the individuals involved usually focuses on their biological and psychological characteristics. The interventions provided often include medicinal and/or psychological treatment and sometimes advice and guidance for family members or other close friends. It is important to note that different types of individual therapies were found to be effective in situations of PTSD. These include Prolonged Exposure Therapy (PE), developed by Edna Foa (Foa, 2011; Nayak, Power & Foa, 2012), based on cognitive behavior principles, and Eye Movement Desensitization and Reprocessing (EMDR), which is used extensively, despite widespread criticism (Engelhard et al., 2010; Hoffman, 2010). Based on this individual analysis, the claim that the percentage of PTSD is on the increase may be accurate. However, analysis from a systemic point of view will go beyond the individual and will raise questions regarding the context in which higher rates of PTSD are found. The systemic view will take into consideration social, cultural and contextual elements, which may increase or decrease the tendency to define specific symptoms or behavior as PTSD. According to the social constructionism (Gergen, 1994) approach, it is necessary to identify the types of relationships, within the particular context, which give rise to the specific narrative and emotions that construct PTSD symptoms. It is also necessary to assess the social narrative that constructs specific feelings, thoughts and behavior as pathology in general and PTSD in particular. The cybernetic point of view (Weiner, 1948) will look for the feedback loop between members within a system that increases or decreases behaviors defined as PTSD, as well as between different professional systems, both medical and psychological, that develop definitions of behavioral and emotional characteristics that construct the PTSD diagnosis.

The following areas of inquiry can provide examples of this direction of systemic analysis:

1   Who is the target population, within a micro or macro system, for this specific information regarding PTSD?

2   What is the purpose of exposing the information? In other words, how will this information impact the different parts of the system (in this case, Israeli society) and the interactions between them?

3   There are several tools available for measuring PTSD, but the outcome sometimes depends on the tool itself rather than on the patient's symptoms. What are the reasons for choosing a specific type of instrument? Could there be a political motive behind this choice? For example, a specific measurement tool that paints a more serious picture of the rate of PTSD might direct policy-makers' attention to the suffering population, leading to the development of intervention programs for its welfare and well-being.

4   Are expressions of traumatic stress widely accepted? Up to the end of the 1970s, expressions of fear and anxiety in response to war or terror attacks were unacceptable in Israeli society. Since then, mainly due to new knowledge acquired in the area of trauma, and greater recognition of the importance of mental health and well-being, the public attitude has gradually changed. Various governmental and NGO services providing mental health help have been developed. During wars or army operations as well as after terror attacks, television and radio advertise telephone numbers that people can call to obtain help and information, teachers discuss fear and anxiety in the classroom, and articles describing the services are published in the written media. All this has legitimized the general acknowledgment of traumatic stress symptoms, especially among non-combatants. Therefore, it may be that it is not the number of people with PTSD that has grown, but the number of people who report it, due to the contextual changes that allow the expression of anxiety.

5   What contextual scientific knowledge exists regarding impact of potential traumatic events and how does it affect mental health providers? As noted in previous chapters, it is only in the last thirty years that the knowledge regarding the PTSD phenomenon has expanded and has received significant visibility in the field of mental health. It may be that the assessment of PTSD was made possible when the community of mental health helpers and social workers developed awareness of the phenomenon. The significant place that PTSD has since acquired in the professional system might have led helpers to look for specific symptoms that would enable them to reach an interdisciplinary consensus. This is despite the research evidence that PTSD is present in only a very small percentage of the population (Bonanno, 2004; Bonanno & Mancini, 2008, 2012).

6   What is the role of those people in the system who suffer from traumatic stress? Do they unconsciously set limits for the system

regarding the level of extra pressure with which it can cope? It is possible that those who take on the "traumatized" role allow other members of the system to assume the role of helpers, which enables them to disconnect from their own fears and anxiety (Shamai, 1994, 2001). Many studies show that women and children are considered to be at higher risk for developing PTSD (Fullerton et al., 2001; Norris et al., 2002; Seedat & Stein, 2000). The results of these studies raise the following questions: What is the specific role of women and children within different human systems that makes them vulnerable to developing symptoms in response to traumatic effect? What are the roles of these symptoms within any specific system? In regard to the women, a possible claim is that being in the role of the "weak" or of "needing protection" supports the social order that perceives men as strong and women as weak, placing men in a powerful position in society, especially in times of war. Do the women unconsciously cooperate with this traditional social order by developing symptoms characterized by the need to be protected, including some which characterize PTSD? The men in the role of protectors are able to deny their own fears and anxiety, and as a result, preserve their well-being. As to the role of children's vulnerability, it is possible that, by expressing feelings of discomfort, anxiety, or anger, they release the parents from experiencing their own feelings of this nature, thus helping them to preserve their parental status. However, through concern for the children's well-being, they can still work through these feelings (Shamai, 2001).

7   Another question that can be asked is: What are the outcomes of this traumatized role for the structure and interaction between the subsystems? For instance, on the national system level, before going ahead with an army operation, many politicians weigh up the population's ability to face the inevitable stress involved.

In sum, PTSD not only reflects the individual, but also symbolizes the distress of the entire system. Therefore, systemic interventions go beyond the individual to the system as a whole. Any systemic intervention will assess the function of the interactions between the parts of the system that are a result of collective or national trauma, and will make use of these interactions in planning and performing intervention.

Every system is part of a larger system and often includes smaller subsystems.

This assumption can be viewed as the basic account for systemic intervention in situations of collective trauma. In these situations, systemic intervention is not only a practical necessity, which relies on the inability to provide mental health help to large numbers of individuals. It also has a theoretical background that perceives each person as related to a system, which is related to a larger system and so on. Therefore, a community that experienced disaster may expect to receive assistance from the larger system, such as the state, and will expect the help provided to be useful to smaller systems within the community, such as the local education or health systems. Although the mutual support between subsystems is positive, it can also be an obstacle to the help process, as apparent in the following examples.

A fire destroyed many houses in a community, and all the residents had to leave their homes for several days. The fire took place during the winter school vacation. The educational psychologists and counselors, who worked together in the local school, met with the children and encouraged them to describe their experiences. They also assessed whether some children needed individual therapy sessions. In addition, they met with the parents of each class to discuss their experiences as parents, as well as their perceptions of their children's difficulties and strengths and provided guidance on request. The educational psychologists met with the teachers before the end of the vacation, to help them plan how to welcome the children back, how to deal with the issue in the different classes and how to relate to children who displayed more distress. This type of intervention was apparently very effective for all concerned. The teachers reported that meeting with the educational psychologists increased their confidence to discuss with their students about the pain and stress created by the fire. They were able to discuss anxiety and fears openly and they indicated that this was helpful not only professionally, but also personally, enabling discussion among their families. The parents also reported finding the meeting with the educational psychologist helpful beyond their parental role—with their personal coping, as spouses and as friends of others in the community. This example illustrates how community intervention with a specific system—the school—impacted other systems in the community, such as families, individuals and their friends. One element that contributed to the success of this intervention was the psychologists, who could be defined as a subsystem within the community education system, which was also part of the overall community system. The intervention did not stop here, however. Since the community was a subsystem of the state, the Ministry of Health sent "experts" to assess the children's mental health. These experts were not acquainted with the teachers, the counselors, the parents, or the children, and their visit created tension with the school system. Their examination of the assessment and intervention performed by the community professionals undermined the position of the community educational psychologist. The state system considered itself to be caring and responsible for its citizens, but this intervention was perceived as not genuine and merely to show that "the state was doing something." From a systemic point of view, before sending experts into a traumatized area, the state needs first to be aware of the structure and processes of the community system, including professional subsystems, and only then make a joint decision about the needs of the community. This act by the state can symbolize the power of one subsystem over another, an issue mentioned in the previous chapters when discussing the characteristics of collective trauma and the role of mental health professionals in situations of collective and national trauma. The issue of use and misuse of power will be discussed further in this chapter when addressing specific descriptions and offering a guide to systemic interventions in various different systems.

A social constructionist perception of this event would focus on the relationships among the people in the community, allowing the educational psychologists to feel competent to perform their work in crisis situations. Social constructionism would also focus on the narratives and emotions of children, parents, teachers and adults as they were constructed during and after the disaster, based on the relationships between the different community subsystems, which were developed into a discourse that shaped narrative and emotion. From the specific illustration, we can assume that the educational subsystem had the community members' trust. It knew how to solve problems effectively in a way that was accepted by parents, children and teachers, resulting in a very small number of children and parents who manifested pathological symptoms.

Systems tend to maintain homeostasis. However, human systems as opposed to mechanical or physical systems respond to expected or unexpected ecological changes.

The idea behind this principle is that human systems, like other systems, tend to maintain stability. Therefore, changes in rules, roles, world-view and power distribution will usually not change until some internal or external event forces the system to act differently in order to exist. In contrast to physical or chemical systems, human systems can make these changes, but this often involves a complicated process that will be carried out only following internal or external pressure.

Taking this principle into consideration can guide both the assessment and the intervention, as it gives some structure to the understanding of systems prior to potential traumatic events and thus, identifies changes necessary to the new situation.

This can be illustrated by the following example. Since the 9/11 terrorist attacks, airport security has been tightened in most locations around the world, especially in the US, in spite of some complaints regarding unnecessary violation of privacy and human dignity. Before the attack on the World Trade Center, the security regulations in airports in the US and most other countries around the world were superficial unless the flight-destination country faced a terror threat, such as Israel or Northern Ireland. The sense of trust and the respect for privacy were perceived as important when the probability of terrorist attacks on airplanes was perceived as very low (despite the occasional exception, such as the Pan American flight from London to New York that was blown up over Scotland in 1988 by Libyan terrorists). In some airports, the system was partially changed and some passengers, especially citizens of countries at war, were checked more thoroughly. It was only after 9/11 that the system responded more drastically to the new ecological situation, and to save human lives, a conscious decision was made to violate certain principles that were fundamental to the homeostasis of American society, such as respect for human privacy.

These changes in the security regulations created a new homeostasis within society, in which the authorities responsible for security received more power. However, despite the criticism, it was accepted by the majority who perceived the threat to life as more important than other principles that structured the society. Analyzing this example from the cybernetic point of view emphasizes the feedback loop; the limited security regulations had been effective for many years and therefore, the system did not have to make any changes. Each new terror incident served as a warning sign, which interrupted the negative feedback loop[1] and resulted in some changes in the security regulations. These changes were minimal, however, and were directed mainly toward people who were not part of the U.S. system (that is, not U.S. citizens) mainly from countries in conflict. These changes were perceived as sufficient to maintain both security and the homeostasis of the system. After 9/11, the negative feedback loop was interrupted by the way civilian airplanes had been used to create the disaster. The fear was communicated and created a discourse regarding the need for more severe action to maintain aviation security, in order to preserve human life and to reduce the probability of the recurrence of such a disaster. The security regulations changed, giving the security system more power, and a new homeostasis was created, which, to an extent, violated some of American society's values in favor of others (preserving human life). The continued discourse regarding possible terrorist attacks, which preserved the sense of fear, maintained the negative feedback loop. Thus, in spite of the inconvenience, the violation of fundamental values of American society regarding privacy and freedom, and the cost of the security regulations, the new security system is still being maintained. From a cybernetic point of view, one may ask whether a positive feedback loop will develop if terror attacks will no longer be a threat. Will the change in discourse and criticism of the present situation call for a reexamination of the necessity to use such strict and costly regulations, leading to yet another change in the homeostasis?

Collective trauma creates a new ecological context. This can mean changes in one or all of the physical, psychological, or sociological contexts. However, in spite of the changes and the ability of human systems to adjust and cope with them, changing homeostasis is often complex and painful, especially if it is not the result of a free decision but of external circumstances often accompanied by some instrumental or psychosocial loss. It requires a sense of hope that the change in behavior or beliefs will lead to something better. In situations of collective trauma, changes in homeostasis are forced on the system and the loss of the previous homeostasis is added to the other cumulative losses. Applying systemic intervention requires acceptance of the mourning of the system's lost or previous homeostasis. After the Holocaust, many Jews who came from religious communities and families became secular or even anti-religious. Many accounted for this by asking where God had been during those years. However, rejecting their religious belief did not prevent them from maintaining many of the Jewish traditions—celebrating the holidays, keeping some of the rituals, singing Jewish prayers and recounting stories of the religious Jewish way of life in their lost homes and communities. Thus, on the cognitive level, they were secular, with a new homeostasis in their life that included their social systems (family, friends, community), but on the emotional level, they were bleeding—remembering and mourning for the old homeostasis.

The concept of equifinality is the idea that various causes can lead to similar solutions and a similar cause can result in different solutions.

The implementation of this idea in systemic interventions in situations of collective and national trauma refers to prejudices held by mental health professionals and social workers while assessing and intervening with different systems. Although some readers might object to the idea that mental health professionals and social workers display prejudice in their professional role, a superficial examination of their comments can expose some of these prejudices: "This is a poor community; therefore, the impact of the traumatic effect might be felt more severely and the people will need more help." "This is a rich community; they will be able to manage; there is no need to invest much time there." "Talk treatment is not effective for these uneducated people." Some of these prejudices might be based on the valid outcomes of research that found, for example, that education and financial resources served as buffers against stress (Hobfoll, 1998, 2001). Nevertheless, the challenge remains regarding how to contain this theoretical information while simultaneously implementing the concept of equifinality and learning from the people about their perceptions of the impact of the traumatic event. In addition, mental health professionals and social workers may be led by a specific intervention method in the belief that it is the most effective or correct way to overcome the traumatic experience, while rejecting and criticizing other intervention options. The concept of equifinality emphasizes the idea that various modes of intervention can lead to success or failure. The mental health professionals' role is to keep an open mind regarding the specific characteristics of the system, the way it functions in the shadow of the traumatic event and the many intervention options. They must then choose the option that best fits the specific system.

Let me illustrate how the concept of equifinality can be implemented in situations of a potential collective traumatic event: During the Second Lebanon War in July 2006, I joined the mental health helping group which volunteered in Nahariyah, a city close to the Israeli border with Lebanon. The city was heavily bombed by Hezbollah for almost a month. I was asked by the team's psychiatrist to find out how residents of a specific apartment block were coping. He had visited the building and found the residents to be "old and apparently very confused," adding that a building across the street had been heavily damaged in one of the missile attacks. When I arrived at the building and knocked on the door of the first-floor apartment, an old couple opened it and said that they were doing well because the younger residents in the building had taken care of everything. I went to see these "younger" residents and discovered that they were both in their eighties. We started talking, and they told me how they had cleaned the communal bomb shelter together with an older resident, who was an artist, who used the shelter as a storeroom for his pictures. As they were the youngest couple in the building, they had made sure that all the neighbors came to the shelter whenever the warning sounded. They had arranged to receive food via the municipal authorities, including hot meals, and they were responsible for its distribution to all the "elderly" neighbors. I accompanied them on their rounds to all these neighbors, who welcomed me and told me about how well-organized this couple had been. I discovered that some of the residents were Holocaust survivors and in spite of their experience of war, they presented functional and emotional resilience. They requested only one thing; that I find out whether they could receive some mattresses from the municipal authorities so that people could lie down in the shelter. This was a reasonable request, which was immediately answered. Thus, contrary to the psychiatrist's assessment, these people were not confused, notwithstanding their advanced age and living opposite a bombed building. Furthermore, the display of social support in the form of the joint effort of cleaning the shelter and obtaining food illustrates that even so-called "vulnerable" systems can function effectively during a potentially traumatic event.

From a cybernetic point of view, it is possible to claim that the good communication between the residents enabled them to prepare the shelter for wartime without offending the artist. The removal of his pictures was done in a caring and respectful manner. The residents had allocated authority to the youngest couple in the building to prepare the shelter and distribute the food. The supportive communication created a feedback loop in which all the residents felt protected and acknowledged.

These assumptions serve as a framework and guidelines for systemic interventions with all sizes and types of human systems. Therefore, despite the different techniques used while providing help to different systems, the assessment and intervention have similar guidelines. The differences between systemic interventions, which are provided to a specific system, are based, first, on the role and size of the system and second, on its contextual characteristics. The similarities and differences between the systemic interventions in regard to the type of system will be described through analyzing systemic interventions with specific systems: nations, communities, and families in situations of collective and national traumatic events.

In this part of the book, I focus mainly on the traditional role of mental health intervention but will refer to some other aspects of intervention that were described in the previous chapter (instrumental interventions and human rights protection). I will also integrate between aspects of supportive, narrative, cognitive-behavioral and psychodynamic approaches to systemic interventions. As I mentioned when describing the concept of equifinality, these are not the only methods of systemic intervention in situations of collective trauma. Others might be effective also, depending on both the system and the characteristics of the social workers and mental health professionals. I would like to stress here, once again, that if the physical needs are not taken care of first, the contribution of mental health assistance might be very limited.

Systemic Interventions With the Nation as a System

I will start this section by illustrating a national ritual that was not initiated by mental health professionals, but by King George V in the United Kingdom in 1919, a year after the Armistice was signed between the Allies of World War I and Germany, at Compiègne in France. This agreement marked the formal cessation of the fighting on the Western Front of World War I. The event took effect at 11 o'clock in the morning and is therefore often described as: "the eleventh hour of the eleventh day of the eleventh month" of 1918. Initially, it was named Armistice Day, and after World War II, its name was changed to Remembrance Day, with the purpose of creating a national remembrance of all soldiers who had given their lives for the freedom of the United Kingdom and Commonwealth nations.

The red poppy flowers have become the principal and most popular symbol of Remembrance Day. The source of this symbol was the poem entitled "In Flanders Fields," written by a Canadian doctor, *Lieutenant Colonel* John McCrae, shortly after losing his friend in the Battle of Ypres. In the poem, McCrae refers to the red poppies, which were the only resilient flowers left growing in the previously beautiful landscape that had been turned into a barren and muddy battlefield. The red poppies symbolize the blood of soldiers killed in armed conflict and this symbol has been adopted by many nations around the world, including the United Kingdom, the Commonwealth Nations and, to a lesser extent, the United States. Remembrance Day in the United Kingdom is known also as Poppy Day, reflecting the strong impact of the symbol. Various official and unofficial ceremonies are held at around this time. In the United Kingdom, for example, the day is usually marked on Remembrance Sunday, the Sunday that falls closest to November 11. Many memorial events take place during this weekend, including church ceremonies and cultural events, with participation of the Queen and other members of the Royal Family. It is important to note that other Commonwealth Nations and France keep the original date of November 11 as a national holiday of remembrance. In the United Kingdom, when the date falls on a weekday, a two-minute silence is observed at 11 o'clock in the morning. In addition, ceremonies are held across the country, including at the National Memorial Arboretum and in London's Trafalgar Square. During the previous month, television news broadcasters wear a poppy pinned to their clothes. Children buy poppies at school for a small sum of money, and wear them up to and during November 11. The proceeds from these sales go to the Royal British Legion, which supports families of those injured or killed. Lessons in school on November 11 are dedicated to this specific day and teachers discuss its meaning, with the students, through stories and artwork. It is important to note that the United Kingdom was the first nation to establish a legacy of a formal public remembrance day for soldiers who were killed in the nation's conflicts. Today, many countries around the globe designate a special memorial day, which may be defined as a national attempt to deal with wars that caused national trauma. The following elements of Remembrance Day might be used when developing national intervention in cases of collective and/or national trauma: The following elements of Holocaust Memorial Day might be used when developing national intervention in cases of collective and/or national trauma.

Sense of Togetherness

The difficult experiences of people in the United Kingdom during War World II, the loss of many soldiers who did not return from wars or came back physically or mentally injured, left many of them and many of their families alone, as if the war was their private issue rather than a national event. Soldiers who survived sometimes feel guilty for remaining alive while their friends were killed. The pain of loss remains with the families and in cases of injured veterans, the constant need to cope can leave them with a sense of loneliness. Dedicating a national Remembrance Day not only reduces the sense of loneliness among the victims, their families and friends, but gives the entire nation the opportunity to thank them and to feel a sense of belonging to a nation that has fought either for its freedom or to defend populations in other places who live under dictatorship regimes. It is well known that entering into a war may cause political disputes within the society. However, these conflicts are put aside during Remembrance Day to honor those who were killed while performing national duty. The sense of national belonging has been found to be a healing variable in situations of collective and national trauma (Possick, Sadeh & Shamai, 2008; Ron & Shamai, 2011; Shamai & Ron, 2009; Shamai & Ritov, 2010; Shamai, 2011). This is because it supports the social identity, which is part of the human self (Brewer, 1991; Turner et al., 1987). The sense of togetherness is especially important in situations of attempted genocide. Survivors of national genocides have usually had terrible experiences: starvation, humiliation, torture, rape, as well as other horrors, both out in the open and in private. Sometimes, people are ashamed of their torment, as if it was they who had been responsible. Most people feel lonely during the agonizing struggle for survival. Thus, when a nation manages to survive, ceremonies marking the genocide encourage the sense of togetherness, and the sense of national belonging may be a step toward collective and national healing.

Working Through the Loss and Ambiguous Loss

The bodies of many soldiers who went to war have never been found and identification was more difficult in the past than it is today. Thus, the families and friends of the missing soldiers assumed that they had been killed, but nevertheless had doubts. These doubts centered on questions of whether the person was taken as a prisoner of war and for some reason had not been released, or that he was physically or mentally injured, and due to memory loss, was alive somewhere without knowing his real identity. The absence of proof regarding the death of loved ones provided fertile ground for developing symptoms of ambiguous loss (Boss, 1999, 2007). To deal with these losses, many countries built a memorial tomb for the unknown soldiers. On a national day of remembrance, they receive, at least, a social identity, as a soldier of the United Kingdom, which might help their families and friends to cope with some of the symptoms of ambiguous loss.

It is important to note that, in cases of genocide, a large percentage of the population might need to work through the ambiguous loss (Boss, 1999, 2007). In many cases of genocide, bodies of the mass murder victims were not identified, many do not have graves and the cause and date of death is often unknown. Memorializing the dead gives individuals the opportunity to acknowledge the death of lost loved ones, as a way of coping with these symptoms. Many people who do not know the precise date of death may adopt this day to mark individual memorials, and they perform the traditional rituals that are customary on the anniversary of a death, such as lighting a candle and saying prayers. On the national level, it gives the feeling that the victims of the mass murders are remembered not only collectively, but as individual human beings. It gives the society, as a nation, the opportunity to work through the unimaginable loss.

Rituals and Spiritual Activities

The use of rituals in psychosocial intervention is known to have a healing impact (Imber-Black, Roberts & Whiting, 1988; Possick, Sadeh & Shamai, 2008). The entire Remembrance Day can be described as a systemic ritual because it includes the entire system (the nation) as well as various types of communities, which are subsystems within the nation. Some aspects of the ritual include the entire nation, such as the official minutes of silence. The ritual activities in the communities can be modified according to their different characteristics. Some groups and communities might add a spiritual aspect to their ceremony, which has been found to be effective in coping with loss and in strengthening the sense of togetherness (Walsh, 1999).

In general, mental health and psychosocial intervention with a nation is mostly instrumental and varies according to the type of the disaster, the country's financial resources and level of human rights awareness. The role of mental health and psychosocial professionals in intervention with the national system is centered mainly on consultations to government ministries regarding the policy of help that is needed, taking into consideration the following seven main areas:

1   Emphasizing the necessity of immediate and/or long-term distribution of basic needs: food, housing, clothes and medical services, which have an impact on the state of physical and mental health. The lack of basic needs causes deterioration not only in the physical condition but has a direct impact on welfare in general and on mental health in particular. For example, when people are hungry, finding food is a source of stress. This might lead them to mistrust others and to develop paranoid thinking ("they know how to find food," "they are taking my share of the food") and/or violent behavior. This causes

the wider population additional anxiety and fear, which, in turn increases the level of stress. A high level of stress was found to impact the level of general health.

2   Preserving human rights: protecting vulnerable and less powerful populations, such as children, women, older persons, the sick, immigrants, excluded communities and tribes, etc., when providing instrumental help and adapting the type of assistance to their specific short-term and long-term needs. Consultation related to the preservation of human rights might be complicated in countries in which they are violated by those with political power. The authorities in these countries might not allow mental health counselors to provide consultation on the national level. To accomplish the goal of providing help to the citizens in need, the helping forces are advised to cooperate with the authorities in order to be allowed to function. Even if only minimal preservation of human rights is possible, such as special care for vulnerable populations, this can still be helpful.

It is noteworthy that totalitarian countries sometimes attempt to hide situations of collective trauma. One example is Myanmar, whose government prevented outside help after Cyclone Nargis. Another example is Syria during the civilian uprising of 2011–12, where the armed forces continued to kill thousands of civilians, including women and children. The role of social workers and mental health professionals is to draw the attention of other countries, the UN and other powers to the conditions under which these populations are living and to call on them to put pressure on the governments of these countries to accept offers of help. Some readers might find this naïve or presumptuous regarding the degree of power available to social workers and mental health professionals. However, systemic interventions are relevant to various types of systems, including the entire global population. Thus, it is the responsibility of professionals who provide help in collective and/or national traumas to be aware of populations around the world who are denied help. Moreover, in many cases, these populations were brought to the attention of the UN and other countries by means of people's insistence through the media and the development of public opinion. These were used as means of convincing powerful countries and the UN to intervene in totalitarian states that forbid the provision of necessary instrumental and mental help.

3   Adapting the type of help and the process of providing needs to the specific culture of the nation and the different groups within it.

4   Supporting the government officials appointed to develop and implement the help policies, taking into account that they might be torn between the needy population and political interests, which may be irrelevant to the type and process of help and to the issue

of human rights. However, systemic help includes the awareness of power issues within the political system and the understanding that it is sometimes important to first join those in power (Minuchin & Fishman, 1981) and that only after developing a sense of trust and creating some alliance, it will be possible to present the short-term and long-term needs. It is important to note that a joining process does not necessarily take long and can be achieved in the first part of the initial meeting. The joining process includes:

a   Listening, with interest, to the story and state of the professional and political people who attend the consultation meeting regarding the traumatic events and the type of help that they appear to want or can offer the hurt population.

b   Communicating sympathy for their pain and acknowledging their responsibility for offering help to the hurt population and highlighting the type of help which, from a professional point of view, seems appropriate to the situation and the population.

c   Empowering policy makers and arousing hope is crucial to the joining process. From a systemic perspective, mental health professionals are aware that after the traumatic event, they may provide counseling to governmental authorities regarding other areas where action should be taken. However, the probability that counselors in other areas, such as engineering, electricity, etc., will perceive empowerment and support to be part of their role is very low. For social workers and mental health professionals, empowering and support is an essential part of their practice. Based on systemic understanding, it is obvious that even the most apparently powerful leaders are often in a very lonely position and need empowerment and support to function effectively.

5   Raising mental health issues that some policy makers may perceive as unimportant or as irrelevant to the policy of help within the specific population. Consultation regarding the impact of a traumatic event on mental health includes:

a   Information about the potential impact of collective traumatic events (see Chapter 2).

b   Information regarding short- and long-term policies for the assessment and treatment of those who developed traumatic symptoms. The information needs to include a description of ways to identify people with traumatic symptoms and the kind of help they need. It requires evaluation regarding the number of professionals who can provide mental health help to trauma victims, such as psychiatrists, social workers, psychologists, counselors, psychiatric nurses and family doctors. Significant parts of the information should be focused on the need for developing special services (medical, welfare, or educational, depending on the specific culture) which can provide medical and/or psychosocial help to those with traumatic symptoms. It should be noted that many countries lack mental health professionals and need voluntary helping forces. In these cases, the information given to policy makers must stress the importance of training and ongoing supervision for the local professionals, which can be based in the centers that provide mental health and psychosocial services.

c   Providing consultation on how to develop policy that focuses on preserving the mental health and psychosocial welfare of the entire nation that directly and indirectly experienced the trauma, including ways of preventing PTSD and of caring for vulnerable populations. Such policy can support programs that can be implemented within larger systems, such as communities, schools, workplaces, etc. In the role of consultation to policy makers, it is important to focus on the importance of such programs, and on their cost and effectiveness rather than on the content, processes and techniques of the intervention programs. This is because the participants in such meetings are generally less interested in the details of such programs than in their accountability.[2] When consulting on issues of psychosocial and mental health policies, it is crucial to refer to the importance of human rights as relevant to national and collective healing.

In addition, it is important to suggest options for developing national memorial events as a way to work through the national traumatic events collectively. Examples are Holocaust Memorial Day in Israel, and May 9 (*Den Pobeda*) in Russia, and previously observed in all the countries of the former Soviet Union (FSU). *Den Pobeda* is the official national holiday to remember the victory over the Nazis, including memorializing the millions of Russians and other FSU combatants and non-combatants who were victims of World War II.

Palestinian Israeli citizens have made an interesting and challenging attempt to create an unofficial recovery ritual in the form of a memorialization of Nakba Day on May 15. As mentioned in Chapter 2, this day symbolizes what the Palestinians perceive as the catastrophe resulting from the 1948 war following the declaration of Israel as an independent state, when many Palestinian Arabs either fled or were expelled from their homes. Many of these deserted villages were subsequently destroyed. On Nakba Day, many Palestinians gathered at the location of the old villages, or close by, if this was not possible because Israeli villages and towns have since been built in these locations. This gathering gives the Palestinians a sense of national identity and of hope for a Palestinian state. Although many of them know that they will not be able to return to their grandparents' or great-grandparents' home, they perceive the act of being together and the sense of longing to be a family and national legacy that must be preserved (Joubran-Saba, 2014). It is noteworthy that the Israeli government has taken steps to prevent this activity, which is perceived as a political protest against the State of Israel and a political attempt to demand the return of the Palestinian refugees, who might pose a threat to the Jewish majority. Social workers and mental health professionals hold two opposing opinions regarding this ritual. Some perceive it as a political act that raises unrealistic expectations among the Palestinians and increases their hatred of the Jews. Others do not perceive the ritual as a threat to Israel or as potentially raising the Palestinians' expectations to resettle in these locations. They perceive it as a recovery ritual and a political act that allows the Palestinians to mourn their loss, to tell the Palestinian narrative, and if this is done together with Jewish participants, can be a seed of reconciliation.

When social workers or mental health professionals suggest that policy makers initiate national rituals, it is essential to emphasize the importance of cultural sensitivity, which requires that special attention be paid to the specific culture of the majority of the population as well as to the different cultures of the country's minorities. It is also crucial to point out that the development of national memorial days is a long-term process before they become rooted in the national culture.

6   When collective trauma leads to rage and hatred between different countries or between populations in the same country, the healing impact of a national reconciliation policy can be suggested and explained to leaders and policy makers. Although the specific details of reconciliatory activities between various groups of citizens are often guided by mental health professionals and are irrelevant to policy makers, the involvement of political leaders in a reconciliation policy might be a crucial prerequisite for its effectiveness. According to Bar-Tal (2000), the reconciliation process depends on several elements, which include the following:

a   An end to the violence or the threat of violence.

b   A desire to turn past conflicts into peaceful relationships.

c   The establishment of relationships between societies of two nations or between groups within one country.

d   An ongoing message conveyed by leaders in which they legitimize diversity, perceiving the other nation or group not as an enemy, but as made up of human beings with whom future relationships can be developed. These messages can be transmitted to the population through the media, educational institutions and joint national activities as well as via activities for specific population groups from different nations or within one nation.

e   The understanding that the reconciliation process might take a long time. Eisikovits (2005) argued that reconciliation means fair coexistence and the ability to sympathize with the other group or nation. By sympathizing, Eisikovits referred to Adam Smith's definition as the ability to project ourselves into circumstances in which others operate (Fleischacker, 2004). It is important to note that, for Smith, it is the projection into the situation of another person or group rather than into the feelings of others, as with empathy. In addition, Eisikovits claimed that reconciliation is context-dependent, meaning that in cases where the two groups or nations are geographically inseparable, such as the black and white populations in South Africa, the Serbian and other Kosovar populations, and the Israelis and Palestinians, sympathy plays a crucial role in the reconciliation process. Hence, in the process of reconciliation between the Argentineans and the British after the Falklands War, a sympathetic attitude was much less important.

A national leader, who showed the world a unique example of a means of reconciliation, calling against revenge and seeking a joint future for the white and black populations in South Africa, was Nelson Mandela. However, Mandela claimed that the ability to reconcile and forgive does not mean forgetting. It means remembering without hitting back or using revenge. Mandela appointed Archbishop Desmond Tutu as chair of the Truth and Reconciliation Commission, which demanded a confession from those who had participated in criminal and abusive activities against blacks during the apartheid era. According to Tutu: "True reconciliation exposes the awfulness, the abuse, the hurt, the truth . . . because, in the end, only an honest confrontation with reality can bring real healing. Superficial reconciliation can bring only superficial healing."[3]

Nonetheless, in many places around the world, where past violence had constituted violation of human rights, the Truth and Reconciliation Commissions turned into truth commissions. Their role was "to investigate a past period of human rights abuses or violations of international humanitarian law" (Hayner, 1994, p. 598) without proceeding to a reconciliation process. True reconciliation requires a national leadership and policy makers who truly believe in its importance as a national healing mechanism and who are ready to invest resources in its development. It is the role of social workers and mental health professionals to consult policy makers and political leaders about the importance of the reconciliation process to national healing and to the national future. In addition, to set a reconciliation process in motion, it is important to specify the necessary actions on the leadership and policy-making levels.

7   Developing monitoring processes to evaluate the implementation and effectiveness of the national mental health interventions. Evaluating mental health interventions is usually a complicated process and is

even more so when trying to evaluate the effectiveness of different activities aimed at the entire nation as a system. It involves questions such as: What do we evaluate? How do we define the impact of the traumatic event on a nation? How do we define the resistance, resilience and well-being of the entire nation? Is it possible to define the effectiveness of national activities, such as memorial ceremonies and other national rituals? What are the activities that call for evaluation on the national level and what are the activities that can be evaluated within smaller systems within a nation, such as communities and organizations? In addition, some essential methodological questions center on the evaluation of systems: Does measuring a system mean obtaining the results from all the individuals in the system and then calculating the average and variance? How can we measure the impact of others on the individual within the context? In small systems, such as couples, several statistical procedures can take this into consideration, but not in large systems.

Social workers and mental health professionals, who consult on the national level, need to consider the cultural and political context in which the monitoring and evaluation are performed. It is possible that, in some political contexts, monitoring and evaluations will not be acceptable unless the outcomes can promise "glory" to the political regime. It is also possible that in some political contexts, either the population will be afraid to take part in the evaluation or their report might be impacted by fear. In countries that are open to evaluation, sensitivity to the cultural and political context is important also. In the consultation process, it is essential to identify the specific issues that are important for evaluation based on the perception of the nation's well-being, culture and history. If possible, it is helpful to suggest additional aspects of evaluation, which are part of the core issues of mental health and psychosocial help, such as monitoring and evaluating how human rights are maintained in various mental health programs, or how a specific population within the nation is included in various programs. In some cases where those in power have difficulty defining the focus of evaluation, the mental health professionals or social workers can facilitate a short brainstorming session to come up with significant areas of evaluation. It is also important to note that many of the mental health professionals and social workers are practice-oriented and might have limited experience in implementing evaluation studies. This does not necessarily mean that they cannot provide consultation and support regarding evaluation issues. Nonetheless, the inclusion of a person with a research background for developing the research design and measurement tools is recommended. It is also worth noting that despite the importance of using evidence-based programs as systemic first aid interventions, it is difficult and almost impossible to evaluate them according to the principles of evidence-based research. Neither the victims nor the helpers have the time or the emotional availability to conduct or participate in research. Therefore, some of the forms of help are evaluated only by an ex-post methodology, which does not give a precise answer regarding the specific effect of the helping program used. In addition, even though some structured protocols of mental health and psychosocial help exist, most of the first aid help provided in situations of collective trauma does not strictly follow these protocols, but is based on the understanding of human needs and professional experience. Therefore, it is often difficult to determine whether the intervention produced effective results because of the structure of the helping program or because of the helper's professional experience. Despite obstacles evaluating helping programs, the mental health counselors should still offer these programs to the policy makers. By pointing out these obstacles, they can highlight one of the most important principles regarding systemic first aid interventions following a collective or national traumatic event; that the interventions themselves and studies attempting to evaluate them never reach perfection.

In sum, interventions on the national level are always systemic because they focus on the nation as a whole entity. Therefore, principles of the system's functioning that relate to interaction, feedback and power need to be taken into account at every stage of development or consultation regarding the intervention.

The consultation process creates a special context that opens up an opportunity for the mental health counselor to communicate to the local and national policy makers that effective and sensitive policy that is implemented to repair the damages caused by the traumatic event can also be an opportunity for developing or increasing the sense of national cohesiveness. Such activity can lead to a sense of patriotism. Citizens can be proud to live in a country whose leaders perceive their role as attending to the hurt population, as opposed to using the traumatic event to increase their control over the population or to implement policies that cause additional pain.

Systemic Interventions With Communities

From a systemic point of view, communities are part of a larger system, such as a nation. Therefore, community intervention needs to be connected to the national authorities in terms of receiving aid and support and receiving information regarding national plans and policies. Social workers and mental health professionals who hold a systemic view will assess the ability of the central regime to provide emergent and long-term help, the ability of specific communities to demand aid, and will work together with the community leaders to look for channels to raise these demands in the appropriate government ministries. The type of connections between the specific community and the national regime modify the characteristics of the community interventions. These connections depend on:

a the type and strength of the central regime;
b the strength of the community and its ability to make demands of the central regime and to fight for them; and
c the damage created by the traumatic event, which can affect one or several communities or can impact the entire country.

Hurricane Katrina and Hurricane Sandy in the United States, and the earthquake and tsunami that caused damage to nuclear power stations in Japan, which increased the level of radiation over a large area, are examples of collective events in which the central regimes were not destroyed and were able to continue to function. The help given to the communities included organized activities initiated and implemented by the central regimes and played significant positive and negative roles both in the short- and long-term rehabilitation.[4] In the earthquake in Haiti, the entire country was hurt, including the governmental systems. The national authorities' ability to function was severely damaged and most of the intervention policies and aids developed from within the communities, mainly by helping forces who arrived from other countries.

In wars, and especially civil wars, it is even more complicated because political agendas are involved which do not necessarily consider the population's welfare. The political regime might sometimes initiate wars against certain groups within the country, such as the case of tribal wars in some African countries. Groups from within the country might initiate wars against the regime, as in the uprising in Syria, which started at the beginning of 2011 and is still ongoing and yet more complicated at the time of writing and has so far lasted for nearly four years. During this time, the army that was operated by the central regime had killed many citizens and destroyed numerous cities. In other cases, such as the war in Yugoslavia during the 1990s, the different nations established their own states, but these new individual regimes lacked the resources to deal with the cruel outcomes of the war. In this situation, many communities were dispersed to different refugee camps and most of the mental health aid was provided by mental health professionals, who related mainly to individuals and families rather than to the camp population as a community. It is possible that in many refugee camps, especially those that existed long-term, community intervention practices were developed. If this was the case, they did not develop a solid conceptualization of the refugee camp as a community—even a temporary community. From a systemic point of view, the refugee camp is considered to be a system. This is because its character is determined not only by the individuals in the camp, but also by the interaction created among them, which has a negative or positive impact on their lives.

The other characteristics of systemic community interventions will be illustrated by two examples, one describing an intervention implemented during a war and the other after a natural disaster. In the summer of 2006 during the Second Lebanon War in Israel, an intervention was implemented involving two communities: a community evacuated from their homes due to heavy bombing, and the hosting community who received them. At the beginning of the war, it was clear to the leaders and members of the community under fire that spending most of their time in bomb shelters would be stressful for mothers and children. Therefore, they asked for aid from a community with similar characteristics, which was located in a different part of the country. The leaders of both communities decided that mothers, children, educational staff and anyone else whose role did not require them to remain in the heavily bombed region would relocate to the more safely situated host community. During the consultation process, it was suggested that the two communities would appoint two or three people to take care of the entire process, which required special organization to provide housing, food, laundry services, etc.

In the second stage, after the basic needs had been provided and the relocated community had settled, a meeting was arranged with appointees from both communities to identify additional requirements, such as psychological and social needs. In this meeting, the relocated community reported how difficult it was for children, teenagers and parents to stay in a confined space without planned activities. The lack of activities increased the sense of uncertainty and resulted in higher levels of stress, which began to be manifest in behavioral problems among the children, increased tension within families that began to project onto the other members of the community and lack of tolerance among the adults. An additional source of stress was the uncertainty regarding the length of time they would have to spend in these inconvenient conditions. At this stage, we decided to find ways to operate the education system for toddlers and kindergarten children as well as informal education for elementary and high school children, as the war took place during the summer vacation. Operating an education system created a routine for the children and the educational staff, which is one of the most important principles in reducing stress, depression and anxiety in times of physical danger and uncertainty. In this meeting, some suggestions were made to create a routine for the adults, including volunteering in the education systems and taking care of the community's physical needs such as doing the laundry and preparing food. Another issue that arose in the meeting concerned the exchange of information between the part of the community that had stayed at home and those who had relocated. As access to reliable official information was found to be one element of community resilience (Norris et al., 2002; Norris, Friedman & Watson, 2002; Norris & Stevens, 2007), the mental health counselors suggested providing a daily source of official information describing the experiences of both parts of the community, in addition to the private telephone conversations between family members in the two locations. The leaders of the relocated community liked this idea and with some humor, imagined all the newsletters on display at an exhibition on the anniversary of the community's establishment. This comment was reinforced by the mental health consultant, who perceived this positive future orientation to be a sign of community resilience.

In addition, some of the parents asked for guidance in answering the children's questions regarding the war, and others who had children in the army, or women whose husbands had been called to reserve duty asked for support to deal with their stress. The host community suggested several social workers who could lead group interventions regarding parenthood in wartime and other support groups for parents and women whose children or partners were serving in the army. Most parents who participated in the group discussions were mothers, and they expressed the yearning for the husbands and fathers who had stayed at home. This issue was brought to the attention of the relocated community leaders and it was decided to organize visits in turn, so that each non-relocated family member could visit his or her family twice a week; once for a few hours in the afternoon and one overnight visit.

For many members of the host community, the encounter with members of the relocated community evoked painful past memories of the War of Independence, fifty-eight years previously, when their community had been under heavy attack, and the women, children and educational staff had been evacuated to other communities for several months (Shamai, 2012). Thus, a meeting between the adults of the two communities was held, to share the stories of both communities. The members of both communities experienced the meeting as an important event that evoked many emotions but also strengthened the ideological perspective shared by many members of both communities. This ideology included strong commitment to the State of Israel and a strong belief in the possibility of peace, despite disappointment with the indirect support of Hezbollah by the Lebanese government following Israel's withdrawal in 2000. This support had enabled Hezbollah to develop its military strength and to attack Israel instead of focusing on the welfare of the Lebanese citizens. The meeting enabled members of the community to reach the highest level in the pyramid of human needs, as defined by Maslow (1954, 1970), namely, giving meaning to the self-existence in a context that provides social support.

When the war was over and the relocated community was about to return home, a short farewell ceremony was held with the two communities.

This gave the relocated community the opportunity to thank the host community for its hospitality and for the host community to give thanks for the opportunity to contribute to the national system. At this point, the contact with the host community ended. On returning home, the relocated community organized a celebration to mark their return to normal life. However, many members wished to give something back to the host community as a way of expressing their strength. In a general meeting called by the community, it was decided to make three gestures:

1   Apples would be sent to each of the host community families for the Jewish New Year,[5] from the relocated community's many apple orchards.
2   The relocated community runs a hotel in a beautiful area of Israel and it was decided that, for the entire year, one room would be left available for members of the host community.
3   The relocated community invited the entire host community for an organized visit several months later.

It is important to note that none of these activities involved any consultation with mental health professionals or social workers, but the ideas can give some additional direction for possible long-term intervention with communities following traumatic events.

As the school year started approximately two weeks after their return home, the teachers held discussions with the children about their experiences during the war and carefully observed the children's behavior to identify any symptoms of traumatic stress. Both the regional department of social services and educational psychology services offered therapeutic intervention to individuals and families in need. Only one family from the relocated community asked for specific intervention due to stress that had developed during the war. Thus, it is possible to assume that the community contributed to the resilience of the individuals within the community and prevented traumatic stress symptoms. This was accomplished through good time organization during the evacuation, effective use of the social workers' suggestions and counseling, and the well-organized process of returning home as well as gestures made to the hosting community.

The second illustration is a description of a community intervention with the population in Sri Lanka following the tsunami in 2004, by Henry Elkeslassy, who was part of the helping forces:

After the tsunami, we found that the people of the village were afraid to go to the ocean. As most of them relied on fishing for their livelihood, this was a real problem because without an income, the routine family and community life was disrupted.

Instead of going out to work, fishing, the men just sat at home or wandered around the whole day with other men, which was a source of many other problems . . . So we met with one of the religious leaders of the village and told him that the relationships with the ocean are like the relationships between married couples. Sometimes anger is expressed, but afterwards, reconciliation occurs and the relationship returns to normal . . . so the ocean got angry, and it is now time to reconcile. The religious leader liked the idea and together, we planned a ritual for the entire population of the village. He invited everyone to the ocean shortly before sunset, and while the people were assembling, the leader and I, and two other people, who were not afraid, decorated a boat with lamps. We then took the boat and sailed in from the ocean. All the people welcomed us and the leader shared our story with them about the ocean's relationship with humans. Then the entire village prayed for peaceful relationships with the ocean . . . The next day, many of the fishermen returned to work and most of the others returned to work in the following days.

Analyzing the two community interventions highlights principles and techniques available for community systemic interventions in situations of collective traumatic events.

1. Emergent Interventions

Keeping the Community Together During Evacuation and Relocation

In many cases, the potential traumatic events that may require the evacuation of populations can be predicted. For example, many communities around the world are located in areas that are prone to natural disasters, such as earthquakes, floods, wildfire, etc., and others are located in the line of fire of ongoing unsolved national conflicts. By conceptualizing the community as part of a larger system, mental health professionals could help to prepare these communities for these events. Thus, connections can be created between communities located in dangerous places with communities located in safer areas. This resembles the concept of "sister cities" and when emergency evacuation is required, the safer communities will host the evacuated population. Some might be sheltered in communal places, such as schools, or depending on the cultural background, families from the host community might invite the relocated families into their homes as guests.[6] Evacuating the community as a group maintains the community structure and facilitates natural social support, which is one of the most important elements in coping with trauma. As one member of the evacuated community described in the parental group meeting:

> every evening, one of us goes crazy, starts crying, complaining; many of us use black humor but all the others know that it is a sign of stress . . . so we listen, but we all join in with the humor and we all start laughing and it's as if we are crazy. We can be like this because we all know each other very well . . . someone from your profession [referring to the mental health professions] might define it as hysterical laughter, but for us, it is just a release of tension.

It is well-known that laughter and humor can be an effective way of reducing stress and other traumatic outcomes impacting both psychological and physiological systems (Grases Colom et al., 2011; Henderson, 2010; Lefcourt, 2003). Based on the previous illustration, it is possible to add the context of natural social support that enables this relief.

In addition, the evacuation might create a joint experience for the community members. If mental health professionals help the community to develop some shared positive memories within the difficult context, this can be a base on which to develop a positive community narrative in the future, which will contribute to strengthening community resilience (Kimhi & Shamai, 2006; Denborough, 2008).

In the evacuation process, special attention must be given to people with special needs, such as those with disabilities, sickness, children who have lost their families, or old people with disability in functioning. For these populations, special attempts are needed to find suitable conditions for their evacuation. Sometimes, these populations need to be evacuated even when the rest of the community is not. The evacuation of these groups is complicated and raises some ethical issues, but in general, it can be said that in places with more resources, where the national system is functioning, such evacuation is possible. For example, children who have lost their families can be sent to relatives or adult acquaintances in safer places, even though this means separating them from their natural physical and social environment. The evacuation of older people is often more difficult. Special care for the old and the sick or for people with disabilities is not always available in the new location. Even if suitable provision is made, adjustment is difficult for the individuals, their families and the staff. These additional changes add to the stress created by the traumatic event.

Creating Community Routine

The importance of creating or restructuring the routine was mentioned in detail in the previous chapter. In this chapter, the focus is on the implementation aspects. The first illustration described how the routine was structured within the non-routine situation. The decision to operate the education system in the hosting community for the children and finding optional activities for the adults served as a distraction from thoughts about the dangers of war and their current inconvenient situation. Among relocated populations and refugees, the daily chaos often results in intensive use of alcohol or drugs, which often leads to violence, especially when people lack basic needs. Developing a routine is usually complicated and sometimes even impossible, especially in refugee camps or when communities are not kept together, but this can be easier to arrange for children than for adults. One main role of mental health professionals is to develop and seek opportunities for such routine activities. These activities can include groups for children, in which they can work through their fear, anxiety and depression through art, drama, or dance therapy; joint groups for parents and children, where they can create a family discussion and deal with painful issues by direct and indirect means (painting, role playing, etc.), groups for parents using a psycho-educational approach, in which parents can share their anxieties and concerns about their children and can receive support and guidance, as well as other organized activities for adults, where they can receive information regarding the situation. Such activities at a specific place and time known to all members of the community can provide some structure for an hour or two during the day. Something constant within the uncertain context creates some basis for a routine that does not often exist following traumatic events.

Not all situations of collective trauma require evacuation, but they can still create disruption in the daily routine. This was the case with most of the population in New York City after the 9/11 terror attack, or in Norway in July 2011, when a Norwegian citizen exploded a car bomb in Oslo, killing 8 people, then later killed 69 youngsters and injured 241 more at a youth camp run by the Norwegian Labor party. Besides the deaths and the changes in transportation in New York City, these events had mainly a psychological and sociological impact on the nations and different communities within the nation. In such situations, it is important to help communities to maintain their routine (education systems, health systems, etc.) and to work through the trauma by means of rituals, discussions and conversations within the natural systems and providing trauma counseling for families and individuals without breaking the routine. The routine allows natural systems within the community to function as social support resources and as a context for working through grief and anger.

To sum up, according to the systemic conceptualization, creating a daily routine helps the community system or the subsystems within it to achieve a new and flexible homeostasis that may be relevant to the new situation.

Informal Community Assembly: Working Through the
Traumatic Experience—Integrating Past and
Future Perspectives

As was described in the first illustration, after the basic needs were met, the members of the evacuated community started to mention higher needs such as guidance in answering the children's questions about the war, and others sought some structured social support where they would be able to share and reflect on their feelings. Based on these requests, the mental health counselor suggested arranging group meetings facilitated by social workers designed to help them work through issues of concern. The topics of these meetings were chosen by the people and the leaders of the evacuated community, with additional subjects for group conversation suggested by mental health and psychosocial helpers.

The choice of the terms "group conversation" and "informal community assembly" over "group work" was not made at random, but reflects the ideology behind this type of community activity. These meetings were not run from a pathological perspective, perceiving the community as a traumatized victim or a hurt population, but as a system that has undergone a difficult and painful experience, which needs to be worked through to continue with life in the future. Thus, the informal community assembly is a concept that refers to the strength of a system. The ability to arrange assemblies and the willingness to take part in them indicates resilience that needs to be taken into account when working with the community. In addition, the "informal community assembly" and "group conversation" allow the individual voices to be heard within the relatively large system of the community. In this way, they resemble the "direct democracy" of ancient Athens, where people discussed policy initiatives directly during the assembly and then were allowed to vote, as opposed to a representative democracy in which people vote for representatives, who then vote on policy initiatives. The former method increases the sense of belonging to the community, which was found to be an important variable in both community and individual resilience (Shamai, 2011; Shamai & Ritov, 2010).

The structure of such conversations is based on two elements that need to be balanced: pain and hope. Lindy and Wilson (2001) coined the term "trauma membrane" referring to a natural coping process that is often adopted after a traumatic experience. It is expressed as the tendency of survivors to put aside the painful experiences and to try and "forget" them, while focusing on concrete and instrumental activities. Therefore, if people describe painful experiences in the assembly, it is important to listen to and acknowledge them, but in the short term, it is recommended not to inquire into the deeper psychological levels of these individuals' experiences. This is mainly because people need to process the traumatic event in small doses (Halpern & Tramontin, 2007; Lindy,

1996), but also because they deal with it in different ways. When implementing systemic intervention, it is the responsibility of the social worker or other mental health professional to assess the impact of such sharing on the entire group. Different groups and different communities can deal with the traumatic experience on different levels, and it has not been proved that focusing on emotional reactions and experiences increases rather than soothes distress (Halpern & Tramontin, 2007; Shalev, 2000; Raphael & Wilson, 2000). However, conversations about the traumatic experience during emergent interventions can be channeled toward aspects of strength and hope, first moving toward the meaning of the construction of the loss (Neimeyer, 2001; Neimeyer & Anderson, 2002). The conversation can be directed toward these issues by introducing the following topics in the discussion:

1 resources of strength that characterized the community before the traumatic event;
2 resources of strength that were discovered since the traumatic event;
3 possibility of using existing strength as a resource for coping in the present and the future;
4 developing a perspective for the future: how people imagine themselves and the community in a month, a year, five years and ten years from the present time; and
5 how the future perspective can be used as a narrative that evokes strength and hope during the daily pain and difficulties in the present.

The informal general assembly creates a space to talk about issues that worry people in a systemic context that enables both natural and planned social support. It is a place in which different voices can be heard—voices that emphasize fear, pain and desperation as well as those that imply strength and hope. In the short term, the traumatic experience tends to overrule the way people think and feel, and it is therefore the role of the mental health professionals, who facilitate these conversations, to give space to all the voices expressed, including those that were hardly mentioned and at very low volume. In addition, informal community assemblies can be a venue for psycho-educational activities, such as providing information and advice for parents or guidance regarding human reactions both during and in the immediate aftermath of collective traumatic events. Such information may enable people who have recently had a collective traumatic experience to define their reaction as "normal," thus reducing anxiety. The informal general assemblies can also be used for conveying general information. The attendance of community members at such assemblies can indicate community strength, as it shows community cohesiveness—the members' willingness for togetherness and joint action, the ability for communication and trust and the ability to search for solutions together with other members of the community.

144

First Assessment of People With Traumatic Symptoms

Although not directly mentioned in the two illustrations, emergent intervention can be used in the initial assessment of children or adults who start to develop traumatic symptoms. First, by receiving information in informal general assemblies or in other community forums regarding reactions to traumatic experiences, the members of the community can be aware of symptoms that often characterize reactions to a traumatic experience. Thus, they are able to ask for emergency mental health consultation, either directly or through other members of the community. Second, in the general assemblies, the mental health professional, who facilitates the meeting, can identify people apparently in need of emergent mental health aid. In the short term, the help is focused on developing social support from family members or friends. It can include one or two counseling meetings for the purposes of support and if needed, medication can be used. From the community's point of view, this is the first stage of assessing whether or not special long-term psychosocial services are necessary, or whether the community's existing welfare and mental health services are satisfactory resources.

Using Rituals and Spiritual Activities

As described in the second illustration, a ritual of community reconciliation with the ocean was used as a way to reduce fear among the majority of the people in the community who made a living from fishing. Community rituals contain the elements of togetherness, which allow the members of the community to relate to the pain through a planned process and to look to the future through promising to perpetuate the memory of those who lost their lives, as well as honoring some of them as heroes. The inclusion of spiritual aspects in rituals, such as joint prayer, provides both a source of strength and a venting ground for many people around the world. People often feel helpless in relation to natural and political processes as a result of collective and national trauma, and many people find strength through religious faith. Spontaneous rituals are not unusual in communities that experienced traumatic events, and these are often motivated by religion, in the form of communal prayers and inspirational speeches by religious leaders.

If the ritual is suggested by mental health professionals, it needs to be planned together with people from the community, who are familiar with the culture and the nature of its members. The mental health professionals can serve as counselors in the planning process and can help to avoid outbursts of uncontrolled emotional reactions shortly after the traumatic event.

Supporting Community Leaders

Both illustrations only hinted at the mental health professionals' work with the community leaders, without providing a detailed description of this work. However, an essential part of the interventions with the leadership system included support and empowerment of the leaders. This aspect of psychosocial and mental health intervention was described also in the previous section focusing on consultations provided to the national policy makers. It is even more crucial for community leaders, as they are physically closer to the hurt population than the national leaders, and may become a target for the population's anger and desperation. The formal and informal leaders of the community often share the same physical and emotional threat as the entire population. Their reaction to the stress created by the trauma is under constant observation and becomes both a source for modeling and a target of criticism. This can be true for all kinds of leaders: formal and informal as well as grass-roots leaders, who took up the position of leadership during or immediately after the traumatic event, as well as members of the community, who were identified by social workers and mental health professionals and were encouraged to take up these positions of leadership (see Chapter 3 "Reestablishing Social Support Within the Community").

The supporting and empowering activities include the following:

1   Creating a safe and containing context, which enables leaders to share their positive and negative feelings that arise in their roles of leadership.
2   Creating an educational context in which processes within the community can be analyzed and understood as "normal reactions" to collective traumatic events rather than attacks on leaders.
3   Creating a communal setting for community leaders and social workers and mental health professionals, where plans for further community activities for coping and adjustment are discussed.

In these settings, it is important to help the leaders develop a systemic view, which enables them to understand situations and to plan activities while taking into consideration the community's systemic background. Such a systemic view includes the ability to identify subsystems within the community including the different ways in which groups can be influential; some can contribute to coping and others can instigate violent activities and threaten other groups in the community. In addition, it enables the leaders to assess community strength from before the traumatic event, to identify boundaries between groups within the community and the type of relationships between leaders and the entire population. As mentioned in the previous section, in spite of the power given to and/or held by community leaders, the leadership role includes a sense of loneliness, which may also be added to the pressure to present a strong image in the face of painful and difficult situations. Thus, the support, empowerment and ability for containment plays an important role in helping communities to maintain or restructure community leadership.

Some of the activities of emergent community systemic interventions (Halpern & Tramontin, 2007) described above can be modified and utilized also in the long term. It is often difficult to draw a clear boundary between the emergent and long-term situation. Some people live in ongoing war situations and under the threat of terror for many years. Refugee camps become the population's permanent place of residence. Certain places around the world have experienced many natural disasters. In most cases, the boundary between the emergent and the long term is determined by physical and instrumental rather than by psychosocial conditions. Sometimes, it seems that the danger has passed, and those who were evacuated return to their homes or start to rebuild them, but the impact of the traumatic event on the community as a unit or on the welfare of individuals within the community does not disappear and continues to have an effect. In these situations, further community interventions are needed.

2. Long-Term Systemic Community Interventions

The first illustrations that described community intervention with an evacuated community included a detailed description of long-term community intervention, referring to the activities performed in the evacuated community after returning home. Two main types of activities were apparent from the illustration.

Community Rituals as a Way of Working Through the Traumatic Event and Integrating it into the Community Narrative

I called the ritual described in the illustration as "Giving back to the host community." It was performed not only as a way to say thank you, but also to experience the sense of community strength and power. It was performed through activities that could be defined as rituals, such as sending the apples for the Jewish New Year from the community farm, organizing a visit for the entire hosting community, and creating a role reversal between the relocated and hosting community by providing a hotel room for free vacations for an entire year. These activities can be defined as rituals because they match the definition of a prescribed form of behavior for special occasions with reference to a specific belief system (Turner, 1967). In the described illustration, the prescribed behavior was initiated by the evacuated community and part of it related to Jewish culture—the apples for the Jewish New Year. One key element of the ritual is its collective dimension that connects with a broader social meaning (Roberts, 1988).

The principles and structure of community rituals are similar to those of the national rituals, but focus on a smaller system. The rituals on the community level can be performed by community ceremonies that include memorialization of the loss, especially of those who were killed in the traumatic event. This acknowledges the attempts of members of the community and to cope with the traumatic situation, through asking people from the community to share their experiences, organizing exhibitions in which members of the community, especially children and youth, can present artwork based on their experience of the traumatic event. In some populations, practical experiences emphasize the role of spirituality as a curative element. Many make use of religious content, such as communal prayer, as a way of integrating painful memories with hope. The community rituals construct the community narrative regarding the traumatic past but also affect the future narrative and community perception. As the community narrative is one important aspect of community resilience (Norris & Stevens, 2007), it is the role of social workers and mental health professionals to highlight even hidden parts of the community narrative that signify strength. If such implications of strength are not included in the narrative, it is useful to ask a direct question regarding strength aspects, as described in the following illustration.

Israel's withdrawal from Lebanon in May 2000 increased the anxiety and stress of the Israeli population living next to the Lebanese border. The main causes of this stress were terrorist infiltration into Israel with the aim of murdering civilians and Hezbollah's close proximity to the border, which made this population a more vulnerable bombing target. The local Department of Social Services decided to implement community interventions with some of the rural communities in the area, which seemed to be in need of support. When planning interventions with one of the villages, almost all the social workers described this community in negative terms focusing on the community's weaknesses. At some point, the person facilitating the discussion asked them to mention at least one aspect of strength in the community. The request was followed by silence. The question was reframed for the social workers, who were asked what the community members would answer if asked the same question. One of the social workers replied that none of the community members would relate to their strengths, but would speak only about their weaknesses. After several more minutes of silence, one of the social workers commented that the women in the community are great cooks and whenever they come to the regional center for senior citizens, they bring their "goodies" for everyone to enjoy. The facilitator of the meeting then highlighted this skill, adding that they are also very generous, because they always bring refreshments to the regional senior citizens' meeting. This led the conversation in a different direction. Suddenly, the social workers remembered situations in which the community members offered help and social support and expressed how warm and welcoming they were. This process indicated that the members of the community were unable to perceive the community as having aspects of strength.[7] The first stage of the planned intervention was designed to create strength and a hopeful narrative with the community members. The social worker who worked with this particular community suggested creating a community celebration for the anniversary of its establishment, incorporating stories of the older generation. These included difficulties and coping in the immigration process to Israel from North Africa, building the village, coping with missile attacks over long periods, as well as with previous terrorist attacks in which some members of one family were killed. The community members and community leaders accepted this idea and they suggested other ways to celebrate the anniversary. The celebration itself was like a ritual that allowed the community to be aware of its strength and resilience that had enabled them to live in the line of fire for so many years. This illustration is an example that integrates concepts from systemic intervention and narrative therapy techniques (Denborough, 2008), which enable the community to work through the traumatic events that have continued to a greater or a lesser degree for almost thirty years, with no certainty of future peace. At the same time, the community is strengthened through the creation of a community narrative that includes aspects of coping with challenges. It is important to note that rituals can be formed with specific groups within the community as well as with the entire community.

A touching experience of a community ritual is described in the works of Brave Heart, aimed at dealing with the historical collective trauma of Native American Indians (Brave Heart, 1998; Brave Heart & De Bruyn, 1998; Brave Heart-Jordan & De Bruyn, 1995). The community rituals were performed in a group, where people of American Indian origin recounted their painful memories of the white people's destruction of their culture. The group was witness to the testimony given by members of the community, while validating the suffering and pain of the people as individuals, families, the community and the tribe. In addition, the people had the option to assemble around a historical community issue and allowed themselves to regain their cultural and social identity with the social support of the other. The healing impact of testimony in front of a group of witnesses has been used in many rituals aimed at healing from historical traumas (Denborough, 2008).

Community Services for Vulnerable or At-Risk Populations

The intervention with the evacuated community described in the first illustration attempted to work through the experience of war and

149

evacuation with the children within the natural education system. These activities were performed by the educators and teachers with the supervision and guidance of the Service of Educational Counseling Psychology. In addition, families and children who needed further help in working through the experience were offered family, individual, or group therapy in the municipal services: in the Family Therapy Clinic, which was part of the Department of Social Services and in the Service of Educational Counseling Psychology. Based on this example, the development of new services or the identification of appropriate existing services for focused or long-term psychosocial help for families and individuals in the community is one initiative of social workers and mental health professionals.

An interesting attempt to provide community services for vulnerable populations is the WAVE Trauma Centre in Belfast, Northern Ireland, where members of both the Catholic and Protestant populations in the city can receive help. The WAVE Centre provides group interventions where various processes of healing take place. These include the use of narrative as a means of remembering and telling the painful experiences in the presence of others who experienced pain, leading to mutual validation of suffering. Music and art are used as means of expressing pain and sadness along with hope. The interventions implemented in the Centre are exposed to the public in Belfast and other parts of Ireland, in the United Kingdom, and other trauma centers around the world through publications by the participants. Two examples are *Injured . . . on That Day* (WAVE, 1999), and *That Night in December* (WAVE, 2009), which both tell the stories of the terrible experience, with the aim of giving a voice also to those who were killed or to those who do not come to the Centre. Other books publicized have art work on the topic. Although many of the therapeutic means that are used in the WAVE Centre are not necessarily based on a systemic approach, the attempt to publicize the outcome of intervention with the traumatic population can be used by the entire community as a guide to coping with the past painful experience that has left symptoms of trauma in the present.

It can be argued that in many areas around the globe that have already experienced or have the potential of experiencing traumatic events, no welfare, psychological and medical resources exist, even though they are necessary. These services can be developed in some places, making use of local professionals, such as teachers, general practitioners, or clergy to provide some counseling for families and individuals in need, while receiving supervision from external mental health helping forces. Furthermore, it is strongly recommended that long-term activities aiming to work through the traumatic experience would be run by people from the natural system. If people who are familiar with the culture serve in family or group counseling roles, they would not perceive some reactions as a "sickness," but as typical behavior following a traumatic event. In some places around the world, the traumatic event was the reason for developing psychosocial and mental health services that were focused, initially, on providing help for the traumatized population and were later used as regular psychosocial services.

The intervention provided by these services is often based on various approaches that were found to be helpful in situations of trauma. The following elements should be taken into consideration when planning services for long-term systemic interventions with people who experienced collective trauma:

1   It is important to understand that most people are resilient and can cope with the traumatic experience by using their natural social and individual strength.
2   People are not living in a vacuum and it is possible that some of them present the unspoken sadness and fear of the closer system. Therefore, it is important to include in the intervention process family members, significant people from the education system (in the case of children) and significant others. Sometimes, this seems complicated, but if the social worker or other mental health professional explains the benefits to the person asking for help, other people are often encouraged to join.
3   Cultural, age-related and gender differences exist in the way they may benefit from interventions. For example, women are more willing to join interventions that involve talking and sharing whereas men receive more benefit from interventions involving physical activities. Thus, systemic interventions need to include techniques that may answer these different preferences. Furthermore, it is important to be aware of power issues within the client system, and therefore, to be respectful of power divisions and at the same time present basic human rights, which include protecting the client system from internal or external violence and humiliation.

In addition to the directions for long-term community intervention mentioned in the illustration, the activities discussed below are also possible.

Initiation and Monitoring of Continued Counseling Regarding Basic/Instrumental Needs

This type of help needs to be initiated by social workers, as it is connected to basic instrumental needs. Through listening to the stories of some people living in the flooded area in New Orleans in the aftermath of Hurricane Katrina and of people from Kiryat Shmona in northern Israel after the heavy bombing during the Second Lebanon War, I learned about the confusion experienced by people whose houses were damaged or destroyed in the traumatic event. First, people needed to go through bureaucratic processes to find out if they were insured, and if they were entitled to receive reparation money from the state, and if they were, whether they would receive the money in advance of any repairs so that they could engage building contractors. Second, most people have no experience in choosing contractors. Following such events, many people offering repair work appear in the damaged area. Some take money from the affected population and do not finish their work, and others are merely posing as contractors and do a quick and inadequate job. Continuation counseling services are used as an information center regarding eligibility for compensation, names of authorized contractors and prices of various types of repairs. These services may operate for a limited amount of time, and are necessary to reduce the stress of coping with the challenge of restoring basic needs such as a place to live. The role of social workers regarding this issue goes beyond initiation of the service; from a systemic view, they are expected to liaise with the service staff, and with the community and national leaders to provide the best care and benefits for the people whose houses and other property were lost or damaged by the traumatic event. Unfortunately, many countries around the world lack resources and have no insurance or compensation policy. In many other countries, the population does not have the resources to pay the contractors and they do most of the repair work themselves. Following traumatic events that resulted in uprooting people from home, initiating such services might be irrelevant. Nevertheless, initiating similar services to provide instrumental help based on the reality of the context is highly recommended for long-term community intervention.

Restructuring the Community Subsystem

Collective traumatic events may increase or decrease the prestige of leaders and directors of various subsystems within the community. Some of these roles are elected and people who lost their prestige might not be re-elected, unless by underhand means, such as threats or blackmail. Sometimes, during the period between the event and the election, the leader, such as the mayor, or a senator, still needs to function. People in these positions do not usually seek help but people in more lowly positions might request some help. Let me illustrate this with an example from the Second Lebanon War, when the director of the Department of Social Services of one of the heavily bombed cities left the city, abandoning the department without a director. For political as well as unknown reasons, the mayor of the city decided to leave her in the role of director, although she lost her leadership prestige among her colleagues and among those clients and citizens who knew about what had happened. In a consultation process aimed at helping her regain authority as director, the social worker consultant met first with her separately, then with the group of workers, and after the separate meetings, arranged a joint meeting. In the separate meeting with the director, the consultant listened to her narrative, which was focused on the reason for her leaving the staff and her role during the war. After listening to her story and inquiring into the meanings she gave to this act, she was asked to tell the story of being a director since she had begun this job. When listening to the story, the consultant highlighted some of the strengths of her activities that were latent in the story and asked how she perceived the future of the department in general and her role as director in particular. The consultant then summarized the entire story, of which the war period was merely a small but relevant part. The director was then asked about her feelings regarding the anger directed toward her by the staff. The director could understand their anger, but noted that the staff would mention her leaving in contexts irrelevant to the issue, particularly when wishing to shirk some of their responsibilities. She was asked whether she would agree to attend a joint meeting with the staff, where both she and they could express their feelings about her leaving during the war and where she would be able to share her reasons for acting in this way. After receiving her consent, a meeting with the staff was held.

The same process was performed with the staff. First, they told the story of the war, expressing their anger and disappointment with the director, contemplating the acceptance of her leadership. This was followed by a request to share their pre-war experiences of the director, which were generally positive. Then they were asked about the role of the department in the short-term and long-term future. After summarizing the story, highlighting the strength of the department's staff and the positive atmosphere at work, the consultant asked the staff members whether they could find a point of reconciliation between themselves and the director, taking into account that she would be continuing in the role and that the town's population needed a strong social services department, especially after the war. This question raised many conflicts among the staff, but most of them finally agreed that for the population's well-being and due to their commitment to their clients, regularization of director–staff relationships was important. However, most of them asked the director to apologize for abandoning them during such a difficult time. The meeting was very emotional on both sides. It started by the director telling her narrative regarding the war, which evoked anger with no signs of empathy. When the consultant asked about empathy toward the director's situation, a tense silence fell around the room. This silence was broken when one staff member said that she had no feelings of empathy toward the director, as all the workers had families in the city and were working under fire, but she was ready to put this aside and focus on future work. Other members concurred, while clarifying that they neither forgave the director nor accepted her accounts for leaving, but did accept her directorship. Although no reconciliation was achieved, the atmosphere in the department was stabilized and the day-to-day tasks were accomplished.

To sum up, while restructuring roles, boundaries, or powers following a collective traumatic event, it is important to view the functioning of the system in a larger time frame, including before and after the event. A long-term view of the system is necessary, to help systems to function in an imperfect reality, meaning that some situations are beyond the community member's current power to change. Thus, they must look at the least bad option and function within it, but not give up the activities that might create change even during or after traumatic events. Systemic community intervention can target either all community members, or specific groups in the community, such as groups of leaders and staff within various community institutions. It also includes developing services for the community population, such as families, who are considered a type of subsystem within the community.

Systemic Interventions With Families

From a systemic point of view, the family and its subsystems (parents/couples and children) is considered to be the basic system of human society. In line with this view, the family is the system in which the essence of pain resulting from a collective traumatic event is located. Different types of loss resulting from collective traumatic events are often centered within the family because of families' specific characteristics and roles. In the case of a mass disaster, people are initially connected to the loss of their own family members and family property and only afterwards to the loss of other families and friends. This is true for families living in different cultural contexts around the globe, as all have certain things in common: families are considered to be a place where individuals are protected and they are the source of socialization; and the family system is a source for developing usually positive, but also negative, intensive emotional connections. From a systemic point of view, it is important to underline the constant interaction between the family and society so that the messages conveyed by the society are appropriate to the characteristics and roles within the family.

The type of collective traumatic event often determines the nature of the harm caused to families. In cases of natural disaster or wars, the entire community might be destroyed, including many of the local families, contrary to terror attacks, where only some families within a community or nation are directly hurt. In some situations, the entire family is exposed to the traumatic events. In others, only one or more of the family members are exposed, but the entire family feels the effects. The type of damage may vary, ranging from severe cases, in which only one family member remains alive, through cases in which one or more family members suffer physical and/or mental injury, through to the loss of property. Thus, systemic intervention with families includes instrumental help along with different types of supportive psychosocial intervention.

The first question one may ask focuses on the uniqueness of systemic intervention in situations of collective trauma. Does it differ from the various interventions in cases of collective disasters described in writing in the last three decades? The answer to this question is somewhat complex, because some parts of the interventions are similar but the ideology, goals and role of the social workers and mental health helpers is somewhat different. Interventions implemented from a systemic point of view emphasize the role of the family as a healing system for its individual members. Thus, the system has a lot of power to provide healing and support to its members, as the individual members are nested within it (Hobfoll, 1998, 2001). The goal of family systemic intervention is to reestablish family structure in a way that leaves room for the experience and the reality in which the family exists. This goal can be reached only if the mental health helper acknowledges the power of the family system and uses this power in the service of healing. Various approaches developed in the field of family therapy may be useful for family systemic interventions in situations of collective trauma (Doherty & McDaniel, 2010; Minuchin, 1974; Boscolo et al., 1987; White & Epston, 1990), with specific tailoring to the specific traumatic events (Boss, 1999, 2007; Figley, 1990; Harkness & Zador, 2001; Landau & Saul, 2004; Walsh, 2007).

Before describing principles and techniques of family intervention in situations of collective trauma, I will provide two illustrations. The first will describe the natural strength of a family to create a healing system, and the second will describe the expectation from a family to be a healing system.

In the first example, Miriam was the only member of her family to survive the Holocaust. As many Jewish children were hidden by Polish families during World War II, she was found by a Jewish organization that searched for Jewish children who had survived the war by hiding in forests, small villages and with farming families. Miriam was sent with a group of children to one of the kibbutzim[8] in what was then still Palestine under the British Mandate (and in 1948 became Israel). She did not know how this came about, but her two uncles, who had immigrated to Palestine as pioneers before the war and who were living on a different kibbutz with their families, discovered that she was alive and was being raised on another kibbutz. They asked the education committee of their kibbutz to adopt Miriam and transfer her to live with them. Unfortunately, the education community refused to accept her, for reasons, which, today, would be unacceptable in the cultural context. For example, Miriam had adjusted very well to the group of children with whom she had arrived from Poland and into the host community, and the move would have involved a separation from this group. Despite the tremendous power of the kibbutz committees of that time, her uncles did not accept the decision and continued their struggle to bring Miriam to live with her extended family. They were ready to leave their community, but before taking this step, they applied to the kibbutzim movement education committee, who supported their request and instructed the local education committee to accept Miriam. Miriam moved to her uncles' kibbutz, where she was informally adopted by one of their families. She was raised as one of their children and was accepted as their older sister.

This description clearly illustrates the power and strength of the family, even in a structured community, where, at that time, the family and the individual took second place to the collective. It is possible to assume that such family strength can be expressed also in a different direction. Let us imagine that those who brought Miriam to Palestine (Israel) would have known that she had relatives in the country and would have put pressure on them to raise her. It is possible to assume that, in such a case, the family would use its power both directly and indirectly to avoid this challenge, as was often the case with other survivors. Therefore, the different ways of expressing the power of the family must be considered when meeting and helping families.

The other example is taken from a therapeutic discussion with Holocaust survivors about 65 years after the Holocaust. Mrs Y., an octogenarian, had survived Auschwitz as a young girl and returned to her hometown after the war. She discovered that her two older brothers and two older sisters had survived, whereas she already knew that her younger brother and her parents had died in the ghetto. Three of her siblings emigrated to the United States, and she and the other sister emigrated to Israel. Looking back in old age, she criticized her eldest brother for allowing the siblings to separate after the terrible war:

> we were all confused, but he was the eldest and he should have taken a stance and told us that we needed to stay together after losing our parents, our brother and many other relatives, and after experiencing the Nazi camps. I wouldn't have minded if it was in America or Israel. At that time, I didn't even know if I was a Zionist. I was a teenager, who had been left alone since the age of 10 and what I wanted was a family . . . and I still feel sad that he didn't insist. So I live in Israel and the sister who came with me moved to the United States five years later, so I stayed here by myself. But none of my other siblings were close. They were spread out over the United States; one lived in the East, one

in the West, one moved to West Canada . . . he should have told us to stay together.

This illustration emphasized the desire for leadership within a family. Mrs Y. expected the older brother to assume the parental position and guide the family. It seems, however, that after all their traumatic experiences, none of the siblings were capable of taking the lead to keep the family united and did not have the necessary strength to guide the family toward a joint decision-making process. At the end of World War II, mental health was not considered crucial to the healing process. It was only years later that mental health help was given to survivors, and usually in individual therapy. In addition, such a large number of nations, communities, families and individuals had been hurt that even if knowledge about the impact of collective traumatic events and appropriate interventions had been widespread, one may wonder whether there would have been enough professionals available to apply it. If family intervention had been implemented at the time, might the family members have reached a different decision? Or was the decision not to stay together really what the family wanted? In other words, helpers adopting a systemic view must understand that the power of a system carries far more weight than the power of theory or practical knowledge, even in cases where the system—in this case, a family system—was significantly hurt.

In the previous section, two general types of systemic intervention with communities in cases of collective trauma were described, one short-term and one long-term. However, when discussing systemic intervention with families, a more complex structure is required, as the levels of intervention may overlap, and the type of loss and damage might be more significant than the passage of time. Therefore, the structure of this section follows several general goals of intervention with families:

1 instrumental help;
2 working through the family members' traumatic experience and working through the loss;
3 restructuring the family system; and
4 writing the family narrative.

Instrumental Help

The following illustration describes one type of instrumental help given to a family after a terror attack in Israel:

One weekend, Mr T. and his wife went out for lunch to one of the restaurants in the city center. Their teenage children had a youth organization activity, and chose not to join their parents.

A few minutes after they started their meal, a loud explosion was heard. Mr T. remembered chaos, people shouting and running out of the restaurant, as well as blood, smoke, dust and destruction. He found himself on the floor, having been thrown by the force of the blast. He started to crawl outside, while calling to his wife. He continued to look for her and call her name, but did not find her. When the police and first aid forces arrived, he was asked to leave the premises. One policeman suggested that he go home and wait and maybe his wife would arrive soon. Mr T. went home and waited there for half an hour. He tried calling his wife, but there was no reply and she did not arrive home. Mr T. began looking for her in the hospitals around the city. When he arrived at the first hospital, social workers approached him and asked him if other people in the family needed to be taken care of while he was looking for his wife. Mr T. told them about his two children and suggested that they would stay with their good friends' families, whose parents they knew very well. The social workers called the two families, who both agreed to take care of the children. Mr T. asked the social workers to guide these families, to tell the children that their father was all right and that he was looking for their mother, who had not yet been found. He also promised that he would call them as soon as he had more news. Mr T. asked the social worker to call his wife's brother to join him in his search and to call his sister to ask her to stay at Mr T.'s home to answer calls by extended family members and friends.[9] After the social workers took care of these initial instrumental needs, Mr T. continued to look for his wife.

This illustration focuses on one important issue included in instrumental first aid—taking care of children and other family members who need 24/7 nursing care. In this example, it was straightforward because the children were teenagers and had close friends, and Mr T. had suitable members of the extended family who could be called on and were ready and available to help. In other cases, in which both parents were injured or killed, social workers had to take care of the children and to place them within the extended family, or if this was not possible, either with foster families or in other institutions. This illustration focuses on a traumatic event that did not destroy the entire community, so that social institutions, such as social services departments, continued to function. Furthermore, the traumatic event happened within a society that had unfortunately become accustomed to such attacks and had developed a trained helping system to take care of first aid and long-term assistance.

In other situations, the helping forces might take several days to arrive, and only then begin to provide first aid, which usually takes the form of community intervention. However, if enough helping forces are available, it is helpful to open first aid centers for families to provide clear information regarding the provision of instrumental needs, such as shelter, food and clothing. It might also be helpful for mental health and psychosocial helpers to reach out and find families who need support in obtaining the instrumental help. Some families might have lost one of the parents. In other families, the parents might be confused and therefore need more attentive care. Some extended families or friends provide this care independent of external intervention, but in some other situations, especially when the damage includes large populations, families tend to take care of their own members first, even at the expense of other families. However, thousands of stories tell of the generosity of people who are willing to help and care for others even in difficult situations. These people serve as a source of strength for the helping forces who seek families to accompany others in acquiring their basic needs. As mentioned several times in this book, it is important to note that the role of psychosocial and mental health professionals in situations of collective and national trauma begins with concern for the provision of basic needs in a way that includes the entire population. Providing basic needs is not part of the role of mental health and psychosocial helpers, but they are responsible for identifying those who, for various reasons, are not able to obtain basic instrumental needs.

Working Through the Traumatic Experience and the Grief

Although families might be open to receiving instrumental help, they might be more suspicious of help that includes mental health aspects. In some societies, mental health help is interpreted as an indication of "craziness" or "sickness." In other societies, it is perceived as an indication of weakness and others merely wish to bury the painful memories, afraid to reawaken them by talking. Adults are more willing to ask for mental health help for their children than for themselves or for other adults in the family. Thus, access might be gained to many families via the children's needs. Adults might report their children's anxieties, fears, sadness, or other symptoms that often characterize depression. Discussing these symptoms with the entire family is a way to help not only the children but all the family members. Coping with these symptoms can be a way of restructuring family functioning by constructing the meaning of the traumatic experience and loss in a way that enables the family to be a supporting and containing system for its members.

It is possible to assume that families might begin by describing symptoms displayed by one or more of their members, mainly the children, resulting from the traumatic events. The family's description often includes an experience of the trauma and grief combined, even though they are theoretically considered to be two different entities. In many cases, however, they might overlap. Systemic intervention means working according to the family's needs and not according to trauma theories that differentiate between the traumatic experience and the grief. For many families, the intervention is the first space in which they can talk and listen to each other. The following example was described by Dr M., a psychiatrist and family therapist from Bosnia, who was working with families and children who had survived the war with the Serbs in the 1990s:

The family included a father and three children—two sons and a daughter of around 12 years old. The father applied for help because of his daughter's anxiety attacks. Shortly after the war, the mother had died of cancer. The daughter had told the father that the anxiety attacks were provoked by thoughts regarding the war. He also mentioned that these attacks had not started immediately after the war, but a month after the mother's death. The father also mentioned that the family had been forced to separate during the war; he had been with the boys while the daughter had been with her mother. This separation had lasted for more than a month and they never talked about this difficult period. About a month after the war, the mother's illness was diagnosed and they tried to care for her while attempting to rebuild their life. They apparently put aside the horrors of the war and channeled their energy into fighting the illness and attempting rehabilitation. Rebuilding their life focused mainly on achieving instrumental needs. The father had to renovate their home that had been destroyed during the war, and find a new job, as well as running the household and raising the children as a single working parent. In addition, the family had to adjust to the new regime, as fewer of their citizens' needs were financed by the state than had been previously.

After listening to the family's description, the psychiatrist responded by telling the family that it is not unusual for people to experience such symptoms following traumatic events, and that they are even more common when the traumatic experience includes loss. She then asked the daughter if she would agree to share the thoughts that come into her mind during the anxiety attacks. The daughter agreed and described an incident in which she and her mother had been separated, during the period of separation from the rest of the family. The father intervened and asked the daughter to tell him what had happened there. In response to this request, the psychiatrist asked the daughter whether she felt ready to recount what had happened at that time and in that setting. The daughter agreed and described the period when the Serbs had separated her and her mother from the father and the brothers, and described what had happened when she was separated from her mother for several hours. Implicit from the story was the daughter's strength and bravery. While she was describing her experience, the look on the father's face changed several times from sadness to pride. When the daughter had finished, the father acknowledged her bravery by telling her how proud he was of her strength to cope with such a difficult situation and her older and younger brothers followed suit. The psychiatrist added to the father's and brothers' response by pointing out that the family's ability to acknowledge pain and strength indicates their mutual warmth and care. The daughter responded by saying that she did not perceive herself as a heroine, but quite the contrary, as she had not been able to save her mother's life in the end. This comment introduced an additional direction for discussion, which focused on the loss.

An analysis of this illustration can point to several processes that are relevant to systemic intervention with families who experienced collective or national trauma. First, it was clear that when people had instrumental and mental targets simultaneously, they tended to put aside their mental pain as much as was possible and focused on basic instrumental needs. This is the reason why many traumatic stress symptoms might appear long after the traumatic event. Furthermore, many people think that repressing the horrors will help them to rid themselves of the trauma, and this is true for many trauma survivors, who have succeeded in encapsulating their memories, leaving themselves free for daily functioning. Having done so, however, many of these people find the strength to create an opportunity to share the horrors with other people.

Second, family intervention can be a context in which the family members can share their experiences. In this example, the psychiatrist offered them this option, while exercising caution and sensitivity by asking the daughter whether this was an appropriate time and context in which to tell the story. Such sensitivity is necessary because in situations of collective trauma, and especially during wars, people can have had experiences that they cannot or do not wish to share with the entire family—such as rape, torture, humiliation. In addition, recounting the traumatic experience might be counterproductive. The father's request to hear the daughter's experience of when they had been separated resembled a request for debriefing, and studies of debriefing show confusing outcomes (Hawker, Durkin & Hawker, 2011; Robinson, 2007; Tuckey, 2007). Positive outcomes were found when the debriefing process focused on cognitive and educational aspects, without entering the emotional level (Adler et al., 2011; Hawker, Durkin & Hawker, 2011; Robinson, 2007; Tuckey, 2007). I do not have the transcript of the intervention process, but based on the psychiatrist's description, the daughter told her story and was not interrupted either by requests to share her feelings and emotional reactions during the traumatic period, or to share her emotional reactions while she was telling her story. This was an opportunity for the daughter to share her experience with people who were close to her, and their listening made them witnesses of her pain. The opportunity to share painful experiences was found to have a healing effect because it validates the victims' perceptions of the horrors they underwent (Adler et al., 2011; Denborough, 2008; Prince, 2009). In narrative therapy, this is defined as "witnessing," but it is used also outside the therapeutic context. One example is the Spielberg project in which Holocaust survivors are interviewed about their experience during the war. Many of the participants reflected that this was helpful because they felt that the interviewer was listening and was interested in their story. They were also reassured that their experience would not be lost—it was videotaped and a copy was given to their family. In the present illustration, the father, brothers and psychiatrists validated the daughter's painful experience by referring to her ability to handle the situation with bravery and strength. The question can be asked here about what can be said to someone who has not acted bravely. According to the daughter's response, she perceived herself as neither brave nor strong. It is possible to assume that by behaving in the way she did, she had been able to survive. In extremely stressful situations, victims seek different means of survival, which might be different than their regular behavior in daily life. However, such behaviors make sense when looked at in relation to the context in which they occurred and are validated as a courageous and legitimate way to survive in immoral situations. This validation provided by listening to the victim's story reduces the sense of shame that they often experience. The perception by significant others, such as family members, of these behaviors as bravery and as a means of survival, allows the victims not to be ashamed of the way they behaved.

Third, from a systemic point of view, mental health helpers may raise the following questions: What was the daughter's emotional role in the family? Was she the one who took it upon herself to bear the anxiety and sadness of the entire family? Did her expression of anxiety release the other family members from dealing with their own anxieties and sadness related to the experience of war? Why was the daughter the one to take over this emotional role? Was this related to gender issues? Were Bosnian men allowed to express their feelings, especially those related to vulnerability? Additional questions may be focused on the onset of the anxiety attacks—a month after the mother's death. Why did the anxiety attacks start only then? Could this have been related to the potentially new emotional or practical role as the single female in the family, which the daughter had taken upon herself, or had been steered toward by others in the family? These issues had to be brought to the family's attention as the therapeutic process progressed. Making the family aware of such issues could provide additional understanding of the "normality" of the daughter's symptoms, besides the explanation offered by the psychiatrist in the session regarding typical responses to traumatic events (Minuchin & Fishman, 1981). The family context after the war could provide additional understanding of the daughter's anxiety—besides the impact of the war, they had to deal with the mother's illness and the pain of losing her. As the only female in the family, it is quite reasonable to assume that the daughter might have attempted to fulfill the traditionally female role. When this proved too difficult, the stress was manifest through anxiety attacks.

Great care must be taken when raising this issue, to avoid being perceived as critical or intrusive. Indirect or general questions can be asked, such as: How are painful feelings expressed in the family? Do different members of the family express these feelings differently? How did the family get organized when they had to rebuild their life while taking care of the sick mother? How did they arrange their daily routine after the mother had died? What was the functional role of each person in the family? Did they talk about the mother? How did they grieve for her? Artistic methods can be used in families with younger children. Therapists can ask the family to draw their fears, or to imagine "hero forces" that can fight and conquer the fear. Connections can be made between these heroes, either to "join forces" against the fears, or to try to communicate and make peace with the fears. Therapeutic techniques used in structured family therapy (Minuchin & Fishman, 1981), narrative family therapy (White & Epston, 1990) and solution-focused family therapy (De-Shazer, 1988) can be used to facilitate the session.

Fourth, at the end of the intervention, the daughter described her guilt feelings for not being able to save the mother from her illness. The literature on the impact of collective trauma describes feelings of guilt often experienced by victims (Hodgkinson & Stewart, 1998). From a systemic point of view, it is possible to assume that the family might be subconsciously carrying some latent feelings of guilt. These surfaced indirectly when the daughter mentioned not having been able to save her mother. When using systemic thinking and systemic intervention, it is possible to ask about the focus of these guilt feelings. As a response to the daughter's comment, she could be asked if she felt responsible for her mother's death. If so, how did she reach this conclusion? Maybe some of the guilt was rooted in the time they were together during the war. One method used intensively in systemic therapy is circular questioning, invented by the Milan group (Boscolo et al., 1987). Circular questioning enables the therapist to bring the spirit of the mother into the therapy room by asking the daughter and the other family members how they think the mother would have responded if she could have heard the daughter expressing her feelings. This can also be an opportunity to begin a discussion about guilt evoked by the experience of collective traumatic events, which might be the cause of traumatic stress symptoms, as well as guilt that might be evoked after the loss of a significant other. In such a discussion, the helper can normalize the appearance of the guilt feelings in the two situations by providing scientific information, as well as by using cognitive techniques, especially by pointing to a contextual irrational belief that causes a sense of guilt (Ellis, 1997; Malkinson, 2007). It is common to find irrational beliefs among survivors. These include the sense that they could have saved other people, but did not try hard enough, or that something bad in their personality enabled them to survive. Returning to the illustration, discussing the issue of guilt between family members can also clarify whether direct or indirect communications within the family evoke these feelings and whether actual blame was put on the daughter or on other members of the family. The goal of family intervention is to turn the family into a support system that can release both the system and its members from these guilt feelings. As guilt feelings often increase anxiety and depression, reducing the guilt by creating family support might result in fewer anxiety attacks.

Let us move on from the illustration, for a while, and focus on families in which only one person was exposed to the traumatic event, such as soldiers who return from war suffering from PTSD. When they return to their families, they might have a low level of tolerance and become angry quickly; they might be depressed and anxious and unable to function on a daily basis. The sense of guilt because of their reactions at home is added to their overall traumatic stress experience. Often, they neither want to ask their family members directly for help because they do not think that they deserve it, nor do they wish to share their war experience with the family. This might be for fear of being misunderstood or that the family members will not be strong enough to contain the terrifying experiences. On the other hand, the family members might not feel capable of helping their suffering relative (Dekel & Monson, 2010; Figley, 1978, 1990). In such cases, family interventions open up these issues for direct communication, reducing some of the guilt feelings and allowing empathic communication between the suffering person and the rest of the family. Reframing (Minuchin & Fishman, 1981) can be used, as well as defining the family as people who continue to fight for their family relationships despite the obstacles. Some battles are lost and others are won, but the mutual support is ongoing.

The fifth process that can be learned from the illustration centers on the family intervention as an option to open up communication between the family members regarding issues that were not openly discussed in daily life. Although I am familiar with only one of the intervention sessions, it is possible to assume that the psychiatrist would have invited the father and the brother to share their own experiences during the time of separation from the mother and the daughter. As mentioned above, this must be approached in a sensitive way because opening up their memories and experiences is counterproductive for some people. Some families find it helpful to perform a ritual that distances the family members from the experience, especially if they developed a negative reaction after telling their story. Some families write down their experiences and placed them in an envelope, which they bury, symbolically placing the experiences outside the family. Other families hide the envelope in their home, for future generations to open and read. (This will be discussed further when addressing family narratives.) When young children are involved, the act can include painting as well as writing. Working through the traumatic experience and the loss is usually a long process, but the family intervention can be short. The principle of systemic intervention is that even a small amount of direction can stimulate the system and help it to establish a healing process.

Restructuring the Family System

Restructuring the family system, and working through the traumatic experience and the loss are often inseparable in the family intervention process. Whereas restructuring the family system focuses mainly on the functional role within families, working through the painful experiences focuses mainly on emotional roles. Nonetheless, functional roles usually have emotional aspects and emotional roles have functional aspects. The process of restructuring the family aims to define roles within the family based on the new conditions and to empower the family members within the new roles. The family from Bosnia initially had to work out how to continue their life under the new regime: Did the father go back to his previous job? Was he still considered to be the powerful head of the family? How did the experience of war impact his self-image as a father and a husband in the specific cultural and family context? And how did this impact his children's perception of him? The role of the mental health professional in the helping process is not only to assess which areas of the father's functioning were damaged, how and whether they could be repaired and how to empower the father. The description of the psychiatrist's session with the family did not provide adequate information regarding the experience of the father and his sons during the war. It often happens that children, especially teenagers, are able to cope more effectively than their parents in traumatic situations, which may result in loss of the parents' power. When working with families, mental health helpers need to assist them to differentiate between the time during and immediately after the traumatic event, and a "'normal" situation. Thus, empowering the father and encouraging him to resume his role is often crucial to the family's functioning. However, the experience gained by the children during the traumatic period can be of benefit to the family, who usually need to cope with many issues to return to a normal life. One direction of family intervention is to explore how the parents can use their children's experience and talents without relinquishing their role as leaders of the family.

Following the death of family members either during or immediately after the traumatic event, as in the above illustration, the family must decide who will be responsible for the roles previously fulfilled by the mother. They cannot all be performed by the daughter or by another child in the family, and although the tasks can be shared, it is important to remember that children still need an adult parental figure in the home. Extended family members, if they exist, can be a source of instrumental and emotional support, and need to be reached by the nuclear family and if necessary with the assistance of the mental health helper.

A restructure in family functioning is needed also when one of the leading figures has been hurt in a collective traumatic event, such as soldiers who return to their families after a war. In many of these situations, the leading figure who remained at home has acquired a lot of power, having become accustomed to functioning alone and making independent decisions. Sometimes, one of the children acquires this power and may turn into a parental child (Minuchin, 1974). In spite of wishing for the father or mother's return, it is not always easy to readjust to sharing on a daily basis, or to a lessening of autonomy. Adjustment takes time and the family must extend its boundaries to enable its returning relative to regain his or her position. This is more difficult when a soldier returns home with painful war experiences and often with varied levels of PTSD. The return home from war usually involves high expectations from both sides. Although the family learned to gain some stability during the time the parent or soldier was away, they still missed him and longed for his return to share the daily tasks. The soldier expects to leave the battlefield behind and to resume his role in what is expected to be a warm family environment. This is often not the case, however. When soldiers come home, they lose the social support system of the friends with whom they experienced the horrors of war. The return home might be accompanied by disappointment characterized by both partners' sense of loneliness. This is fertile ground for ongoing family battles, in which the children are torn between the parents (Figley, 1978; Hogancamp & Figley, 1983).

A crucial goal of intervention with these families is the restructuring and rebalancing of the family system. It is important to provide information regarding family reunions after wars, including the impact of war experiences on soldiers. This can reduce the level of anxiety that one is "not normal." The family is also in great need of help in restructuring its daily life, taking into consideration the impact of the war on the ability of parent/partner/soldier to resume the previous role and of the other partner to relinquish some of the power gained during that time. This requires careful assessment that provides a picture of the present management of daily life, including role implementation, decision-making processes, communication around daily functioning, and the sense of the ability to request and receive help. In addition, it is important to find out whether the family can become an emotional support system for the person who has experienced the war. Physical and/or mental injury might prevent the return to the same role or level of functioning, and the mental health helper can assist in finding ways to restructure roles and decision-making processes in which the returning person can continue to function and regain family respect. Based on systemic thinking, it is helpful to identify support systems in the environment, such as from extended family or from other families who have undergone similar processes.

The ability to help among families who underwent similar experiences has been studied previously (Possick, Sadeh & Shamai, 2008) and was used in the context of mental health intervention in several situations of collective trauma (Boss, 2002). The most common access to this source of help was through multi-family groups, where the entire family joins a support group for families dealing with similar experiences and difficulties. In such a group, people not only share their difficulties but discover that they are neither "different" nor "strange," but are facing difficulties typical to many families in the same situation. The families share different coping strategies, which others can adopt in their own coping process. This sharing can enrich problem-solving processes and can lead to others finding creative ways to deal with their difficulties (Reid, 1978). Children who take part in these meetings have the option of participating in the discussion, or of spending time doing activities, such as arts and crafts, with other children. They are still within earshot of the discussion, even if they are occupied with other things, and learn that their family members are not "bad," "angry," or "crazy," but are coping with situations typical to families who have shared similar experiences. In some of these meetings, the mental health helper facilitating the discussion might ask the children to express their point of view and make suggestions. Giving the children the opportunity to be heard, which might rarely happen in the midst of the daily tension at home, has two functions. First, it can provide a way for them to ventilate their feelings within a supportive context. Second, it opens up communication channels between parents and children in a safe context, where both children and parents can be supported by the other group participants, as well as by the mental health professionals who can use techniques for increasing communication skills (Stuart, 2004). Third, children are often creative and might have original ideas that could help the family.

To sum up, family restructuring is a complex task, as it moves between functional or even instrumental issues, while touching the emotions under the surface. When families come for help, they tend to raise mainly functional issues of one family member or the impact of the functional issues on relationships. However, to deal with these issues, they must work through the painful feelings attached to the need to restructure the family's roles and decision-making processes. It goes without saying that addressing these feelings means relating to the painful experiences of the traumatic event.

Writing the Family Narrative

Writing the family narrative seems to be a part of working through the traumatic stress and loss. According to systemic thinking, however, the family narrative needs to include the family's overall experience, which includes instrumental, functional and emotional aspects. The content and structure of the family narrative relates to its essence and goals.

The Essence of the Narrative

What is the essence of the narrative? Does it emphasize only weakness and a negative attitude toward the coping process? Does it emphasize only heroism? Or does it provide a comprehensive view in which weakness and heroism are integrated in the shadow of the traumatic experience? A narrative that is saturated with descriptions and words that criticize some or all of the family members diminishes the family's ability to find the necessary strength for the coping process. A narrative focused solely on heroism prevents working on pain, anger, rage, criticism and other negative aspects. An integrative narrative allows the family to be in touch with its strength as well as with the negative feelings experienced during the traumatic event.

An integrative narrative is created through the following stages (White & Epston, 1990). First, the mental health professional listens to the family members' descriptions of the difficulties that led them to ask for help and how they connected the difficulties with the traumatic event. Second, once the helper has received some hints about the family's experience of the traumatic event, he or she can make further inquiries about the family's experience. At this stage, the family can bring different descriptions because they were in different places during the event or because they have different views regarding the event. Third, the helper tells the family what he or she has heard from them, in a similar way to how the family members told the story. However, differences and agreements within the family story can be identified. The impact of collective trauma can confuse the timing and sequence of events, and it is important to retell the family narrative in the order in which things happened. Organizing the timeline of events can help the family members to make sense of incidents that occurred either during or after the traumatic event. For example, some might think that they were abandoned by their families, whereas the families had actually had no means of making contact. To edit the family narrative according to the time sequence, the helper may ask some clarifying questions about the order of events. Retelling the story to the family using the family's language and metaphors has a witnessing effect; the story was heard attentively by another person, who accepts the experiences of the different family members. After telling the story, the family is asked to reflect on the way it was told and to clarify apparent inaccuracies. In the fourth stage, the family members retell their narrative led by the helper's questions, which are designed to assist the family to re-edit its story in an integrative way, emphasizing the weak and painful parts along with parts describing strengths. Below are some of the optional questions to ask families whose story is saturated with negative descriptions: You described the reaction of some or all of the family members using words such as "helpless" and "paralyzed." Were there moments when the reactions were different? How do you explain these reactions? Can they be explained differently? Based on what was happening around you (the context), can these behaviors be perceived differently than under normal circumstances? How? What did you like about the way the family functioned or about family relationships during the difficult time? What do you like about your family relationships in the present?

The following are optional questions for families whose narrative includes only the heroism perspective: Is there anyone in the family who does not perceive him or herself as a hero/heroine? What will happen if different perspectives will be raised? Will this diminish the heroism, which was obviously expressed in your behavior during and after the traumatic event? Disasters such as the one that your family experienced often evoke feelings of anger or rage, sadness and even helplessness. I wonder if any of you felt these emotions and how they impacted your behavior. What is it about your family that maintained the sense of capability even during the difficult period? And how did this help you to overcome feelings of helplessness or anxiety in certain situations?

At this stage, family members can listen to each other's different perspectives on various incidents, sometimes for the first time. In the fifth stage, the helper retells the story again, editing it according to the information provided by the family. Based on this information, it is possible to enrich the narrative with more details, more points of view and perspectives of the family members. This process gives a place to the sense of helplessness together with strength, and to fear, anxiety and sadness along with a sense of power. The sixth stage of helping to create the family narrative goes beyond the essence of the narrative and depends on its goals.

The Goals of the Family Narrative

What are the goals of family narrative? Does the family use the narrative as a way to survive and as a defense tool that helps them cope with the daily difficulties and justifies their decision-making processes? If this is the case, it is possible to find a rigid narrative saturated with descriptions either criticizing or praising the behavior of family members. Any deviation from this story is not accepted. As people arrange their lives according to their stories, rigid narratives may limit problem-solving and decision-making options and general creativity that is needed to cope with the impact of collective trauma. A rigid narrative that focuses on criticism might also damage the sense of hope that is always needed when coping with difficulties. Therefore, the fifth stage of writing the family narrative, the helping process, includes questions regarding the future: How do the family members see their life five, ten, fifteen years on? What will be good for the family? What will make them into a happy family? What might still be difficult? What are the family's current strengths that can impact the future? At this stage, the mental health helper assists the family members in writing their future narrative. Contemplating the relatively distant future allows the family members to channel their imaginations and release some of the present troubles that might also reduce the level of stress.

Another goal of family narrative is to create a family story as a legacy to be passed down to future generations. This is a natural human desire. The mental health helpers may ask family members what they especially wish to convey to their future generations about the family regarding the collective traumatic event and how this can be done. This also provides an opportunity to memorialize lost family members, by recounting and discussing the different family members' experiences with the deceased. The sixth stage is an active phase of intervention, when the family and the mental health helper actually write the family narrative. The narrative can include drawings by the children or by other family members as well as photographs. Some families choose to dedicate the document to the memory of family members who died in the traumatic event. The mental health helper might present the family with his or her own written impressions and acknowledgment of the family's coping. As was found in practice, this type of formal acknowledgment gives strength and support to the family (Boscolo et al., 1987; Denborough, 2008; Shamai, Sharlin & Gilad-Smolinski, 1994). The process can be ended as a ritual, in which both the family members and the mental health professionals share their experiences during the writing of the family narrative. If the family wishes, these rituals can include several minutes in which they remember lost family members, but the ritual must be structured according to the family's wishes. The idea will not suit all families, and some might reject it, or even react to the suggestion with cynicism or anger.

Interventions with families in situations of collective and national trauma are often titled, in the professional literature, as interventions with families and individuals. However, most of the interventions described focus on the individual, while the family is perceived only as a supportive background to contain the individual's pain. As was mentioned at the beginning of this chapter, several of these individual interventions have been empirically evaluated and have been found to be effective (Engelhard et al., 2010; Hoffman, 2010; Nayak, Power & Foa, 2012; Foa, 2011). However, it is rare to find interventions that work with the family as a unit that needs to rebuild itself as a functional and emotional system. The uniqueness of the systemic intervention is the ability to look at the wider picture that includes the entire family, even if only one or a small number of family members exhibit symptoms. The systemic view of interventions in situations of collective and national trauma does not ignore the need for individual medical or psychosocial help, but always relates to the suffering of individuals as impacted by the context and as impacting the context of family, community and nation. In addition, this is a practical view, because in many places around the globe, mental health services for individuals are limited and the natural system in the environment might provide some of the necessary help. However, it should be noted that families can receive medical and individual psychosocial help together with the family systemic intervention. This individual help can be discussed during the family intervention, especially if the family shows some resistance to the medical or individual psychosocial help. In such cases, the mental health helper can be a source of information regarding the type of medical or individual psychosocial help and if necessary, can act as mediator between the family and the psychiatrist, psychologist, or social workers providing the individual intervention.

Concluding Comments About Systemic Interventions

Systemic interventions in situations of collective and national trauma were described according to the different systems: nation, community and family (see Table 4.1). However, these interventions are interrelated: To develop appropriate policies to help the victim population, the national authorities are informed of the needs of communities, families and individuals. Based on this information, national helping policies can be planned and provided to the hurt population (see Figure 4.1). Based on systemic thinking, it is possible to assume that the implications of the systemic interventions reach beyond the three target systems (nation, community and families). They may affect larger systems, including the cultural system. As discussed in Chapter 2, collective and national traumatic events may impact the culture also because their consequences interact with norms, values, belief systems and narratives that are an

Table 4.1 Summary of goals, tasks and techniques of systemic intervention

Systemic Intervention on the National Level	Systemic Intervention on the Community Level	Systemic Intervention on the Family Level
Goals	Goals	Goals
1 Helping the national system to regain homeostasis after the traumatic event	1 Helping the community system to regain homeostasis after the traumatic event	1 Helping the family system to regain homeostasis after the traumatic event
2 Restructuring the national system: Supporting the development of national policy that will take into account the experience of the traumatic event	2 Developing connection with the national regime	2 Family working through the loss
3 Collectively working through the national loss	3 Collectively working through the community loss	
Tasks	Tasks	Tasks
Providing consultation to politicians and policy makers on the following issues:	Emergent interventions:	1 Helping the family to obtain the instrumental help (such as basic needs)
1 The necessity of providing basic needs in the short- and long-term	1 If necessary, arranging joint community evacuation	2 Working through the traumatic experience and the grief
2 Preserving human rights: focusing on vulnerable and at-risk populations	2 Developing or supporting formal and informal leadership system	3 Restructuring the family system (helping to define roles, supporting parents' role and leadership, acknowledging children's experiences, identifying effective family decision-making processes)
3 Raising the issues of mental health needs resulting from the traumatic event	3 Providing accurate information regarding instrumental help, such as places and times of distribution of basic needs	
	4 Preserving human rights: focusing on vulnerable and at-risk populations	

4 Being involved in planning mental health policy: Providing information regarding the information needed from subsystems (states, municipal regions, etc.) to learn about the needs of the populations, and developing, monitoring and evaluating mental health services

5 Suggesting activities that enhance public mental health, such as providing accurate information to the public, establishing a national memorial ceremony, creating sense of togetherness and reconciliation

Techniques

1 Systemic joining with the different politicians, leaders and policy makers; giving space for the different voices and opinions

2 Explaining possible impacts of collective traumatic events on mental health

---

5 If possible, providing information regarding the damages and plans for the short term

6 Helping to create community routine

7 Initial assessment of people with traumatic symptoms

Long-term intervention:

1 Collective working through the community loss

2 Developing and maintaining mental health and welfare services for vulnerable and at-risk populations

Techniques

1 Systemic joining with the different formal and informal leaders in the community; giving space for the different voices and opinions

2 Psycho-educational techniques: Providing information regarding impact of collective trauma and its effect on communities, families and individuals

2 Focusing on strength, using reframing and defining phenomena in relation to the traumatic context

---

4 Enhancing sharing of experiences and emotion regarding the traumatic event

5 Writing the family narrative

Techniques

1 Systemic joining with all family members

2 Reframing and normalizing the traumatic symptoms

3 Supporting communication between family members, especially regarding the traumatic event

4 Circular questioning

5 Using narrative techniques

6 Creating family rituals

(continued)

Table 4.1 (continued)

Systemic Intervention on the National Level		Systemic Intervention on the Community Level		Systemic Intervention on the Family Level	
3	Listening to and empowering national leaders and policy makers, who often need to maintain a "strong" position for the public and might feel lonely in their roles	3	Supporting and empowering community formal and/or grass-roots leaders	7	Psycho-educational techniques: Providing information regarding impact of collective trauma and its effect on families and individuals (adults/children)
4	Recognizing and acknowledging activities that enhance psychosocial welfare and mental health, such as national rituals, memorialization ceremonies and reconciliation rituals	4	Guiding and training of community leaders, religious leaders, teachers, physicians, etc.		
		5	Organizing community assembly/conversation groups within community		
		6	Using collective community rituals to work through the loss and for memorialization		
		7	Using narrative techniques to write the community narrative		
		8	Using art techniques (painting, drama, music, etc.) to work through the loss		

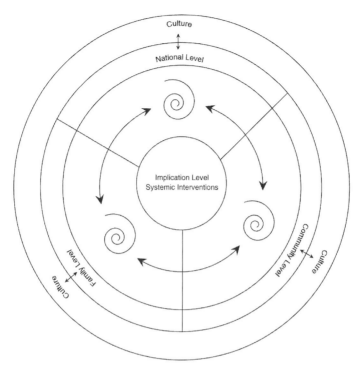

Figure 4.1 Interactions between levels of systemic interventions in situations of collective and national trauma.

integral part of the culture. As a result, beliefs, values and narratives inherent within the culture may be changed, while new beliefs, narratives and values may be added. Since the systemic interventions and their implications are part of the construct of the traumatic event, they may also impact the culture within which they were implemented. In addition, it should be remembered that the cultural values, norms and beliefs color the implementation of the interventions. The goals of all levels of intervention include instrumental and emotional help using some similar techniques, such as providing information and support, facilitating communication, working on loss and ambiguous loss, and rituals for memorializing the dead, as well as specific techniques tailored to the size and structure of the system. Some of the goals and techniques are used in other types of interventions that are not based on systemic thinking. However, the difference in use depends on the way the assessment and the goals of intervention are constructed. Therefore, it is possible to find similar use of techniques in a different context of intervention, which is what makes the difference in implementing the intervention process. I end this chapter by repeating an empirical fact: Most systems and individuals are resilient and can find sources of help within their natural social systems, without the interventions of psychosocial and mental health helpers (Bonanno, 2004). In addition, natural systems usually have more power than the helping system. Therefore, any intervention that is implemented should take into consideration both the power of the system and human strength, even when symptoms related to traumatic stress and grief are expressed. Even if systems appear to be stuck as a result of the collective traumatic event, this is not the case. Sometimes, they just need the intervention to function like an enzyme, which helps the system to develop strategies to cope with the challenges it has to face (Boscolo et al., 1987).

Notes

1 The negative feedback loop maintained homeostasis, while the positive feedback loop shook the homeostasis.
2 The content, process and techniques used in various systems will be described in detail in the following sections of this chapter.
3 Retrieved from: http://www.goodreads.com/author/quotes/5943.Desmond_Tutu.
4 It is beyond the scope of this book to evaluate the efficacy of the short- and long-term interventions implemented by the U.S. and Japanese governments. However, it is important to mention that such interventions were implemented and had positive as well as negative impacts on the communities that were coping with the situations.
5 Apples and honey are traditionally eaten on the Jewish New Year.
6 In Israeli culture, it is common for families to open their houses to families who have been evacuated during emergencies. This is organized through the media and through special centers established for this purpose. This happened also in the United Kingdom during the Blitz in World War II, when people from rural areas invited families and children from London to stay with them. In many cultures, however, hosting evacuated people in private houses means violating the sense of privacy.
7 This assumption was found to be true in a study that examined the resilience of several communities living close to the Lebanese border (Kimhi & Shamai, 2004).
8 Plural of kibbutz, which is a collective community existing only in Israel, integrating Zionism and socialism.
9 During the Second Intifada (2000–4), Israel experienced large numbers of terror attacks at an intensive rate. Following an attack, people usually called their families and friends who lived close to the location of the attack, or who might have been in the area. The large numbers of calls in a very short time often resulted in the collapse of the telephone system.

5

IMPACT OF
INTERVENTIONS ON
THE HELPERS' SYSTEM

Compassion Fatigue and Secondary Traumatization

I came home at 3 a.m. after being with A. [a man whose son had been killed and his wife seriously injured in a terrorist attack] for about 11 hours . . . his son had not been found in any of the city's hospitals and he had been asked to come to the morgue. I waited for him in the cab that took us there . . . and he came with his brother . . . there was such silence . . . I started to introduce myself and my role but he stopped me angrily . . . I tried to develop some contact with him but he didn't respond . . . this attitude changed when we entered the morgue. It was shocking . . . meeting with all the victims' families and knowing that they were waiting to hear that their son, daughter, spouse, or whoever, was dead. He started talking to me. I don't even remember how he started or whether I was the one who asked something . . . after identifying his son's body, he came out of the room and walked toward me in tears and let me support him . . . On the way back home, there was the same silence in the cab. I escorted him home and we started talking about the funeral arrangements and about how he was going to tell his wife and the other children about the loss of the youngest son, their brother. I made some suggestions and together, we figured out the best way to tell the family. He wanted to do it alone, without my being present . . . He started telling me about his family and about the son who had been killed. I stayed with him for about an hour until his sister arrived . . . I came home and could not sleep, I had to feel my children, to touch them, physically, I felt it in my body, in my hands . . . as if I had to feel that they were alive. So I did crazy things. I got into my eldest son's bed, and he threw me out; so did my daughter and my youngest son. So I went to my own bed. My husband had no choice but to accept me. It took me several weeks to return to normal life . . . and even today, after more than a year, you interview me and I can't stop crying.

This quote is from an interview conducted as part of a research project to study how social workers, who were assigned to help direct and indirect victims of national and collective traumatic events—in this specific case, a nationalist terror attack in Israel—cope with helping, on the professional and personal level (Ron & Shamai, 2011; Shamai & Ron, 2009). This citation describes a phenomenon that was studied and described over the last three decades, referring to the negative and painful consequences of indirect exposure to a traumatic event through helping someone close who has experienced trauma.

The phenomenon has several names, but all of them, as Arvay (2001b) claimed, referred to the same concept. McCann and Pearlman (1990) and Pearlman and Saakvitne (1995) coined the term "vicarious traumatization" to describe painful and negative consequences. Figley (1988) used the term "secondary victimization," and later, "secondary traumatic stress disorder" (STSD) and "compassion fatigue" (Figley, 1988, 1995a, 1995b, 1995c). STSD and PTSD have identical symptoms (*DSM*, 2013). The difference lies in the type of exposure to the traumatic event: PTSD is a result of direct exposure, whereas exposure resulting in STSD is an indirect effect of the empathic care provided to traumatized persons. Here, I will use the term "secondary traumatic stress disorder" (STSD), because this describes the essential characteristic of the phenomenon that exists only in a systemic context. Secondary traumatization implies some relation to primary traumatization and these relationships are the cause of the development of secondary traumatization. Secondary traumatization occurs in systems that include two separate roles—one of the caregiver and the other of the victim of a traumatic event. The interactions between the two roles in the system are characterized by the caregiver's attentiveness to the victim's experiences and descriptions of the traumatic event while attempting to ease the victim's pain. The caregiver might then identify with the victim's suffering, and begin to imagine experiences and feelings similar to those of the victim, thus developing symptoms of secondary traumatization. When this happens, the functioning of the help-system is no longer intact.

The studies that have explored secondary traumatization focused on the symptoms characterizing the phenomenon and on the specific variables related to the development of STSD, such as the worker's caseload, personal and professional experience, and exclusive exposure to traumatized clients (Arvay & Uhlemann, 1996; Ghahramanlou & Brodbeck, 2000; Hyman, 2001; Lind, 2000; Myers & Wee, 2005; Wee & Myers, 2002). The phenomenon was not found to be unique to the professional mental health helpers, but was observed also among those caring for a family member with PTSD (see Chapter 2) (Figley, 1989a, 1989b, 1995a, 1995b, 1995c; Figley & McCubbin, 1983; Solomon et al., 1992). The aim of this chapter is to highlight systemic aspects nested in the phenomenon of secondary traumatization and to present possible systemic interventions designed to prevent and/or treat STSD among social workers and mental health helpers in situations of collective trauma.

Various Impacts of Collective or National Trauma on Psychosocial and Mental Health Helpers

The impact of collective and national trauma on psychosocial and mental health helpers will be described according to the phenomenological tradition in the following three domains: space, time and significant others (Van den Berg, 1972). This analysis follows the way the phenomenon of collective and national trauma was analyzed in the first chapter of this book. The type of exposure of helpers to the traumatic event or to its consequences refers to the space domain. Therefore, the following issues are addressed: Where do the helpers and victims meet? What is the level of damage to which the helper is exposed? What are the physical conditions like in the place in which the help is given? Do the helpers stay in the damaged area? In what physical conditions do the helpers live while providing help?

The timing of the help relates to the time domain: Is it immediately after the traumatic event or several days or weeks after its occurrence, or several months or years after the traumatic event? The duration of the help: Is it short-term versus long-term help?

The significant others domain includes similarities and differences between the helpers and the victims, and the social support and acknowledgment given to the helpers by their colleagues, supervisors, directors, formal institutions and political figures. Based on the interactions between the different types of situations described in these three domains, it is possible to identify potential implications for the mental health and psychosocial helpers of victims of collective and/or national trauma (see Table 5.1).

For example, psychosocial helpers, who were not exposed to the traumatic event, but who arrived as helping forces shortly afterwards, might be affected. These helpers are usually part of international and/or national organizations such as the United Nations World Health Organization (WHO), the Red Cross, the United States Federal Emergency Management Agency (FEMA) and many NGOs that operate around the world. These organizations send delegations of helpers who stay and provide help to the victims for a relatively short time (usually up to a month) and if

Table 5.1 Level of exposure (space domain), length of intervention (time domain) and similarities/differences between victims and helpers (significant others domain) as possible antecedences of STSD

Space Domain	Time Domain	Significant Others Domain
Level of Exposure to Traumatic Event	Time of Arrival at the Damaged Area and Length of Intervention	Similarities vs. Differences Between Victims and Helpers
Direct exposure: • Being present at place and time the traumatic event occurred Indirect exposure: • Arrival at the location of the event shortly after (from several hours to one or two weeks) • Arrival at the location of the event after first aid has been provided • Long-term help—ongoing help to victims not necessarily in the area, or after the damaged area was partly or fully rehabilitated Mixed exposure: • Shared situation • Ongoing traumatic event (refugee camps—victims can continuously arrive at the camp after camp routine was already established)	Time of arrival at the damaged area: • Related to the level of exposure Length of intervention: • First aid—psychosocial/mental health intervention • Short-term psychosocial/mental health intervention • Long-term psychosocial/mental health intervention	Similarities between helpers and victims: • Shared situation: helpers and victims are from the same collective and are targets of the same traumatic event • Helpers and victims are from the same collective but are not targets of the same traumatic event • Helpers and victims are not from the same collective but share the same values Differences between helpers and victims: • Helpers and victims are from different collectives and hold completely different cultural values (such as helpers from Western culture and victims from traditional cultures or Third World countries)

further help is needed, they are replaced by another group of helpers from the organization. These groups of helpers might be directly exposed to difficult and horrifying outcomes of the original traumatic event.

These groups provide mainly emergent help (described in Chapter 4 as "short-term interventions"). One may wonder whether the negative impact on these helpers can be defined as secondary traumatization. This is because, while providing the help, they might be exposed to traumatic experiences, such as exposure to corpses or injured bodies, areas of destruction, etc. In cases such as these, their reactions might be more accurately defined as primary traumatic stress. The development of either PTSD or STSD among these helpers is prevented by perceiving and operating the helper's delegation as a *task system*, indicating social support within the system as essential for preserving the helpers' self-welfare, which is necessary for empathic listening to victims' pain and needs.

Based on systemic theory, it is important to define clear roles within the system, and to divide tasks in a way that gives members enough time for physical rest, as physical tiredness reduces the ability to cope emotionally (Pearlman, 1999). In addition, it is important to be aware of the differences between the helpers' coping abilities and to assign their roles based on their emotional and physical state. It is reasonable to assume that social workers and mental health helpers who join such helping delegations are resilient. However, helpers may still differ in resiliency levels and providing intensive help in a traumatic context may cause these differences to surface. The attitude of the system's members (the helping delegation) toward the variance in each other's emotional and physical coping ability impacts the cohesive atmosphere in the delegation, and therefore, can be used as a systemic buffer against direct and indirect exposure to the traumatic event. Thus, adopting an accepting attitude by acknowledging and respecting individual differences in resiliency levels will result in increased cohesiveness in the delegation, while maintaining individual boundaries. Such an atmosphere within the system encourages social support among the delegation's members, allowing them to be open and to share feelings and thoughts regarding their personal helping experience. This can be an effective means of ventilation, reducing the possibility of developing traumatic stress. In addition, such an accepting atmosphere within the system encourages helpers to express their thoughts regarding help strategies and tactics within the specific context, enhancing their assistance to the victims. It can be assumed that if a system accepts the variance between its members, then problem-solving and conflict resolution processes will be possible when necessary. Characteristics such as these within a system reduce additional stress that may develop among the helping delegation due to the overwhelming effect of providing emergent help, thus allowing helpers to focus on the helping process. In contrast, helping delegations that are unable to accept variance in their members' emotional and physical state are characterized by low levels of cohesiveness, low tolerance of individual needs and low tolerance to listening to and accepting different ideas regarding the helping context. Systems of this nature may result in high levels of internal criticism, and difficulties in problem solving and conflict resolution. All this reduces the social support within the helping delegation. The helpers are left alone with their own difficult experiences, including those experienced within the delegation, which increases the probability of developing traumatic stress. Thus far, the description of help has referred to two dimensions: the space dimension (type of exposure) and the time dimension (time and duration of help). The third domain—significant others—refers to the similarities and differences between the helpers and the victims, and may determine the impact of the help on the helpers.

The help delegation can be composed of people from the same culture and nation as the victims' collective, as was the case with many of the mental health helpers in the US following 9/11, Hurricane Katrina and Hurricane Sandy, or following terror attacks and wars in Israel. The similarity and the frequent sense of having the same national belonging create special closeness between the victims and the helpers. This intensifies to such a degree that the helpers' empathy turns into actual identification with the victims. In several places, this phenomenon has been called *a shared situation* or *a shared reality*, referring to events in which the helpers are part of the collective and were either directly or indirectly exposed to the same potential traumatic event (Shamai, 1998, 2001, 2002; Shamai & Ron, 2009; Wee & Myers, 2002). Thus, it is possible to claim that if, in such situations, traumatic stress develops among helpers, it cannot be defined simply as secondary traumatic stress, but as a combination between the two syndromes.

Since we are focusing on mental health and psychosocial helpers, it is possible to assume that helping in a *shared reality* occurs mainly in countries that have developed solid welfare and mental health systems that can provide emergent and/or long-term help to their citizens. The probability of developing traumatic or secondary traumatic stress among workers in these places depends, to a certain extent, on the sense of the helper's self-security, including that of the helper's family. In a study conducted in Israel with emergent psychosocial helpers in situations of nationalist terror attacks, it was found to be effective for social workers to establish that their own family members were unharmed before providing help to victims in a professional capacity (Shamai & Ron, 2009). It was interesting to discover that some of the emergent psychosocial helpers held the superstitious belief (despite being aware of its irrationality) that helping other victims would protect them from potential harm (Shamai & Ron, 2006). Although no one who held this belief indicated that it was a buffer against developing traumatic stress, it is possible to assume that its subconscious integration into the belief system is one of the variables that may determine the helpers' degree of vulnerability to developing traumatic stress (Janoff-Bulman, 1989). Among the beliefs that psychosocial helpers reported as relevant to coping with the traumatic experience of helping in a shared reality was the sense of belonging to the collective or the nation, including the sense of patriotism (Shamai & Ron, 2006). This sense of patriotism was found to exist regardless of the helpers' political orientation. For example, helpers who supported the Israeli government's policy toward the Palestinians perceived their act of helping the victims of nationalist Palestinian terror as a way of supporting this policy. Their resilience to the painful experience of having to cope while helping the victims was their way of demonstrating that the society under terror would not break down. Helpers whose political orientation was against the government policy perceived their help to the terror victims as a way to legitimize criticism of the government for not proceeding with peace negotiations—which, in their opinion, was the only effective way of stopping nationalist terror. Although the use of political orientation as a buffer belief against painful helping experiences seems relevant in situations of national terror and war, it was surprising to find that helpers used this in other shared traumatic realities, such as in the aftermath of natural disasters. When I joined and acted as consultant to a group of emergent psychosocial helpers, both during and immediately after a fire in the Carmel Mountains in Israel in December 2010, I witnessed discussions between helpers in which those who were opposed to the government identified with and supported the citizens' anger regarding the government's responsibility for the outcomes of the fire. Some were motivated to social activism that would force the government to take responsibility for the lack of firefighting equipment and for the malfunctioning of the police and the fire brigade. Other helpers, who usually supported government policy, claimed that "such things can happen," and that "overcoming such fires takes even longer in Australia and California." These helpers minimized the traumatic experience.

It was not only in Israel that I found political orientation and sense of belonging serving as a buffer against traumatic experiences among psychosocial helpers (Shamai, 2011). In discussions with emergent mental health and psychosocial helpers from the US after 9/11 and Hurricane Katrina, both elements were discernible in their processing of the helping experience. This was merely an impression I received, however, and further study is required to determine the role of national and social belonging as well as of political orientation in constructing the mental health and psychosocial helpers' experience in situations of shared reality. Nonetheless, if helpers use their sense of belonging and political orientation as buffers against the painful experience, it is important to incorporate them in preparation programs and summarizing activities.

It is important also to note that both concepts are systemic. Sense of belonging refers to systems of which the helper feels a part, such as national and community systems or help organizations. Political orientation refers to each individual's attitude toward political leaders within the systems of national and local government. Both sense of belonging and political orientation are part of the individual's social self-identity (Brewer, 1991). Due to the importance of both concepts in the construction of the helper's identity and as a buffer against painful collective events, it is important to focus on both concepts in preparation programs for mental health and psychosocial helpers and in the activities summarizing the help. This can be achieved by referring to the various systems to which the helpers belong and the meaning of these system in the helping process, as well as to the individual's sense of belief when providing help to victims of collective trauma.

A different aspect of the significant other's domain refers to mental health and psychosocial helpers, who are not part of the same collective or the same cultural orientation. Differences between helper and victim can be used as a way of creating distance that may be used as a buffer against the helpers' painful experience. Thoughts, such as "it can happen only in this kind of area . . . not where I am living . . . not to my type of population" often cross the helpers' minds. Such thoughts are not necessarily negative if the helpers succeed in splitting between these thoughts and their ability to be attentive to the victims' pain and needs. My personal and professional experience in Israel contradicts the psychodynamic orientation that often perceives splitting as denial or repression. From my experience, a certain level of denial or repression may be effective for adjustment and coping. Furthermore, denial and repression are not necessarily prerequisites for developing a delayed traumatic response; most of the helpers succeed in using them as an effective defense mechanism that allows them to function professionally and personally, while containing the pain and working it through spontaneously. This does not mean that some summarization of the help should not be performed. This can be relevant for both the individual helpers as well as for the helping systems to which they belong.

Other types of help provided by mental health professionals and social workers are interventions that are offered much later, allowing some distance from the traumatic event. Such help can be provided several months or even years later, and can constitute either short- or long-term interventions. All these types of help take place far from the glamor of the media and public interest, and lack the glory and social recognition earned by providing immediate help. Both the lack of recognition and the nature of the necessary interventions, provided mainly to systems whose difficulties have not been overcome by existing resources or emergent aid, are potential sources for the development of secondary traumatic stress among the helpers.

Although the nature of interventions provided by mental health professionals and social workers are fixed to some extent, recognition and acknowledgment of the helpers' work depends entirely on the attention and goodwill of political leaders, and leaders of professional, community, national and international institutions and organizations.

Recognition can be perceived as a component of emotional social support (Boszormenyi-Nagy & Krasner, 1986), which confirms, for the helpers, that their work is needed and valued by society or by people in power in professional or other relevant institutions and organizations (Catherall, 1999; Flannery, 1990; Gonen, 2008; Shamai & Ron, 2006). Many studies found social support in general and emotional social support in particular to be moderators of traumatic stress (Catherall, 1999; Ron & Shamai, 2011; Shamai & Ron, 2006; Stamm, 1999, 2002). Therefore, it is important to find ways to provide helpers with this type of support, even if the "voice of the trauma" has lessened and consequences of the traumatic event have "disappeared" from the public discourse and from the focus of institutions responsible for victims' rehabilitation.

Recognition is a systemic concept, by nature. It is granted within micro or macro systems, usually by people or institutions with professional, political, or social power over individuals and groups who acknowledge this power. Therefore, recognition by those with political or professional power is usually appreciated by those who receive it. This recognition is often perceived as an indication of their support of the helpers' professional activities.

It is important to note that one of the most exhausting and often frustrating types of help centers on long-term interventions with individuals suffering from PTSD and their families. Although some PTSD interventions are effective, such as Prolonged Exposure therapy (PE) (Foa, 2011), as well as some family interventions for the relatives of PTSD individuals (Figley, 1990), healing is not achieved in many cases; in others, some healing occurs only after long-term intervention with many periods of disappointment. These long-term experiences of working with individuals and systems suffering from ongoing pain can lead to STSD among the helpers, characterized by symptoms of burnout (Adams, Matto & Harrington, 2001; Adams, Figley & Boscarino, 2008). Although some researchers claim that STSD represents a phenomenon distinct from burnout (Adams, Figley & Boscarino, 2008; Arvay, 2001b; Figley, 1995a, 1995b, 1995c), both constructs encompass several similar symptoms (Adams, Matto & Harrington, 2001; Adams, Figley & Boscarino, 2008) and are often described as outcomes of stress experienced by helping professionals. Nevertheless, the similarities and differences between STSD and burnout have scarcely been specified, and the particular conditions leading to each syndrome have not been identified (Butollo, 1996; Kushnir & Melamed, 1992; Vicarcy, Searle & Andrews, 2000). Adams,

Figley and Boscarino (2008) suggested the concept of compassion fatigue as a construct of both STSD and burnout. Compassion fatigue is measured using two subscales, one of STSD and the other of burnout (Adams, Boscarino & Figley, 2006, 2008). It seems that helpers administering long-term interventions some time after the traumatic event, mostly with the severe cases and in individual therapy contexts, might experience both STSD and burnout symptoms, and their reactions might therefore be better defined as compassion fatigue.

To sum up, although helping victims of collective trauma can be rewarding, it might also carry some negative implications. These depend on the helping system's characteristics and the help context, referring to the type of exposure, duration and location of help and similarities and differences between the victims, which were described in three domains: space, time and significant others. As these negative implications, which may be termed either STSD or compassion fatigue, developed mainly within a system (the helping system nested within the helping organization within a specific traumatic context), it makes sense that the type of actions for preventing or healing these negative implications will be based on a systemic view.

Systemic Interventions for Preventing and Healing STSD

In this section, I will refer to actions for the prevention and treatment of STSD that are in use in many mental health and psychosocial organizations that provide help in situations of collective trauma. I will focus on the systemic aspects of these actions, and will suggest narrative techniques, where relevant. The actions will be presented according to the time axis:

1   preparation of mental health and psychosocial helpers for the helping task;
2   supporting helpers during the helping process;
3   ending and summarizing the helping process; and
4   providing appropriate help to helpers with STSD.

Preparing Psychosocial and Mental Health Helpers for the Helping Task

One buffer against STSD among helpers is training and experience (Halpern & Tramontin, 2007; Myers & Wee, 2005). Therefore, training to provide mental health help in situations of collective trauma has become commonplace in many organizations, including academic institutions around the world. In some places, it is a prerequisite for joining help delegations. The content of these training programs is somewhat similar and covers areas such as the impact of collective traumatic events on individuals and communities, normal versus extreme reactions to the experience, types of vulnerable populations and types of psychosocial first aid. These include supportive techniques, assessment of psychosocial conditions, assessing traumatic and stress responses, stress and crisis-management theory and techniques, coping skills, impact of media and accurate information, and cognitive-behavioral and psycho-educational techniques in situations of collective trauma. Unfortunately, elements of systemic interventions are not directly included in most of these programs. The importance of using a systemic approach in the training program goes beyond the type of help that can be provided to the victims. It constructs the helping system in such a way that creates a safe and supportive context for the helpers. In other words, it refers to the structure of the helping system and to how it lends itself to providing the best type of help for victims. Since helping in situations of collective trauma generally involves teamwork rather than "private practice," the team structure, the different roles and interaction between the team members need to be included in the training and preparation. During the training process, it is important to provide the trainees with information regarding the structure of the helping team, and to explain the importance of the helpers' system as a source of personal and professional support. In addition, there is a need to describe issues characterizing psychosocial interventions under extremely stressful conditions, which can be a source of conflict within the professional teams. Possible causes of an increase in such conflicts should be discussed, such as power issues among the team members, unclear role definitions that confuse the boundaries between different leaders and team members and undefined responsibilities. Hence, fewer interactions that allow problem-solving processes take place, although these are needed in the process of helping victims of collective trauma, both for the quality of the help and the welfare of the helpers.

Another issue that is hardly discussed in the existing training program is the helpers' sense of belonging to a specific collective, which can be a nation, a culture, a community, a profession, or an organization. Focusing on the sense of belonging defines the helper as part of a system rather than as a disconnected individual, and clarifies beliefs and social commitments that the helpers can use as a frame of reference at difficult times, both during and after the helping process. This can be used as a buffer against the overwhelming experience of helping victims of collective trauma.

Focusing on the importance of the helpers' system in the training process is not enough, however. It is worth taking several minutes to review this issue, either when forming a delegation prior to starting a helping mission, and during preparation exercises in an existing organization whose goals include interventions in situations of collective trauma. This is illustrated by the following detailed description by Ms N., a social worker from the Social Services Department in Haifa:

> After the first terror attack, there was some chaos . . . after the second and third attacks, we were better organized . . . after the first attack, we were divided into . . . three teams, each one attached to one of the city's hospitals. The role of these teams was centered on providing information to people who were looking for their family members. We cooperated with the social services of these hospitals treating the victims, and they informed us of their names and in which department they could be found. We also cooperated with the teams in the other hospitals so as to give the families accurate information regarding the location of their relatives. Part of our role was also to calm people down. Sometimes, it would take hours to identify victims who were in the operating rooms. Those searching were anxious, and they would sometimes behave violently, yelling and cursing, and we needed to calm them down so that they could give us identifying information about the missing people that would help us to identify them. We had a list of pre-prepared questions to help the hospital staff identify people, but getting this information out of terrified and anxious people was difficult . . . People who are hospitalized and who need mental health help are taken care of by the hospital staff but the family team takes care of their family members during the hospitalization . . . most of the social workers were attached to the family team, in which pairs of social workers were attached to a family in need of help. They might have been families in which both parents were injured and it was necessary to find someone to take care of the children; they might have been families in which someone needed to stay in hospital with one or more injured family members and it was necessary to find someone to take care of the rest of the family, or even to accompany people to the morgue to identify a body . . . we formed a protocol with information to be taken from the family and we were trained in how to do this. The pair of social workers attached to a family that had suffered a death helped with the funeral and the *shiva* arrangements.[1] During the week of the *shiva*, a social worker from the National Insurance Institute made the initial connection with the family, thus ending the role of the municipal department of social services.

The third team was the "morgue team," who referred to themselves as the *sayeret* [elite military combat unit]. The choice of the military vocabulary indicates the special courage that this role requires. If the police announced fatalities in the attack, the team went directly to the morgue to wait for the families to come to identify the bodies. These families were terrified and anxious, grasping for hope for a miracle—that their loved one would be found in one of the hospitals, or longing for the phone call that would tell them that he was safe and well and had just returned home . . . but most of them know that this was the end . . . Since the condition of most of the bodies prolonged the identification process, some of the relatives reacted angrily and the role of both the morgue team and the family team was to calm them down, support them and to be with them. The morgue team was in contact with the pathologist, and liaised with the family to provide additional information to help identify the body . . .

The fourth team was the management team. They remained in contact with all the other teams, as well as with other services, such as the police, hospitals, educational psychology service, etc., and coordinated the entire helping process. It is important to note that during preparation, there was a clear division between us and the educational psychologists. The educational psychologists were responsible for helping or guiding parents or relatives as to how to tell their children about the loss of one or more siblings, or of one or both of their parents. They guided teachers in how to discuss the issue with students who had lost friends in the attack. While working within the local school, community workers from the department of social services intervened with the community, as necessary.

. . . so we each knew our role and we could get organized very quickly if needed. But before starting the help, the team leader briefly went over our tasks, roles and protocols, reminding us of the most important things that should and should not be done. Although each of us knew all these things, the short preparation helped us enter into the sad and difficult situation and to reconnect between us, since in our daily work, each team included social workers from various departments in the city, or even if social workers were from the same department, they may have had different roles and minimal professional contact during regular daily activities.

Ms N.'s elaborate description illustrates how systemic preparations were made by assigning each of the social workers in the city to different teams and by defining the tasks and roles within them. However, in spite of these preparations, each team leader recreates the helping system each time before beginning the action, while remembering two specific basic elements: tasks and roles, as well as setting some boundaries regarding "things that should and should not be done."

Although several institutions, such as the Red Cross, provide training for mental health professionals and social workers, in many situations, helpers are involved in providing help without having received previous training or experience in working with victims of collective trauma. In such cases, accompaniment for the untrained and inexperienced helpers is crucial both during and after the helping process. However, professional accompaniment is not available in every situation, and therefore, special attention should be given at the end of the process. Narrative techniques can be used, such as writing or telling the story of the help, in a way that focuses on:

1   strength aspects that enabled the helper to provide the help;
2   outline of professional and personal learning through the help process;
3   problems that the helper succeeded in solving despite the lack of experience;
4   questions and thoughts related to professional issues that were raised during the helping process;
5   whether and how the professional experience gained during the help to the victims of the traumatic event contributes to the helper's professional and personal growth; and
6   the future story—how the helpers will tell their experience to children, grandchildren or friends twenty or thirty years after the collective event.

As providing help without having received the relevant training might be an overwhelming experience, it might be helpful to tell or to write the story in the presence of supervisors, who can provide support sometimes just by asking guiding questions to help construct the story and to arrange the different events in order. Acknowledging the inexperienced helper's work is crucial in such situations.

Supporting Helpers During the Helping Process

As mentioned previously in this chapter, support is a systemic concept, as it occurs within a system of at least two people, in which one provides and the other receives, or within systems in which mutual support exists between the members. Professional support can be either formal or informal. Among the types of formal support is supervision, usually provided by experienced helpers to less experienced helpers, or acknowledgment of the helpers' work provided by a person in power, who is recognized by the professional system. Therefore, it can be assumed that formal support represents the power division within a system: people with more experience and knowledge support the less experienced. Following Foucault (1980), who claimed that knowledge and its uses is a basis of power within society, it is possible that actions expected to be supportive turned into power conflicts within systems, which did not clarify the divisions between specific roles and the type of interactions between them. In such cases, the system has less ability to function as a safe resource for its members and to provide the needed professional and personal support during the helping process.

The informal support refers to spontaneous conversations among helpers (for example, during breaks or in other settings), when they share their experiences and discuss their difficulties and hesitations. These sharing conversations can happen within systems built on mutual trust between the members and where collegial relationships are perceived not just as professional relationships, but as having characteristics of friendship, such as warmth, caring and a genuine desire to know how the other is coping with the difficult and painful task. It is the atmosphere in the system that enables such relationships, which is often the outcome of leadership that gives space to different opinions, professional views and professional experience, as well as knowing how to make painful and unpopular decisions when needed.

In general, it is possible to focus on two main types of systems that call for different ways of providing help during the helping process: The first refers to delegations that are sent to help victims and stay on location as a group while help is still needed, or to a specific service that provides first aid help, such as the one described by Ms N. from the Department of Social Services in Haifa. The second help-system structure refers to social or mental health services that provide long-term help—mainly therapeutic interventions with victims of collective trauma. The similarities between the types of support given to helpers working in both structures of the system is the accepting and caring atmosphere, with space given to differences such as helpers' personality types, helpers' reactions to the traumatic situations, levels of professional experience, perceptions of professionals issues, personal and professional beliefs, etc. Making room for these differences means respecting the members of the help team and giving voice to their narratives. This, in itself, might serve as social support during the period of help. It is important to note that giving a voice to differences does not mean avoiding the need to decide on one way to act or for group leaders to use their power when needed. This can still be accomplished in a supportive manner if the different voices are heard first, and the reason for the decision is explained. The differences between the two structures of help systems refer to the type of help and the condition under which it is provided.

In first aid delegations or existing first aid services, the role and task of each helper needs clarification before the start of the helping process, and a couple of members should be assigned to be ready to answer professional and personal questions raised during the helping process. If the help lasts for more than one day, it is important to find even a short time to summarize the work that was done, to voice professional problems and suggest solutions. It is also important to assign an experienced member to assess whether one of the helpers needs specific support or some time off for resting. The help given in such situations is very intensive and, in most cases, lasts for many hours. It requires special attention to task divisions among the members in a way that allows each member enough time for physical rest. Physical weakness due to lack of sleep and food may reduce the helpers' ability to cope with their tasks. These are basic needs that may seem irrelevant to the helping process, but as mentioned when describing the type of first aid help given to the victims, without supplying basic needs, the helpers would not be able to function on levels that require them to interact socially, communicate hope and have the power to help others in traumatic situations.

The other type of helpers' system refers to those psychosocial or mental health services that provide long-term help to victims of collective trauma. As mentioned earlier, this help may be exhausting, because the cases of those people who apply for help are more severe, since their personal resilience and/or the natural social support did not succeed in helping overcome the traumatic experience. These helpers are at risk of developing burnout in addition to secondary traumatization (Shamai & Ron, 2006). Beyond the help given to the individual helper, such as supervision or recommendations for self-care (Figley, 1995b; Harris & Linder, 1999; Pearlman & Saakvitne, 1995), the system in which the helpers work plays a crucial role in providing opportunities for sharing with peers (Catherall, 1995; Gonen, 2008; Shamai & Ron, 2009, Stamm, 1999, 2002), in directors' recognition of their professional functioning (Gonen, 2008; Ron & Shamai, 2011, Shamai & Ron, 2009) and in developing a sense of belonging to the special system and its tasks. Enhancing the sense of self- and system-esteem based on the helpers' important work increases the ability to cope with the ongoing and sometimes never-ending work. In addition, taking care of the helpers' basic needs, such as time out from work, a reasonable caseload and relaxing system activities are as important as the supervision, recognition and social support.

Ending and Summarizing the Helping Process

Ending and summarizing the helping process is relevant mainly to short-term first aid helpers, whose interventions with the victimized population are usually very intensive. Ending and summarizing means creating a boundary around the experience of help. Such a boundary does not mean burying the memories and images of the experience, but putting them in a capsule that remains closed most of the time without interfering with the helpers' daily activities or detracting from their ability to function normally. For some readers, the use of the words "ending and summarizing" may have associations with the term "debriefing," including all the doubts raised by this process. From a systemic point of view, I prefer to define the ending and summarizing process as creating the narrative of the helping process, focusing on the individual narrative and the group (organization, delegation, etc.). The narrative includes the following elements:

- *Reasons for joining the helping forces:* What brought the helper to join mental health or psychosocial helping forces?
- *Description of the helping process:* What happened during the helping process, with emphasis on facts: What did the helper do? What did they witness the other helpers from the group doing? How did the victims respond to the help? How did the victims' responses to the aid change or modify the helper's intervention during the helping process?
- *Strength aspects:* How did the helper cope with personal and professional difficulties and painful experiences that arose throughout the helping process? How did the helping team cope with difficulties and helpful experiences that arose in the helping process? Which coping abilities and strengths did the helpers notice in themselves during the helping process? Which coping abilities and strengths did the helper notice among the team or specific members within the team during the helping process?
- *Personal and professional growth:* How did the helping process contribute to the helper's personal and professional growth? How did the helping process contribute to the team's cohesiveness and professional abilities?
- *Meaning of providing help:* What was the meaning that the helpers attached to their role as helper in situations of collective trauma: personal meaning, collective meaning, political meaning, etc.? How and when did the meaning attached to the helping process help the helpers to cope with painful and difficult reactions to the experience? Was the meaning attached to the helping process reflected by the reasons for joining the helping process? If so, how?
- *Future narrative:* In this part of the summary, the helpers are asked to build a future story and to imagine how this experience of helping will be integrated into their life story. The invitation to tell the future story is presented in the following way: Try to imagine yourself in ten, twenty, or forty years from now. You may be sitting with your children, grandchildren or friends, and you are telling them about your life. How will the story about this helping experience be told?

Thinking about the future may put the painful meeting with victims of collective trauma in a broader context of life and, besides this and other experiences, might evoke a sense of strength, the ability to cope and to contribute to others and a sense of empowerment at being involved in a professional task that requires special expertize and resiliency. This method of summarizing can be performed once a year with staff of services or organizations, who provide long-term help to victims of trauma. It is important to include the narrative of the organization, focusing on the way the staff wishes to convey it to future generations of social workers or mental health professionals.

In sum, the phenomenon of STSD has been studied for more than three decades. No one can deny its presence among mental health and psychosocial helpers. STSD is an outcome of a helping system that includes helpers and victims. The existence of buffers against the outbreak of STSD depends mainly on the way organizations (systems) construct their preparation for providing such help, how the teams that work together develop a supportive and accepting atmosphere, how leaders share responsibilities without ignoring them, and how the individual helper can feel safe within the helping team. However, some questions must be asked regarding the number of helpers who suffer from STSD and the intensity of the traumatic symptoms—questions that need further research and challenge the thinking regarding this phenomenon. Let me share two findings from a study of social workers from Israel, who were providing short- and long-term help following terrorist attacks. One finding refers to the impact of the help. Most of the participants in the study reported that, from several days to a week after providing the help, they experienced some traumatic experiences which disappeared fairly quickly, mainly through informal sharing with their peers, family support and simply returning to their routine (Shamai, 1998; Shamai & Ron, 2009). This process is consistent with the general population's reaction to traumatic events (Bonanno, 2004). As claimed by Bonanno and other researchers of PTSD and resilience, only a small percentage of the general population develop PTSD. It is possible to assume that mental health professionals and social workers who choose to work in organizations dealing with victims of collective traumatic events are basically resilient. Therefore, the probability of developing STSD is relatively low and among those who do, the recovery rate is relatively high. Another issue refers to the method of measuring STSD. In a list of questions regarding traumatic stress, we found (Ron & Shamai, 2011; Shamai & Ron, 2009) that the participants perceived their experience of intrusive thoughts, regarding the victims whom they had helped, as empathy and professional caring rather than as symptoms of trauma. It is possible that these findings refer to specific contexts and systems, and therefore cannot be generalized, but they definitely raise the need for further inquiry into STSD.

Note

1 *Shiva* (literally "seven" in Hebrew) is the week-long mourning period in Judaism for first-degree relatives. Starting immediately after the funeral, family members traditionally gather in one home (preferably the home of the deceased) for the seven days and receive condolence visits.

6

EVALUATION OF
SYSTEMIC INTERVENTIONS
IN SITUATIONS OF NATIONAL
AND COLLECTIVE TRAUMA

The search for evidenced-based studies that evaluated systemic intervention in situations of collective and national trauma produced hardly any results. Some individual interventions with victims, especially those using cognitive behavior techniques that targeted traumatic stress, have been empirically evaluated (Foa, 2011; Meadows & Foa, 2000; Nayak, Power & Foa, 2012). However, the lack of empirical evaluations with families, communities, organizations and larger systems is conspicuous. Most of the existing publications regarding family, community and organizational interventions describe various experiences of working with systems after traumatic events. Nevertheless, only very few include quantitative or qualitative evaluations, not to mention evidence-based interventions that have additional methodological requirements (Campbell, 1991; Shadish, Cook & Campbell, 2002; Thompson, 2003). In this chapter, I prefer to be "politically incorrect" and instead of using the cliché that often appears at the end of many publications about the need for "empirical evaluation," or "further research," I will try to account for the lack of systematic evaluation research and will propose some directions in which such evaluations could be encouraged.

Difficulties in Performing Systematic Evaluations
of Systemic Interventions in Situations of
Collective and National Trauma

There are several main reasons for the paucity of systematic evaluations of systemic interventions in situations of collective and national trauma. They are all related to the context in which these interventions take place. The first two are derived from the lack of time available to collect data that will serve as a baseline for the study. The first reason relates to the intervention characteristics. Many systemic interventions are implemented under emergent situations. It is therefore impossible to postpone the emergent help to collect data for a detailed systematic assessment, which would provide a baseline for comparison with post-intervention measures. The second reason refers to recruiting participants, who have just experienced a traumatic event. Those familiar with evaluation research are aware of the difficulties involved in recruiting participants for psychosocial clinical research, especially when the potential participants are still strongly impacted by the traumatic event, and need all their time and energy to cope with the new situation. It can be assumed that the majority of the mental health and psychosocial helpers would perceive any postponement of the emergent intervention as unethical, both for recruiting participants and for developing a baseline, which includes the active participation of the affected population. Since these evaluative activities have significant ethical shortcomings in general, they are scarcely used in situations of collective trauma, and I wholeheartedly agree with this approach.

Some conservative supporters of evidence-based practice might criticize this lack of baseline policy, stating that any mental health or psychosocial intervention cannot be started in the absence of an assessment process. As described in detail in Chapter 4, when working in emergent situations, the mental health helpers and social workers do perform assessments. However, these assessments are characterized by a general picture, and descriptions of the systems' strengths, weaknesses and harm to mental health can be useful when starting the emergent intervention. This is in lieu of specific, more detailed information, as is needed in the classical traditional evaluations in which the methodology is the basic guide for implementation (Alkin, 2012a; Carden & Alkin, 2012; Campbell & Stanley, 1966).

The third reason for the lack of evaluations relates to the sampling process. The classical-traditional evaluations, as well as interventions that are defined as fully evidence-based (Thompson, 2003), require at least two comparison groups that will be randomly designed (Campbell, 1991; Campbell & Stanley, 1966). This definitely cannot be the case when providing help in situations of collective trauma. From an ethical and humanistic point of view, it is unacceptable to provide help only to those systems (families or communities) who either asked for help or who agreed to receive assistance when approached by the helping services. It is also unacceptable to delay the provision of help to the control group for purposes of comparison with the experimental group before and after treatment.

The fourth reason refers to the type of help provided. In most cases, helping interventions provided to systems in situations of collective trauma is not always implemented in full adherence to the fixed protocol. During implementation, they are very often adjusted according to how the situation evolves, through additional episodes of the traumatic event, or the development of new risks following the original event. One example is the damage caused to the Fukushima nuclear power plant in

Japan by the tsunami in 2011, which led to the need for rapid evacuation of a large population who had just begun to cope with major loss and damage already inflicted by the tsunami. In other cases, the interventions are changed at the request of clients, or because of cultural differences, and/or the size of the helping teams and are subject to financial resources. In addition, intervention with systems is often more complicated and includes several goals, unlike many post-trauma interventions with individuals, which focus on overcoming specific symptoms, such as PTSD, depression, or anxiety. Thus, the classical evaluations based on strict and defined intervention are almost impossible to implement.

The fifth reason refers to the pre-event condition of a specific system. Classical evaluation attempts to show that the measured outcomes can be attributed to a specific intervention. Let us assume that a baseline measured after the traumatic event shows similarity between several systems, and that the intervention goals are similar, as well as the provided intervention. Is it possible that the outcomes achieved are due to the pre-event condition and not to the specific intervention implemented in the system? Is it possible that the system's resources and narrative as constructed before the traumatic event intensifies or lessens the outcomes? This can work in several directions. A system with positive esteem and a history of strength might make better use of the help and achieve better outcomes than a system with a negative narrative and poor functioning even before the traumatic event. However, it is also possible that systems with negative esteem, and with few and limited resources before the traumatic event might be "accustomed" to difficulties, and therefore might adjust more easily and/or benefit from any type of help. These are only two of what, I assume, are several possibilities referring to the pre-event condition and not necessarily to the program itself. Thus, classical evaluation might fail to attribute the outcomes only to the chosen intervention.

The sixth reason refers to financial resources. Planning and implementing a valid evaluation requires financial resources, which are often at the bottom of the list of goals in situations of collective trauma. Providing instrumental and psychosocial help are considered more crucial. In most cases, there is a lack of financial resources even for these purposes, and all the more so when it comes to funding evaluation. In other cases, the amount of funds allocated to evaluation is not sufficient to implement a valid evaluation.

Campbell (1991) and many other researchers (e.g., Gribbons & Herman, 1997; Shadish, Cook & Campbell, 2002) addressed classical and traditional evaluation, which utilizes experimental designs as the "true experiment." However, even those who strongly support the true experimental design as the fundamental and best method of evaluation recognize its limitations (Gribbons & Herman, 1997; Lipsey & Freeman, 2004). There is an ongoing debate regarding the most accurate type of evaluation from which to gather information about the effectiveness of a specific intervention (Cook et al., 2010). Alkin (2012b), Carden and Alkin (2012), Christie and Alkin, (2012) and Patton (1994) present wider perspectives and types of evaluations, in which the classical experimental and quasi-experimental designs were only one of the options, and they were characterized by steadfast emphasis on methodological concerns (Alkin, 2012b; Carden & Alkin, 2012). In his proposal of developmental evaluation, Patton (1994) referred to several types of evaluations, and named the classical evaluations "summative evaluations." He described their aim as to judge the extent to which desired goals have been attained and whether the measured outcomes can be attributed to a specific intervention so that it can be generalized to other similar conditions. The six difficulties described above clearly explain why it is almost impossible to implement evaluations of systemic interventions in situations of collective and national trauma. However, these difficulties do not sufficiently account for the lack of evaluations, especially due to the significant developments in evaluation theory in the last two decades, which recognize the limitations of classical evaluations utilizing experimental or quasi-experimental designs. Therefore, there is an option to go beyond the traditional experimental design and to take other crucial elements into account, such as participation of clients or help providers in the process of evaluation, the complexity of interventions, and ongoing changes in intervention plans.

Beyond Classical Evaluation: Possible Directions for Evaluating Systemic Intervention in Situations of Collective Trauma

In this section, I will present different views of evaluations that seem more relevant to situations of collective and national trauma, and that are definitely friendlier to both social workers and mental health helpers as well as to the recipients of the help. One important principle will characterize the suggested ways of evaluation in situations of collective trauma: it will require the evaluators to accept imperfection and to make evaluative judgments based on partial data. I base this requirement on my own interpretation of Alkin's analysis (Alkin, 2012a; Christie & Alkin, 2012), with which he would not necessarily agree. Christie and Alkin emphasized the different roots and foci of the different evaluation theories (models). They described three branches of evaluation theories, of which only one focuses on and highlights the role of methodology. The other two branches do not ignore the role of methodology, but place other elements inherent in evaluation in the center.

The second branch focuses on a value judgment of the evaluation including aspects that need to be taken into account when evaluating a specific program (Scriven, 1991). Whereas Scriven claimed that this judgment should be made by the evaluators, others, such as Alkin (2012b) and Lincoln and Guba (2012), highlighted the role of the context, including participants of a specific program that is being evaluated, whose judgment of the value of a program or parts of the program could be considered to be most relevant.

The third branch refers to the users, mainly those who ordered the evaluation. Later researchers, such as Patton (1994), extended this to anyone potentially empowered by the information provided by the evaluation. In the case at hand, they include social workers and mental health helpers, the population suffering from collective trauma, and policy makers who assess the type of mental health help required.

Based on Christie and Alkin's (2012) classification, I would like to propose that any model that will be used in evaluating systemic intervention in situations of collective trauma will emphasize the second and third branches. Thus, the value judgments of what to evaluate, and identifying the most important aspects of a helping program for study should take the specific context into account. For example, in a traditional religious society, evaluating the impact of spiritual or collectivistic aspects of an intervention might be more relevant, whereas in a modern secular Western society, the individualistic aspects within systemic intervention might be evaluated. Others might be more curious and inquire into the role of social support in the systemic intervention with Western vs. traditional systems.

As to the branch that refers to users, evaluation of systemic intervention gives rise to many challenges. For example, regarding community intervention in situations of collective and national trauma—who will use the evaluation? Are these the social workers or mental health professionals, who planned or implemented the intervention? Are they the formal leaders of the community, the grass-roots leaders, or ordinary members of the community? It may be claimed that the users are those who finance the interventions; either policy makers on the national level or leaders of NGOs, who contribute to the helping forces in various disaster situations. Similar questions can be asked regarding interventions on the family level. Are the users those who plan and implement the intervention? Are they the parents, the spouses, or the children? Are they members of the extended family? This becomes even more complex when evaluating systemic interventions on the national level. The nature of systemic intervention calls for various voices of evaluation. This can be better described using the metaphor of a puzzle, which reveals the entire picture only when all the pieces are in place. Moreover, the picture can be fully understood only by studying the position of each piece and its relation to all the others.

It is possible to argue that proposing such directions for evaluation complicates the process even further and increases the complexity of data collection. However, I would like to propose some suggestions to improve the data collection process, which enable the performance of evaluation in situations of collective and national trauma:

1   Emphasize achievements rather than insisting on a baseline. This requires clear definition of the program goals including those that are added during the intervention. Through information from the professional helping forces and members of the various systems regarding the extent of achievement of the program goals, the effective and ineffective elements of the program can be identified, even though this method of data collection might raise doubts regarding the validity of the evaluation, such as whether the achievement of the goals be attributed to the intervention program or merely to spontaneous recovery. This deficit in the methodology design can be partly reduced by comparing the information provided by the different informants, helpers and various groups from the population that received the help.

2   Means of data collection: People who experience collective trauma often refuse to participate in any kind of research, stressing that they hate the fact that some people will take advantage of the situation, even for the benefit of science or for the sake of helping others. However, many people are very willing to describe their experience of the event, including their experience of the help they received. Hence, the use of data collection techniques that are based on listening to narratives might increase their motivation to participate. The same is true for the social workers and mental health helpers. It is no secret that practitioners hold an ambivalent attitude toward research; almost all of them acknowledge the importance of research in developing and evaluating helping programs, but only a small number use empirical knowledge in their practice or even attempt to evaluate their help empirically, including cooperation with others' attempts. However, like their clients, mental health helpers are pleased to share their experience of helping in situations of collective and national trauma. Therefore, they are more likely to be willing to cooperate when they feel that their helping story is being heard. In addition, it will increase the participants' sense that their experience is valuable, and might serve as part of the healing process, which in turn increases the ethical level of the evaluation. It is true that conducting interviews with clients and helpers is more expensive than distributing questionnaires. This is because researchers often perceive questionnaires to be more objective and valid. There is no clear-cut solution to the dilemma of interviews vs. questionnaires. The gathered data from whichever method is chosen can be analyzed using both quantitative and qualitative techniques, thereby presenting

a wider picture of the helping process while strengthening the validity of the study (Patton, 1986, 1990, 1994).

3   Many articles describe systemic interventions in situations of collective and national trauma. These valuable descriptions and their analysis can highlight the aspects and elements of systemic interventions found to be effective in situations of collective and national trauma. The analysis cannot be performed according to regular meta-analysis because most of these descriptions do not provide "numbers." However, content analysis or qualitative analysis can give some direction regarding the effect of systemic interventions in general as well as some specific techniques or strategies that were learned from implementing such interventions. It is true that such analysis cannot compare specific differences between the programs, and currently, we have no solution for this. Knowing the context of collective traumas, I wish to avoid such clichés as "further research is needed." Instead, I prefer to claim that just as the helping process in situations of collective and national trauma is always "imperfect," the evaluations of such processes will be imperfect also. This imperfection needs to be accepted, and, depending on the context (the type of the event, the hurt population, etc.), creative ways should be sought to perform such evaluations in spite of their deficits.

4   Long-term systemic interventions, especially those that start and continue sometime after the traumatic event, have greater evaluation potential, since some of the emergent difficulties requiring mental health help might have already received preliminary assistance. Based on the existing literature, individual treatments for specific symptoms, such as PTSD, were evaluated. The evaluated treatments include cognitive behavioral therapies (Meadows & Foa, 2000) and pharmacological treatments (Shalev & Bonne, 2000). The lack of evaluation of systemic interventions might be due to their complexity, which is characterized by multiple goals, multiple participants and multiple techniques. It is possible that developmental evaluation (Patton, 1994), which perceives the evaluation process to be flexible to changes in the intervention goals and techniques, as well as qualitative evaluation (Patton, 1986), might be more appropriate for systemic intervention with families, communities and societies experiencing the impact of collective trauma.

In spite of the lack of evidence-based systemic interventions in situations of collective and national trauma, it is important to note that most of these interventions are based on findings of various studies regarding the impact of traumatic events. For example, most of the interventions include aspects of social support, providing information, opening communication channels within and between systems, empowering leaderships (either within the family system, or within the community or national systems), increasing the sense of belonging, creating a narrative, and highlighting elements of commitment, control and resiliency. All these aspects were found to be impacted by collective traumatic events and were found to be relevant in increasing resiliency and the ability to cope (e.g., Antonovsky, 1991; Bonanno, 2008; Bonanno & Mancini, 2008; Denborough, 2008; Kimhi & Shamai, 2004; Kobasa, 1982; Lahad & Ben Nesher, 2005; Lahad, Shacham & Niv, 2000; Lazarus & Folkman, 1984; Norris & Stevens, 2007; Norris et al., 2008; Walsh, 2007; White & Epston, 1990). The interventions centered on the search for instrumental and psychological resources as compensation for those lost in the traumatic events (Hobfoll, 1998, 2001), as well as aspects of trauma, focused on therapies that were found to be effective (e.g., Lahad, Shacham & Niv, 2000; Meadows & Foa, 2000). In addition, systemic interventions take into account the crisis and loss created by the traumatic event and include in their program aspects that allow systemic working on the loss, ambiguous loss and guilt while using various techniques, depending on the social context (e.g., Boss, 1999, 2007; Figley, 1990; Hodgkinson & Stewart, 1998; Malkinson, 2007; Possick, Sadeh & Shamai, 2008; Walsh, 1999). Thus, it is possible to claim that, even if systemic interventions have been scarcely evaluated, they have been planned and developed based on outcomes of both quantitative and qualitative studies. These interventions are not entirely evidence-based, but make some contribution within an imperfect context for evaluation.

REFERENCES

Aarts, P. G. & Op den Velde, W. (1996). Prior traumatization and the process of aging: Theory and clinical implications. In B. A. van der Kolk, A. C. McFarlane & L. Weisaeth (Eds.), *Traumatic stress: The effect of overwhelming experience on mind, body and society* (pp. 359–77). New York: Guilford.

Abramowitz, S. A. (2005). The poor have become rich, and the rich have become poor: Collective trauma in the Guinean Languette. *Social Science & Medicine, 61,* 2106–18.

Adams, R. E., Boscarino, J. A. & Figley, C. R. (2006). Compassion fatigue and psychological distress among social workers: A validation study. *American Journal of Orthopsychiatry, 76,* 103–8.

Adams, R. E., Figley, C. R. & Boscarino, J. A. (2008). The Compassion Fatigue Scale: Its use with social workers following urban disaster. *Research on Social Work Practice, 18,* 238–50.

Adams, K. B., Matto, H. C. & Harrington, D. (2001). The Traumatic Stress Institute Belief Scale as a measure of vicarious trauma in a national sample of clinical social workers. *Family in Society, 82,* 363–71.

Adger, W. (2000). Social and ecological resilience: Are they related? *Progress in Human Geography, 24,* 347–64.

Adler, A. B., Bliese, P. D., McGurk, D., Hoge, C. W. & Castro, C. A. (2011). Battlemind debriefing and battlemind training as early interventions with soldiers returning from Iraq: Randomization by platoon. *Sport, Exercise, and Performance Psychology, 1,* 66–83.

Afana, A. H., Pedersen, D., Rønsbo, H. & Kirmayer, L. J. (2010). Endurance is to be shown at the first blow: Social representations and reactions to traumatic experiences in the Gaza strip. *Traumatology, 16,* 73–86.

Ainslie, R. C. (2013). Intervention strategies for addressing collective trauma: Healing communities ravaged by racial strife. *Journal of Psychoanalysis, Culture & Society, 18,* 140–52.

Alkin, M. C. (2012a). Comparing evaluation points of view. In M. C. Alkin (Ed.), *Evaluation roots: A wider perspectives of theorists' views and influences. 2nd Edition* (pp. 3–10). Thousand Oaks, CA: Sage.

Alkin, M. C. (2012b). Context-sensitive evaluation. In M. C. Alkin (Ed.), *Evaluation roots: A wider perspectives of theorists' views and influences. 2nd Edition* (pp. 283–92). Thousand Oaks, CA: Sage.

Allport, G. W. & Postman, L. (1947). *The psychology of rumor*. Oxford, England: Henry Holt.

Alphonse, M., George, P. & Moffat, K. (2008). Redefining social work standards in the context of globalization: Lessons from India. *International Social Work, 51*, 145–58.

Anderson, H. & Goolishian, H. (1992). The client is the expert: A not knowing approach to therapy. In S. McNamee & K. J. Gergen (Eds.) *Therapy as social construction* (pp. 25–39). Thousand Oaks, CA: Sage.

Antonovsky, A. (1979). *Health, stress, and coping*. San Francisco, CA: Jossey Bass.

Antonovsky, A. (1987). *Unraveling the mystery of health*. San Francisco, CA: Jossey Bass.

Antonovsky, A. (1991). The structural sources of salutogenic strength. In C. Cooper and S. R. Payne (Eds.), *Personality and stress: Individual differences in stress process* (pp. 67–104). New York: Wiley.

Antonovsky, A. & Sourani, T. (1988). Family sense of coherence and family adaptation. *Journal of Marriage and Family Therapy, 50*, 79–92.

Apfel, R. J. & Simon, B. (1996). *Minefields in their hearts: The mental health of children in war and communal violence*. New Haven, CT: Yale University Press.

Arendt, H. (1976). *Eichmann in Jerusalem: A report on the banality of evil*. Harmondsworth, NY: Penguin Books.

Arvay, M. J. (2001a). Shattered beliefs: Reconstitution the self of the trauma counselor. In R. A. Neimeyer (Ed.), *Meaning reconstruction and the experience of loss* (1st edn., pp. 213–30). Washington, DC: American Psychological Association.

Arvay, M. J. (2001b). Secondary traumatic stress among trauma counselors: What does the research say? *International Journal for the Advancement of Counseling, 23*, 283–93.

Arvay, M. J. & Uhlemann, M. R. (1996).Counselor stress and impairment in the field of trauma. *The Canadian Journal of Counseling, 30*, 193–210.

Azaryauo, M. (1997). Geographical Myth of Hadar 11th: From Tel Hai to Biria and to Eilat. *Ofakim Begeographia*, Vol. 46–7, 9–20 (in Hebrew).

Banac, I. (1984). *The national question in Yugoslavia: Origin, history, politics*. Ithaca, NY: Cornell University Press.

Bar-Tal, D. (2000). From intractable conflict through conflict resolution to reconciliation: Psychological analysis. *Political Psychology, 21*, 351–365

Bartov, O. (2000). *Mirrors of destruction: War, genocide, and modern identity*. Oxford, UK: Oxford University Press.

Becker, C. S. (1992). *Living and relating*. Newbury Park, CA: Sage.

Ben-Arzi, N., Solomon, Z. & Dekel, R. (2000). Secondary traumatization among wives of PTSD and post–concussion: Distress, caregiver burden and psychological separation. *Brain Injury, 14*, 728–36.

Bengston, V. L. (2001). Beyond the nuclear family: The increasing importance of multigenerational bonds. *Journal of Marriage and the Family, 63*, 1–15.

Berenbaum, M. (2005). Some clarification on the Warsaw ghetto uprising: Based on interviews with Marek Edelman and Simcha Rotem. In E. J. Sterling (Ed.), *Life in the ghetto during the Holocaust* (pp. 17–25). Syracuse, NY: Syracuse University Press.

Berenz, E. C., Vujanovic, A. A., Coffey, S. F. & Zvolensky, M. (2012). Anxiety sensitivity and breath holding duration in relation to PTSD symptom severity among trauma exposed adults. *Journal of Anxiety Disorders, 26*, 134–49.

Berger, R. (2015). *Stress, trauma and posttraumatic growth: Social context, environment and identities.* New York: Routledge.

Berger, R. & Paul, M. S. (2008). Family secrets and family functioning: The case of donor assistance. *Family Process, 47*, 553–66.

Bhui, K. et al. (2006). Mental disorders among Somali refugees: Developing culturally appropriate measures and assessing socio-cultural risk factors. *Social Psychiatry Psychiatric Epidemiology, 41*, 400–408.

Bleich, A., Gelkopf, M. & Solomon, Z. (2003). Exposure to terrorism, stress-related mental health symptoms, and coping behaviors among a nationally representative sample in Israel. *JAMA, 290*, 612–20.

Bohem, A., Enosh, G. & Shamai, M. (2010). Expectations of grassroots community leadership in times of normality and crisis. *Journal of Contingencies and Crisis Management, 18*, 184–94.

Bonanno, G. A. (2004). Loss, trauma, and human resilience: Have we underestimated the human capacity to thrive after extremely aversive events? *American Psychologist, 59*, 20–28.

Bonanno, G. A. (2008). Resilience in the face of potential trauma. In S. O. Lilienfeld, J. Ruscio & S. J. Lynn (Eds.), *Navigating the mindfield: A user's guide to distinguishing science from pseudoscience in mental health* (pp. 239–48). Amherst, NY: Prometheus Books.

Bonanno, G. A. & Mancini, A. D. (2008).The human capacity to thrive in the face of potential trauma. *Pediatrics, 121*, 369–75.

Bonanno, G. A. & Mancini, A. D. (2012).Beyond resilience and PTSD: Mapping the heterogeneity of responses to potential trauma. *Psychological Trauma: Theory, Research, Practice and Policy, 4*, 74–83.

Boscolo, L., Cecchin, G., Hoffman, L. & Penn, P. (1987). *Milan systemic family therapy.* New York: Basic Books.

Boss, P. (1999). *Ambiguous loss: Learning to live with unresolved grief.* Cambridge, MA: Harvard University Press.

Boss, P. (2002). Presentation describing the work done by the presenter and colleagues with union families who lost one of their members in September 11, 2001, attacks. Presented at American Family Therapy Academy 24th annual meeting, New York.

Boss, P. (2007). Ambiguous loss theory: Challenges for scholars and practitioners. *Family Relations, 56*, 105–11.

Boszormenyi-Nagy, I. (1987). *Foundations of contextual therapy: Collected papers of Ivan Boszormenyi-Nagy, MD.* New York: Brunner/Mazel.

Boszormenyi-Nagy, I. & Krasner, B. (1986). *Between give and take: A clinical guide to contextual therapy.* New York: Brunner/ Mazel.

Bowen, M. (1978) *Family therapy in clinical practice.* New York: Aronson.

Bower, M. (1978). *Family Therapy in Clinical Practice.* Northvale, NJ: Jason Aronson.

Brave Heart, M. Y. H. (1998). The return to the sacred path: Healing the historical unresolved grief response among the Lakota. *Smith College Studies in Social Work, 68*, 287–305.

Brave Heart, M. Y. H. (2004). The historical trauma response among natives and its relationship to substance abuse: A Lakota illustration. In M. Phillips & E. Nebelkopf (2004). *Healing and mental health for Native American: Speaking in red.* (pp. 7–18). Walnut Creek, CA: AltaMira Press.

Brave Heart, M. Y. H. & De Bruyn, L. M. (1998). The American Indian holocaust: Healing historical unresolved grief. *American Indian and Alaska Mental Health Research: The Journal of the National Center, 8,* 60–82.

Brave Heart-Jordan, M. & De Bruyn, L. M. (1995). So she may walk in balance: Integrating the impact of historical trauma in the treatment of Native American Indian women. In J. Adleman & G. Enguidanos (Eds.), *Racism in the lives of women: Testimony, theory, and guides to anti-racist practice* (pp. 345–68). New York: Haworth Press.

Breslau, N. (2009). The epidemiology of trauma, PTSD, and other posttrauma disorders. *Trauma, Violence & Abuse, 10,* 198–210.

Breslau, N., Davis, G. C., Peterson, E. L. & Schultz, L. R. (2000). A second look at comorbidity in victims of trauma: The posttraumatic stress disorder-major depression connection. *Biological Psychiatry, 48,* 902–9.

Breton, M. (2001). Neighborhood resiliency. *Journal of Community Practice, 19*(1): 21–36.

Brewer, M. B. (1991). The social self: On being the same and different at the same time. *Personality and Social Psychology Bulletin, 17,* 475–82.

Brewin, C. R. (2003). *Posttraumatic stress disorder: Malady or myth?* New Haven, CT: Yale University Press.

Breznith, S. (1967). Incubation of threat. *Journal of Experimental Research in Personality, 2,* 173–9.

Budden, A. (2009). The role of shame in posttraumatic stress disorder: A proposal for a socio-emotional model for DSM-V. *Social Science & Medicine, 69,* 1032–9.

Butollo, W. H. (1996). Psychotherapy integration for war traumatizatio: A training project in central Bosnia. *European Psychologist, 1,* 140–6.

Cadell, S., Regehr, C. & Hemsworth, D. (2003). Factors contributing to posttraumatic growth: A proposed structural equation model. *American Journal of Orthopsychiatry, 73,* 279–87.

Cairns, E. & Wilson, R. (1989). Mental health aspects of political violence in Northern Ireland. *International Journal of Mental Health, 18,* 38–56.

Cairns, E. & Wilson, R. (1991). Northern Ireland: Political violence and self-reported physical symptoms in a community sample. *Journal of Psychosomatic Research, 35,* 707–11.

Calhoun, L. G. & Tedeschi, R. G. (1998). Posttraumatic growth: Future directions. In R. G. Tedeschi, C. L. Park & L. G. Calhoun (Eds.), *Posttraumatic growth: Positive change in the aftermath of crisis* (pp. 215–38). Mahwah, NJ: Lawrence Erlbaum Associates.

Calhoun, L. G. & Tedeschi, R. G. (2006). The foundations of posttraumatic growth: An expanded framework. In L. G. Calhoun & R. G. Tedeschi (Eds.) *Handbook of posttraumatic growth* (pp. 1–23). Mahwah, NJ: Lawrence Erlbaum Associates.

Campbell, D. T. (1991). Methods for the experimenting society. *American Journal of Evaluation, 12,* 223–60.

Campbell, D. T. & Stanley, J. C.(1966). *Experimental and quasi-experimental designs for research.* Chicago, IL.: Rand McNally.

Caplan, G. (1964). *Principles of preventive psychiatry.* New York: Basic Books.

Caplan, G. (1974). *Support systems and community mental health: lectures on concept development.* New York: Behavioral Publications.

Carden, F. & Alkin, M. C. (2012). Evaluation roots: An international perspective. *Journal of Multi Disciplinary Evaluation, 8,* 102–18.

Carr, L. (1932). Disasters and the sequence-pattern concept of social change. *American Journal of Sociology, 38,* 207–18.

Carver, C. S. & Antoni, M. H. (2004). Finding benefit in breast cancer during the year after diagnosis predicts better adjustment 5 to 8 years after diagnosis. *Health Psychology, 23,* 595–8.

Catherall, D. R. (1995). Coping with secondary traumatic stress: The importance of the therapist's professional peer group. In B. H. Stamm (Ed.), *Secondary traumatic stress: Self-care issues for clinicians, researchers, and educators,* (pp. 80–94). Baltimore, MD: The Sidran Press.

Catherall, D. R. (1999). Family as a group treatment for PTSD. Group treatments for post-traumatic stress disorder. In B. H. Young & D. D. Blake (Eds.), *Group treatments for post-traumatic stress disorder* (pp. 15–34). Philadelphia, PA: Brunner/Mazel.

Chakrabarti, S. & Kulhara, P. (1999). Family burden of caring for people with mental illness. *British Journal of Psychiatry, 174,* 463.

Charles, L. L. (2010). Family therapists as front line mental health providers in war-affected regions: Using reflecting team, scaling questions, and family members in a hospital in Central Africa. *Journal of Family Therapy, 32,* 27–42.

Christie A. C. & Alkin, M. C. (2012). An evaluation theory tree. In M. C. Alkin (Ed.), *Evaluation roots: A wider perspectives of theorists' views and influences. 2nd Edition* (pp. 11–58). Thousand Oaks, CA: Sage.

Clauss-Ehlers, C. S. & Lopez-Levi, L. (2002). Violence and community, terms in conflict: An ecological approach to resilience. *Journal of Social Distress and Homeless, 11,* 265–78.

Cohen-Silver, R., Holman, A., Macintosh, D. N., Poulin, M. & Gil Rivas, V. (2002). Nationwide longitudal study of psychological responses to September 11. *JAMA, 288,* 1235–44.

Cook, T. D., Scriven, M., Coryn, C. L. S. & Evergreen, S. D. H. (2010). Contemporary thinking about causation in evaluation: A dialogue with Tom Cook and Michael Scriven. *American Journal of Evaluation, 31,* 105–17.

Cree, V. E. (2000). *Sociology for social workers and probation officers.* London: Routledge.

Cuijpers, P. & Stam, H. (2000). Burnout among relatives of psychiatric patients attending psycho-educational support groups. *Psychiatric Services, 51,* 375–9.

Danieli, Y. (1982). Families of survivors of the Nazi Holocaust: Short term and long term effects. *Series in Clinical & Community Psychology: Stress & Anxiety, 8,* 405–21.

Danieli, Y. (1998). *International handbook of multigenerational legacies of trauma.* New York: Plenum Press.

Dasberg, H. (1987). Psychological distress of Holocaust survivors and offspring in Israel, forty years later: A review. *Israeli Journal of Psychiatry Relate Science, 24*, 243–56.

DeBruyn, L. M. (1978). Native American child rearing in the city. Unpublished manuscript.

de Jong, J. T. V. M. (2002). Public mental health, traumatic stress and human rights violations in low-income countries: A culturally appropriate model in times of conflict, disaster and peace. In J. de-Jong (Ed.), *Trauma, war, and violence: Public mental health in socio-cultural context* (pp. 1–92). New York: Kluwer Academic/ Plenum Publishers.

de Jong, J. T. V. M., Komproe, I. H., Van Ommeren, M., El Masri, M., Araya, M., Khaled, N., van de Put, W. & Somasundaram, D. (2001). Lifetime events and Posttraumatic Stress Disorder in 4 post-conflict settings. *JAMA: Journal of the American Medical Association , 286*, 555–62.

Dekel, R. & Baum, N. (2010). Intervention in a shared traumatic reality: A new challenge for social workers.*The British Journal of Social Work, 40*, 1927–44.

Dekel, R. & Goldblatt, H. (2008). Is there intergenerational transmission of trauma? The case of combat veterans' children. *American Journal of Orthopsychaitry, 78*, 281–9.

Dekel, R. & Monson, C. M. (2010). Military-related post-traumatic stress disorder and family relations: Current knowledge and future directions. *Aggression and Violent Behavior, 15*, 303–9.

Dekel, R. & Solomon, Z. (2006). Secondary traumatization among wives of Israeli POWs: The role of POWs' distress. *Social Psychiatry and Psychiatric Epidemiology, 41*, 27–33.

Denborough, D. (2008). *Collective narrative practice: Responding to individuals, groups, and communities who have experienced trauma.* Adelaide, Australia: Dulwich Centre Publications.

De-Shazer, S. (1988). *Clues: Investigating solutions in brief therapy.* New York: Norton.

DeVries, M. W. (1995). Trauma in cultural perspective. In B. A. van der Kolk, A. C. McFarlane & L. Weisaeth (Eds.), *Traumatic stress: The effects of overwhelming experience on mind, body and society* (pp. 398–413). New York: Guilford.

Doherty, W. J. & McDaniel, S. H. (2010). *Family therapy.* Washington, DC: American Psychological Association.

DSM Diagnostic and statistical manual of mental disorders (3rd edn.) (1980). Washington, DC: American Psychiatric Association.

DSM Diagnostic and statistical manual of mental disorders (4th edn.) (1994). Washington, DC: American Psychiatric Association.

DSM Diagnostic and statistical manual of mental disorders (DSM-5) (2013). Washington, DC: American Psychiatric Association.

Dyson, M. E. (2006). *Come hell or high water: Hurricane Katrina and the color of disaster.* New York: Basic Civitas.

Elliott, M. (2003). Mother nature: Political reformer. *Time Asia, 161*, 59.

Ellis, A. (1997). *Stress counseling series a rational emotive behavior approach.* London: Cassell.

Engelhard, M., van den Hout, M., Janssen, W. & van der Beek, J. (2010). Eye movements reduce vividness and emotionality of "flashforwards." *Behavior Research and Therapy, 48,* 442–7.

Eisikovits, N. (2005). *Sympathizing with the enemy: A theory of political reconciliation.* Ann Arbor, MICH: UMI Dissertation Services

Erickson, K. T. (1978). *Everything in its path: Destruction of community in Buffalo Creek Flood.* New York: Simon & Schuster.

Everly, G. S. Jr. & Mitchell, J. T. (2000). The debriefing "controversy" and crisis intervention: A review of lexical and substantive issues. *International Journal of Emergency Mental Health, 2,* 211–25.

Falls, C. (1941) *The nature of modern warfare.* New York: Oxford University Press.

Fay, M. T., Morrissey, M. & Smyth, M. (1999). *Northern Ireland's troubles: The human cost.* London: Pluto Press.

Fazel, M., Wheeler, J. & Danesh, J. (2005). Prevalence of serious mental disorder in 7,000 refugees resettled in western countries: A systematic review. *The Lancet, 365,* 9467.

Figley, C. R. (1978). Psychosocial adjustment among Vietnam veterans: An overview of the research. In C. R. Figley (Ed.), *Stress, disorders among Vietnam veterans: Theory, research and treatment* (pp. 57–70). New York: Brunner/Mazel.

Figley, C. R. (1988). Victimization, trauma and traumatic stress. *Counseling Psychologist, 16:* 635–41.

Figley, C. R. (1989a). *Treating stress in families.* New York: Brunner/Mazal.

Figley, C. R. (1989b). *Helping traumatized families.* San Francisco, CA: Jossey-Bass.

Figley, C. R. (1990). *Helping traumatized families.* New York: Brunner/Mazal.

Figley, C. R. (Ed.). (1995a). *Compassion fatigue: Coping with secondary traumatic stress disorder in those who treat the traumatized.* New York: Brunner/Mazal.

Figley, C. R. (1995b). Compassion fatigue: Toward a new understanding of the costs of caring. Secondary traumatic stress: Self-care issues for clinicians, researchers, and educators. In B. H. Stamm (Ed.), *Secondary traumatic stress: Self-care issues for clinicians, researchers, and educators* (pp. 3–28). Baltimore, MD: The Sidran Press.

Figley, C. R. (1995c). Compassion fatigue as secondary traumatic stress disorder: An overview. In C. R. Figley (Ed.), *Compassion fatigue: Coping with secondary traumatic stress disorder in those who treat the traumatized* (pp. 1–20). New York: Brunner-Routledge.

Figley, C. R. (Ed.) (2002). *Treating compassion fatigue.* New York: Brunner-Routledge.

Figley, C. R. & McCubbin, H. I. (Eds.) (1983). *Stress and the family, vol. II: Coping with catastrophe.* New York: Brunner/Mazel.

Flannery, R. B. (1990). Social support and psychological trauma: A methodological review. *Journal of Traumatic Stress, 3,* 593–610.

Fleischacker, S. (2004). *Adam Smith's Wealth of Nations: A Philosophical Companion.* Princeton, NJ: Princeton University Press.

Foa, E. B. (2011). Prolonged exposure therapy: Past, present and future. *Depression and Anxiety, 28,* 1043–47.

Foucault, M. (1980). Truth and power. In C. Gordon (Ed.), *Power/knowledge selected interviews and other writing 1972–1977* (pp. 107–33). Brighton, UK: Harvester.

Frankel, V. (1970). *Man's search for meaning: An introduction to logotherapy.* Boston, MA: Beacon Press.

Frazier, P., Conlon, A. & Glaser, T. (2001). Positive and negative life changes following sexual assault. *Journal of Consulting and Clinical Psychology, 69,* 1048–55.

Friedlander, S. (2007). *Nazi Germany and the Jews: The years of extermination, 1939–1945.* New York: HarperCollins.

Friedman, M. J. & Marsella, A. J. (1996). Posttraumatic Stress Disorder: An overview of the concept. In J. A. Marsella, M. J. Friedman, E.T. Gerrity & R. M. Scurfield (Eds.), *Ethnocultural aspects of posttraumatic stress disorder* (pp. 11–32). Washington, DC: American Psychiatric Association.

Fullerton, C. S., Ursano, R. J., Epstein, R. S., Crowley, B., Vance, K., Kao, T. C., Dougall, A. & Baum, A. (2001). Gender differences in posttraumatic stress disorder after motor vehicle accidents. *American Journal of Psychiatry, 158,* 1486–91.

Gample, Y. (1988). Facing war, murder, torture, and death. *Psychoanalytic Review, 45,* 499–509.

Garbarino, J. & Kostelny, K. (1996). What do we need to know to understand children in war and community violence. In B. Simon & R.J. Apfel (Eds.), *Minefield in their hearts: The mental health of children in war and communal violence* (pp. 33–51). New Haven, CT: Yale University Press.

Garbarino, J., Kostelny, K. and Dubrow, N. (1991). *No place to be a child: Growing up in a war zone.* Lexington, MA: D. C. Heath and Company.

George, M. (2010). A theoretical understanding of refugee trauma. *Clinical Social Work, 38,* 379–87.

Gergen, K. J. (1994). *Realities and relationships: Soundings in social construction.* Cambridge, MA: Harvard University Press.

Gergen, K. J. (2000). *The Saturated Self: Dilemmas of identity in contemporary life.* New York: Basic Books.

Geron, Y., Malkinson, R. & Shamai, M. (2005). Families in the war zone: Narratives of "Me" and the "Other" in the course of therapy. *AFTA Monograph Series, 1,* 17–25.

Geving, R. (2003). *Dad, you have asked me.* Mishmar-Haemek, Israel: Private publication of the Geving family (in Hebrew).

Ghahramanlou, M. & Brodbeck, C. (2000). Predictors of secondary trauma in sexual assault trauma counselors. *International Journal of Emergency Mental Health, 4,* 229–40.

Gilad, D. & Lavee, Y. (2010). Couple support schemata in couples with and without spinal cord injury. *Rehabilitation Counseling Bulletin, 53,* 106–16.

Gilbar, O. & Ben Zur, H. (2002). *Cancer and the family caregiver: Distress and coping.* Springfield, IL: Charles C. Thomas Publisher.

Gilbart, C. (1998). Studying disaster: Changes in the main conceptual tools. In E. L. Quaranteli (Ed.), *What is a disaster? Perspectives on the question* (pp. 11–18). London and New York: Routledge.

Gonen, R. (2008). The way social support given during and after intervention with terror victims and their families is experienced by the social workers. Unpublished MA thesis, supervised by Prof. Michal Shamai, Ph.D., School of Social Work, University of Haifa, Israel.

Grabowski-Kouvatas, L. D. (2006). Toward a better understanding of urban African American girls' perceptions of trust. *Dissertation Abstract International: Section B: The Sciences and Engineering, 67 (3–4),* 1700.

Grases-Colom, G., Trías, A., Cristina, S. C. & Cristian, Z. O. J. (2011). Study of the effect of positive humor as a variable that reduces stress: Relationship of humor with personality and performance variables. *Psychology in Spain, 15,* 9–21.

Gribbons, B. & Herman, J. (1997). *Utilization-focused evaluation* (2nd edn.). Newbury Park, CA: Sage.

Gutman, Y. & Manbar, R. (1984). *The Nazi concentration camps: Structure and aims. The image of prisoner. The Jews in the camps.* Jerusalem, Israel: Yad Vashem.

Halling, C. S., Schindler, D. W., Walker, B. W. & Roughgarden, J. (1995). Biodiversity in the functioning of ecosystem: An ecological synthesis. In C. Perrings, K.G. Maler, C. Folke, C.S. Halling & B.O. Jansson (Eds.), *Biodiversity loss: Economic and ecological issues.* Cambridge, MA: Cambridge University Press.

Halpern, J. & Tramontin, M. (2007). *Disaster mental health: Theory and practice.* Belmont, CA: Thompson Brooks/Cole.

Harkness, L. & Zador, N. (2001). Treatment of PTSD in families and couples. In J. P. Wilson, M. J. Friedman & J. D. Lindy (Eds.), *Treating psychological trauma and PTSD* (pp. 335–53). New York: Guilford.

Harris, C. J. & Linder, J. G. (1999, 2nd edn.). Communication and self care: Foundational issues. In B. H. Stamm (Ed.), *Secondary traumatic stress: Self-care issues for clinicians, researchers, and educators* (pp. 95–104). Baltimore, MD: The Sidran Press.

Hawker, D. M., Durkin, J. & Hawker, D. S. J. (2011). To debrief or not to debrief our heroes: That is the question. *Clinical Psychology & Psychotherapy, 18,* 453–63.

Hayner, P. B. (1994). Fifteen Truth Commissions: 1974 to 1994—A comparative study. *Human Rights Quarterly, 16,* 597–655.

Helsloot, I. & Ruitenberg, A. (2004). Citizen response to disasters: A survey of literature and some practical implications. *Journal of Contingencies and Crisis Management, 12,* 98–111.

Henderson, V. (2010). Humor as a defense mechanism in war veterans. In S. S. Fehr (Ed.), *101 interventions in group therapy* (Rev. edn.) (pp. 515–18). New York: Routledge/Taylor & Francis Group.

Hewitt, K. (1998). Excluded perspectives in the social construction of disaster. In E. L. Quaranteli (Ed.), *What is a disaster? Perspectives on the question* (pp. 75–92). London and New York: Routledge.

Hilberg, R. (1996). *The politics of memory: The journey of a Holocaust historian.* Chicago, IL: Ivan R. Dee.

Hill, R. (1949). *Families under stress: Adjustment to the crises of war separation and return.* Oxford, England: Harper.

Hill, R. (1958). Generic features of families under stress. *Social Casework, 39,* 139–50.

Hobfoll, S. E. (1998). *Stress, culture, and community: The psychology and philosophy of stress.* New York: Plenum.

Hobfoll, S. E. (2001). The influence of culture, community, and the nested-self in the stress process: Advancing conservation of resources theory. *Applied Psychology: An International Review, 50,* 337–69.

Hobfoll, S. E., Hall, B. J., Canetti-Nisim, D., Galea, S., Johnson, R. J. & Palmieri, P. A. (2007). Refining our understanding of traumatic growth in the face of terrorism: Moving from meaning cognitions to doing what is meaningful. *Applied Psychology: An International Review, 56,* 345–66.

Hodgkinson, P. & Stewart, M. (1991). *Coping with catastrophe: A handbook of post disaster psychological after care.* London: Routledge.

Hoffmann, A. (2010). The inverted EMDR standard protocol for unstable complex post-traumatic stress disorder. In M. Luber (Ed.), *Eye movement desensitization and reprocessing (EMDR) scripted protocols: Special populations* (pp. 313–28). New York: Springer Publishing.

Hogancamp, V. E. & Figley, C. R. (1983). War: Bringing battle home. In C.R. Figley & H. I. McCubbin (Eds.), *Stress and the family, Volume II: Coping with catastrophe* (pp. 148–65). New York: Brunner/Mazel.

Horwitz, G. J. (1990). *In the shadow of death: Living outside the gates of Mauthausen.* New York : Free Press.

Hyman, O. (2001). Perceived social support and symptoms of secondary traumatic stress in disaster workers. Unpublished doctoral dissertation, School of Social Work, Adelphi University, Garden City, NY.

IASC (Inter-Agency Standing Committee) (2007). *IASC guidelines on mental health and psychosocial support in emergency settings.* Geneva, Switzerland: IASC.

IASFM (The International Association for the Study of Forced Migration). Retrieved from www.forcedmigration.org.

Imber-Black, E. (1993). Secrets in families and family therapy: An overview. In E. Imber-Black (Ed.), *Secrets in families and family therapy* (pp. 3–28). New York: Norton.

Imber-Black, E. (1998). *The secret life of families.* New York: Bantam Books.

Imber-Black, E., Roberts, J. & Whiting, R. (1988). *Rituals in families and family therapy.* New York: Norton.

Ink, D. (2006). An analysis of the House Select Committee and White House reports on Hurricane Katrina. *Public Administration Review, 66 ,* 800–807.

Janoff-Bulman, R. (1985). The aftermath of victimization: Rebuilding shattered assumptions. In C. R. Figley (Ed.), *Trauma and its wake* (pp. 15–35). New York: Brunner/Mazal.

Janoff-Bulman, R. (1989). Assumptive worlds and the stress of traumatic events: Application of the schema construct. *Social Cognition, 7,* 113–36.

Janoff-Bulman, R. (1992). *Shattered assumptions: Towards a new psychology of trauma*. New York: Free Press.

Joubran-Saba, F. (2014). Intergenerational transmission of the experience of the Palestinian refugees who remained within the borders of the State of Israel in 1948. Unpublished MA thesis, supervised by Prof. Michal Shamai, Ph.D., School of Social Work, University of Haifa, Israel.

Joyce, P. A. & Berger, R. (2007). Which language does PTSD speak? The "Westernization" of Mr. Sánchez. *Journal of Trauma Practice, 5*, 53–67.

Ka-Tzetnik (1989). *Shivitti: A vision*. San Francisco, CA: Harper & Row.

Kamya, H. (2009). Healing from refugee trauma: The significance of spiritual beliefs, faith community, and faith-based services. In F. Walsh (Ed.), *Spiritual resources in family therapy* (2nd edn.) (pp. 286–300). New York: Guilford.

Kaniasty, K. (2012). Predicting social psychological well being following trauma: The role of post disaster social support. *Psychological Trauma: Theory, Research, Practice and Policy, 4*, 22–33.

Kaniasty, K. & Norris, F. H. (1995). In search of altruistic community: Pattern of social support mobilization following Hurricane Hugo. *American Journal of Community Psychology, 23*, 447–77.

Kaniasty, K. & Norris, F. H. (2004). Social support in the aftermath of disasters, catastrophes, acts of terrorism: Altruistic, overwhelmed, uncertain, antagonistic, and patriotic communities. In R. Ursano, A. Norwood & C. Fullerton (Eds.), *Bioterrorism: Psychology and public health interventions* (pp. 200–229). New York: Cambridge University Press.

Keane, T. M., Marshall, A. D. & Taft, C. T. (2006). Posttraumatic stress disorder: Etiology, epidemiology, and treatment outcome. *Annual Review of Clinical Psychology, 2*, 161–7.

Kelly, G. A. (1955). *The psychology of personal constructs*. New York: Norton.

Kermish, J. (1986). *To live with honor and die with honor!: Selected documents from the Warsaw Ghetto Underground* (Archives "O.S." "Oneg Shabbath"). Jerusalem, Israel: Yad Vashem.

Kessler, R. C., Sonnega, A., Bromet, E., Hughes, M. & Nelson, C. B. (1995). Posttraumatic Stress Disorder in the national comorbidity survey. *Archives of General Psychiatry, 52*, 1048–60.

Kessler, R. C., Berglund, P., Demler, O., Jin, R., Merikangas, K. R. & Walters, E. E. (2005). Lifetime prevalence and age of onset distributions of DSM-IV disorders in the National Comorbidity Survey Replication. *Archives of General Psychiatry, 62*, 592–602.

Kimhi, S. & Shamai, M. (2004). Community resilience and the impact of stress: Adult response to Israel's withdrawal from Lebanon. *Journal of Community Psychology, 32*, 439–451.

Kimhi, S. & Shamai, M. (2006). Are women really at higher risk than men? Gender differences among teenagers and adults in their response to threat of war and terror. *Women & Health, 43*, 1–19.

Kleim, B. & Ehlers, A. (2009). Evidence for a curvilinear relationship between posttraumatic growth and posttrauma depression and PTSD in assault survivors. *Journal of Traumatic Stress, 22*, 45–52.

Klein, M. (1946). Notes on some schizoid mechanism. *International Journal of Psychoanalysis, 27*, 99–110.

Klein, M. (1975). *The writing of Melanie Klien. Vol. I: Love, guilt and reparation.* London: Hogarth Press.

Kobasa, S. C. (1982). The hardy personality: Toward a social psychology of stress and health. In G. S. Sanders & J. Suls (Eds.), *Social psychology of health and illness* (pp. 1–25). Hillsdale, NJ: Erlbaum.

Krakowski, S. (1984). *The war of the doomed: Jewish armed resistance in Poland, 1942–1944.* New York: Holmes and Meier

Kretsch, R., Benyakar, M., Baruch, E. & Roth, M. (1997). A shared reality of therapists and survivors in a national crisis as illustrated by the Gulf War. *Psychotherapy: Theory, Research, Practice, Training, 34,* 28–33.

Krystal, H. (1968). *Massive psychic trauma.* New York: International Universities Press.

Kulig, J. (2000). Community resiliency: The potential for community health nursing theory development. *Public Health Nursing, 17,* 374–85.

Kulig, J. & Hanson, L. (1996). *Discussion and expansion of the concept of resiliency: Summary of think tank.* Lethbridge, Canada: University of Lethbridge, Regional Center of Health Promotion and Cummunity Studies.

Kupelian, D., Kalayjian, A. & Sanentz, K. A. (1998). The Turkish genocide of the Armenians: Continuing effects on survivors and their families eight decades after massive trauma. In Y. Danieli (ed.), *International handbook of multigenerational legacies of trauma* (pp. 191–210). New York: Plenum Press.

Kurzem, M. (2008). *The mascot: Unraveling the mystery of my Jewish father's Nazi boyhood.* New York: Plume Books.

Kushnir, T. & Melamed, S. (1992). The Gulf War and its impact on burnout and well-being of working civilians. *Psychological Medicine, 22,* 987–95.

Lahad, S. & Ben Nesher, U. (2005). From improvisation during the traumatic situation to the development of guidelines for interventions: Communities' coping with terror events—preparation, intervention and rehabilitation. In E. Somer & A. Bleich (Eds.), *Mental health in terror's shadow: The Israeli experience* (pp. 259–70). Tel Aviv, Israel: Ramot Publication-Tel Aviv University (in Hebrew).

Lahad, S., Shacham, Y. & Niv, S. (2000). Coping and community resources in children facing disaster. In A. Y. Shalev, R. Yehuda & A. C. McFarlane (Eds.), *International handbook of human response to trauma* (pp. 389–95). New York: Kluwer Academic/Plenum Publishers.

Landau, J. (2007). Enhancing resilience: Families and communities as agents for change. *Family Process, 46,* 351–65.

Landau, J. & Saul, J. (2004). Faciliating family and community resilience in response to major disaster. In F. Walsh & M. McGoldrick (Eds.), *Living beyond loss* (pp. 285–309). New York: Norton.

Landau, J., Mittal, M. & Wieling, E. (2008). Linking human systems: Strengthening individuals, families, and communities in the wake of mass trauma. *Journal of Marital & Family Therapy, 34,* 193–209.

Langston, C. (1992). Too close to the tremors of the earth. In S. K. Majumdar, G.S. Forbes, E. W. Miller & R. F. Schmalz (Eds.), *Natural and technological disaster: Causes, effects, and preventive measures* (pp. 49–61). Easton, PA: Pennsylvania Academy of Science.

Lazarus, R. S. & Folkman, S. (1984). *Stress, appraisal and coping.* New York: Springer.

Lechner, S. C., Carver, C. S., Antoni, M. H., Weaver, K. E. & Phillips, K. M. (2006). Curvilinear associations between benefit finding and psychosocial adjustment to breast cancer. *Journal of Consulting and Clinical Psychology, 74,* 828–40.

Lefcourt, H. M. (2003). Humor as a moderator of life stress in adults. In C. E. Schaefer (Ed.), *Play therapy with adults* (pp. 144–65). Hoboken, NJ: Wiley & Sons Inc.

Legters, L. H. (1988). The American genocide. *Policy Studies Journal, 16,* 768–77.

Lepore, S. J. & Revenson, T. A. (2006). Resilience and post traumatic growth: Recovery, resistance and reconfiguration. In L. G. Calhoun & R. G. Tedeschi (Eds.), *Handbook of post traumatic growth* (pp. 24–46). Mahwah, NJ: Lawrence Erlbaum.

Levi, P. (1986). *Survival in Auschwitz; and, the reawakening: Two memoirs.* New York: Summit Books.

Levi, P. (1987). *The wrench.* London: Michael Joseph.

Levi, P., Gordon, R. & Belpoliti, M. (2001). *The voice of memory: Interviews 1961–1987.* New York: New Press.

Lilienfeld, S. O. (2007). Psychological treatments that cause harm. *Perspectives on Psychological Science, 2,* 53–70.

Lincoln, Y. S. & Guba, E. G. (2012, 2nd edn.). The roots of fourth generation evaluation: Theoretical and methodological origins. In M. C. Alkin (Ed.), *Evaluation roots: A wider perspectives of theorists' views and influences.* Thousand Oaks, CA: Sage.

Lind, E. W. (2000). Secondary traumatic stress: Predictors in psychologists. Unpublished doctoral dissertation, Seattle, WA: Seattle Pacific University.

Lindy, J. (1996). Psychoanalytic therapy of posttraumatic stress disorder: The nature of the therapeutic relationship. In B. A. van der Kolk, A. C. McFarlane & L. W. Weisaeth (Eds.), *Traumatic stress: The effect of overwhelming experience on mind, body and society* (pp. 525–36). New York: Guilford Press.

Lindy, J. D. & Wilson, J. P. (2001). Respecting the trauma membrane: above all, do no harm. In J. P. Wilson, M. J. Friedman & J. D. Lindy (Eds.), *Treating psychological trauma and PTSD* (pp. 432–45). New York: Guilford.

Lipsey, W. M. & Freeman, H. E. (2004). *Evaluation: A systematic approach* (7th edn.). Thousand Oaks, CA: Sage.

Lipstadt, D. E. (1994). *Denying the Holocaust: The growing assault on truth and memory.* New York: Penguin.

Lisitza, S. & Peres, Y. (2008). *A measurement of perceived community resilience: Research report.* Israel Ministry of Welfare and Social Services: Department of Individuals and Social Services—The service of community work (in Hebrew).

Malkinson, R. (2007). *Cognitive grief therapy: Constructing a rational meaning to life following loss.* New York: Norton.

Mallimson, K. E. (2006). *Survivor guilt and posttraumatic stress disorder 18 months after September 11, 2001: Influences of prior trauma, exposure to the event, and bereavement.* Dissertation Abstracts International: Section B: The Sciences and Engineering.

Manne, S., Ostroff, J., Winkel, G., Goldstein, L., Fox, K. & Grana, G. (2004). Posttraumatic growth following breast cancer: Patient, partner, and couple perspectives. *Psychosomatic Medicine, 66,* 442–54.

Marks, N. F. (1998). Does it hurt to care? Caregiving, work–family conflict, and midlife well-being. *Journal of Marriage & the Family, 60,* 951–66.

Marsella, A. J. (2010). Ethnocultural aspects of PTSD: An overview of concepts, issues, and treatments. *Traumatology, 16,* 17–26.

Maslow, A. H. (1954). *Motivation and personality.* New York: Harper & Row.

Maslow, A. H. (1962). *Toward the psychology of being.* Princeton, NJ: Van Nostrand.

Maslow, A. H. (1970). *Motivation and personality.* New York: Harper & Row.

McCann, I. & Pearlman, L. A. (1990). *Psychological trauma and the adult survivor: Theory, therapy, and transformation.* Philadelphia, PA: Brunner/Mazel.

McCubbin, H. I., Hamilton, I. & Patterson, J. M. (1983). The family stress process: The double ABCX model of adjustment and adaptation. *Marriage & Family Review, 6,* 7–37.

McDaniel, S., Hepworth, J. & Doherty, W. (1992). *Medical family therapy.* New York: Basic Books.

McFarlane, A. C. & van der Kolk, B. A. (1996). Trauma and its challenge to society. In B. A. van der Kolk, A. C. McFarlane & L. Weisaeth (Eds.), *Traumatic stress: The effect of overwhelming experience on mind, body and society* (pp. 3–23). New York: Guilford.

Meadows, E. A. & Foa, E. B. (2000). Cognitive behavioral treatment for PTSD. In A. Y. Shalev, R. Yehuda & A. C. McFarlane (Eds.), *International handbook of human response to trauma* (pp. 337–46). New York: Kluwer Academic/ Plenum Publishers.

Mendelssohn, F. (2008). Transgenerational transmission of trauma: Guilt, shame, and the "heroic dilemma." *International Journal of Group Psychotherapy, 58,* 389–401.

Mikulincer, M., Florian, V. & Solomon, Z. (1995). Marital intimacy, family support, and secondary traumatization: A study of wives of veterans with combat stress reaction. *Anxiety Stress and Coping, 8,* 203–13.

Miles, I. A. (2008). Cultural mistrust, academic outcome expectations, and values among African American adolescent males. In C. Hudley & A. E. Gottfried (Eds.), *Academic motivation and the culture of school in childhood and adolescence: Child development in cultural context* (pp. 146–64). New York: Oxford University Press.

Miller, D. S. & Rivera, J. D. (2008). *Hurricane Katrina and the redefinition of landscape.* Lanham, MD: Lexington Books.

Minuchin, S. (1974). *Families and family therapy.* Cambridge, MA: Harvard University Press.

Minuchin, S. & Fishman, H. C. (1981). *Family therapy techniques.* Cambridge, MA: Harvard University Press.

Minuchin, S., Montalvo, B., Guerney, B., Rosman, B. & Schumer, F. (1967). *Families of the slums.* New York: Basic Books.

Mitchell, G. D. (1985). *A new dictionary of sociology.* London: Routledge & Kegan Paul.

Morgan, J. D. (2002). *Social support: A reflection of humanity.* Amityville, NY: Baywood Pub.

Mullaly, B. (2007). Oppression: The focus of structural social work. In B. Mullaly, *The new structural social work* (pp. 252–86). Don Mills, Canada: Oxford University Press.

Myers, D. & Wee, D. F. (2002). Strategies for managing disaster mental health worker stress. In C. R. Figley (Ed.), *Treating compassion fatigue* (pp. 181–212). New York: Brunner-Routledge.

Myers, D. (2005). *Disaster Mental Health Services: A primer for practitioners.* New York: Brunner-Routledge.

NASW Codes of Ethics (2008). Retrieved from http://www.naswdc.org/pubs/code/default.asp.

Nayak, N., Power, M. B. & Foa, E. B. (2012). Empirically supported psychological treatments: Prolonged exposure. In G. J. Beck & D. M. Sloan (Eds.), *The Oxford handbook of traumatic stress disorder* (pp. 427–38). New York: Oxford University Press.

Neimeyer, R. A. (2001). Meaning reconstruction and loss. In R. A. Neimeyer (Ed.), *Meaning reconstruction and the experience of loss* (pp. 1–9). Washington, DC: American Psychological Association.

Neimeyer, R. A. & Anderson, A. (2002). Meaning reconstruction theory. In N. Thompson (Ed.), *Loss and grief: A guide for human services practitioners* (pp. 45–64). London: Palgrave.

Nelson Goff, B. S., Crow, J. R., Reisbig, A. M. J. & Hamilton, S. (2007). The impact of individual trauma symptoms of deployed soldiers on relationship satisfaction. *Journal of Family Psychology, 21,* 344–53.

Nessman, R. (2005). For Israel, the wounds of the Holocaust remain fresh. Retrieved from www.highbeam.com/doc/1P1-104672417.html.

Noriega, J. (1992). American Indian education in the United States: Indoctrination for subordination to colonialism. In M. A. Jaimes (Ed.), *The state of Native America: Genocide, colonization, and resistance* (pp. 371–402). Boston, MA: South End Press.

Norris, F. H. & Stevens, S. P. (2007). Community resilience and the principles of mass trauma intervention. *Psychiatry Interpersonal and Biological Processes, 70,* 320–28.

Norris, F. H., Friedman, M. J. & Watson, P. I. (2002). 60,000 disaster victims speak: Part II. Summary and implications of disaster mental health research. *Psychiatry: Interpersonal & Biological Processes, 65,* 240–60.

Norris, F. H., Stevens, P. S., Pfefferbaum, B., Wyche, K. F. & Pfefferbaum, R. L. (2008). Community resilience as a metaphor, theory, set of capacities, and strategy for disaster readiness. *American Journal of Community Psychology, 41,* 127–50.

Norris, F. H., Friedman, M. J., Watson, P. I., Bryne, C. M., Diaz, E. & Kaniasty, K. (2002). 60,000 disaster victims speak: Part I. An empirical review of the empirical literature, 1981–2001. *Psychiatry: Interpersonal & Biological Processes, 65,* 207–39.

O'Keefe, P., Westgate, K. & Wisner, B. (1976).Taking the naturalness out of the natural disaster. *Nature, 91,* 260.

Osborn, R. N., Hunt, J. G. & Jauch, L. R. (2002). Toward a contextual theory of leadership. *The Leadership Quarterly, 13,* 797–837.

Osofsky, J. D. (1997). *Children in violent society.* New York: Guilford.

Parad, H. J. (1966). *Crisis intervention: Selected readings.* New York: Family Service Association of America.

Parad, H. J. (1990). *Crisis intervention, book 2: The practitioner's sourcebook for brief therapy.* Milwaukee, WI: Family Service America.

Parker, C. F., Stern, E. K., Paglia, E. & Brown, C. (2009). Preventable catastrophe? The Hurricane Katrina disaster revisited. *Journal of Contingencies and Crisis Manangement, 17,* 206–17.

Pastor, L. H. (2004). Culture as causality: Examining the causes and consequences of collective trauma. *Psychiatric Annals, 34,* 616–22.

Patton, D. & Johnston, D. (2001). Disasters and communities: Vulnerability, resilience and preparedness. *Disaster Prevention and Management, 10,* 270–77.

Patton, M. Q. (1986). *Utilization-focused evaluation* (2nd edn.). Newbury Park, CA: Sage.

Patton, M. Q. (1990). *Qualitative evaluation and research methods* (2nd edn.). Newbury Park, CA: Sage.

Patton, M. Q. (1994). Developmental evaluation. *Evaluation Practice, 15,* 311–19.

Paul, M. S., Berger, R., Berlow, N., Rovner-Ferguson, H., Figlerski, L., Gardner, S. & Malave, A. F. (2010). Posttraumatic growth and social support in individuals with infertility. *Human Reproduction, 25,* 133–41.

Pearlman, L. A. (1999). Self care for trauma therapists: Ameliorating vicarious traumatization. In B. H. Stamm (Ed.), *Secondary traumatic stress: Self care issues for clinicians, researchers, and educators* (pp. 51–64). Baltimore, MD: Sidran.

Pearlman, L. A. & Saakvitne, K. W. (1995). *Trauma and therapist: Counter-transference and vicarious traumatization in psychotherapy with incest survivors.* New York: Norton.

Perkins, D. & Long, D. (2002). Neighborhood sense of community and social capital: A multi level analysis. In A. Fisher, C. Sonn & B. Bishop (Eds.), *Psychological sense of community: Research, applications and implications* (pp. 291–318). New York: Plenum.

Pfefferbaum, B. J., DeVoe, E. R., Stuber, J., Sciff, M., Klein, T. & Fairbrother, G. (2005). Psychological impact of terrorism on children and families in the United State. *Journal of Aggression, Maltreatment and Trauma, 10,* 277–88.

Phifer, J. E. (1990). Psychological distress and somatic symptoms after natural disaster: Differential vulnerability among older adults. *Psychology and Aging, 5,* 412–20.

Picou, S. (2009). Review essay: The shifting sands of post-Katrina disaster sociology. *Sociological Spectrum, 29,* 431–8.

Porfirieu, B. N. (1998). Issues in the definition and delineation of disasters and disasters areas. In E. L. Quaranteli (Ed.), *What is a disaster? Perspectives on the question* (pp. 56–72). London and New York: Routledge.

Possick, C., Sadeh, R. A. & Shamai, M. (2008). Parents' experience and meaning construction of the loss of the child in a national terror attack. *American Journal of Orthopsychiatry, 78,* 93–102.

Prince, R. (2009). The self in pain: The paradox of memory. The paradox of testimony. *American Journal of Psychoanalysis, 69,* 279–90.

Purdie-Vaughns, V., Steele, C. M., Davis, P. G., Ditlmann, R. & Crosby, J. R. (2008). Identity contingency threat: How diversity cues signal threat or safety for African-Americans in mainstream settings. *Journal of Personal and Social Psychology, 94,* 615–630.

Quaranteli, E. L. (1998). Epilogue: Where we have been and where we might go. In E. L. Quaranteli (Ed.), *What is a disaster? Perspectives on the question* (pp. 234–73). London and New York: Routledge.

Raphael, B. (1986). *When disaster strikes: How individuals and communities cope with catastrophe.* New York: Basic Books.

Raphael, B. & Wilson, J. P. (2000). Introduction and overview: Key issues in the conceptualization of debriefing. In B. Raphael & J. P. Wilson (Eds.), *Psychological debriefing: Theory, practice and evidence* (pp. 1–14). New York: Cambridge University Press.

Read, P. P. (1993). *Ablaze: The Story of the Heroes and Victims of Chernobyl.* New York: Random House.

Reid, W. J. (1978). *The task-centered system.* New York: Columbia University Press.

Resick, P. A. & Miller, M. W. (2009). Posttraumatic stress disorder: Anxiety or traumatic stress disorder? *Journal of Traumatic Stress, 22,* 384–90.

Riessman, C. K. (2001). Analysis of personal narratives. In J. F. Gubrium & J. A. Holstein (Eds.), *Handbook of interviewing* (pp. 695–710). London: Sage.

Roberts, J. (1988). Setting a frame: Definitions, functions, and typology of rituals. In E. Imber-Black, J. Roberts & R. Whiting (Eds.), *Rituals in families and family therapy* (pp. 3–46). New York: Norton.

Robinson, J. W. (1994). Ten basic principles of leadership in community development organizations. *Journal of the Community Development Society, 25,* 44–8.

Robinson, R. (2007). Commentary on "Issues in the debriefing debate for the emergency services: Moving research outcomes forward." *Clinical Psychology: Science and Practice, 14,* 121–3.

Rolland, J. (1994). *Helping families with chronic and life-threatening disorders.* New York: Basic Books.

Ron, P. & Shamai, M. (2011). Challenging the impact of ongoing national terror: Social workers in Israel. *Social Work Research, 35,* 36–45.

Saakvitne, K., Tennen, H. & Affleck, G. (1998). Exploring thriving in the context of clinical trauma theory: Constructivist self–development theory. *Journal of Social Issue, 54,* 279–99.

Sagi-Schwartz, A., van Ijzendoorn, M., Joels, T. & Scarf, M. (2002). Disorganized reasoning in Holocaust survivors: An attachment perspective. *American Journal of Orthopsychiatry, 72,* 194–203.

Sagi-Schwartz, A., van Ijzendoorn, M., Grossmann, K. E., Joels, T. Scarf, M., Koren-Karie, N. et al. (2003). Attachment and traumatic stress in female Holocaust child survivors and their daughters. *American Journal of Psychiatry, 160,* 1086–92.

Sagy, S. & Antonovsky, A. (1992). The family sense of coherence and the retirement transition. *Journal of Marriage and the Family, 54,* 983–94.

Saul, J. (2013). *Collective trauma, collective healing: Promoting community resilience in the aftermath of disaster.* New York: Routledge.

Schuster, M. A., Stein, B. D., Jaycox, L., Collins, R. L., Marshall, G. N., Elliott, M.N., Zhou, A. J., Kanouse, D. E., Morrison, J. L. & Berry, S. H. (2001). A national survey of stress reactions after September 11, 2001, terrorist attacks. *New England Journal of Medicine, 345,* 1507–12.

Scriven, M. (1991). *Evaluation thesaurus* (4th edn.). Newbury Park, CA: Sage.

Sears, S. R., Stanton, A. L. & Danoff-Burg, S. (2003). The yellow brick and the emerald city: Benefit-finding, positive reappraisal coping, and posttraumatic growth in women with early stage breast cancer. *Health Psychology, 22,* 487–97.

Seedat, S. & Stein, D. J. (2000). Trauma and post-traumatic stress disorder in women: A review. *International Clinical Psychopharmacology, 15,* 25–33.

Segev, T. (1994).*The seventh million: The Israelis and the Holocaust.* New York: Hill and Wang.

Sewpaul, V. (2006). The global-local dialectic: Challenges for Africa scholarship and social work in a post-colonial world. *British Journal of Social Work, 36,* 419–34.

Shadish, W. R., Cook, T. D. & Campbell, D. T. (2002). *Experimental and quasi-experimental designs for generalized causal inference.* Boston, MA: Houghton Mifflin.

Shah, S. A. (2010). "To do no harm" spiritual care and ethnomedical competence: Four cases of psychosocial trauma recovery for the 2004 tsunami and 2005 earthquake in South Asia. In Brenner, G. H., Bush, D. H. & Moses, J. (Eds.), *Creating spiritual and psychological resilience: Integrating care in disaster relief work* (pp. 157–78). New York: Routledge/Taylor & Francis Group.

Shalev, A. Y. (2000). Stress management and debriefing: Historical concepts and present patterns. In B. Raphael & J. P. Wilson (Eds.), *Psychological debriefing: Theory, practice and evidence* (pp. 17–31). New York: Cambridge University Press.

Shalev, A. Y. & Bonne, O. (2000). Pharmacological treatment of trauma-related disorders. In A. Y. Shalev, R. Yehuda & A.C. McFarlane (Eds.), *International handbook of human response to trauma* (pp. 363–78). New York: Kluwer Academic/Plenum Publishers.

Shamai, M. (1994). Family intervention by phone during the Gulf War. *Journal of Marital & Family Therapy, 20,* 327–33.

Shamai, M. (1998). Therapists in distress: Team supervision of social workers and family therapists who work and live under political uncertainty. *Family Process, 37,* 245–59.

Shamai, M. (2001). Parents' perception of their children in a context of shared political uncertainty. *Family and Child Social Work, 6,* 249–60.

Shamai, M. (2002).Comparing parents' perception of their children in a context of shared uncertainty: The case of Jewish settlers in the West Bank before and after the Oslo Peace Agreement. *Child & Adolescent Social Work Journal, 19,* 57–75.

Shamai, M. (2005). Personal experience in professional narratives: The role of helpers' families in their work with terror victims. *Family Process, 44,* 203–15.

Shamai, M. (2011). The sense of national belonging as a buffer against stress resulting from national terror: Some possible inferences regarding the sense of not belonging. In G. M. Ruggiero, S. Sassaroli, Y. Latzer & S. Suchday (Eds.), *Perspectives on immigration and terrorism* (pp. 120–26). Amsterdam, Netherlands: IOS Press, in ccoperation with NATO Emerging Security Challenges Divisions.

Shamai, M. (2012). Life narratives of adults who experienced war during childhood: The case of the attack and bombing of Kibbutz Mishmar-Haemek in 1948. *Traumatology, 18,* 35–49.

Shamai, M. & Kimhi, S. (2007). Teenagers' response to threat of war and terror: The impact of gender and social systems (friends and family). *Community Mental Health Journal, 43,* 359–75.

Shamai, M. & Kimhi S. (2006). Exposure to threat of war and terror, political attitudes, stress and life satisfaction among teenagers in Israel. *Journal of Adolecence, 29,* 165–76.

Shamai, M. & Levin-Megged, O. (2006). The myth of creating an integrative story: The therapeutic experience of Holocaust survivors. *Qualitative Health Research, 16,* 692–713.

Shamai, M. & Ritov, T. (2010). Past and present, individual and systemic sense of belonging as a buffer against fear: Non-combatants on the fire line. Presented in the 32nd Annual Meeting of the American Family Therapy Academy: "Public Issues, Private Lives." Boulder, CO, June 2010.

Shamai, M. & Ron, P. (2006). Social workers in context of ongoing terror: Influence of terror on professional and personal functioning within psychosocial interventions. Final Research Report, No. 901–2003 Report period: 10/2003–4/2006. Submitted to the Israel Science Foundation.

Shamai, M. & Ron, P. (2009). Helping direct and indirect victims of national terror: Experiences of Israeli social workers. *Qualitative Health Research, 19,* 42–53.

Shamai, M., Itay-Askenazie, M. & Mol, N. (2006). Emotional outcomes of exposure to terror among couples in which one of the spouses was a victim of terrorism. Presented in the 29th Annual Meeting of the American Family Therapy Academy: "Hope and transformation: Strengthening families, communities and our selves in challenging times." Chicago, IL, June 2006.

Shamai, M., Kimhi, S. & Enosh, G. (2007). The role of social systems on personal reaction to threat of war and terror. *Journal of Social and Personal Relationships, 24,* 747–64.

Shamai, M., Sharlin, S. & Gilad-Smolinski, D. (1994). A threat to divorce as a tool for keeping the homeostasis within FED population. *Contemporary Family Therapy, 17,* 195–207.

Shamai, M., Enosh, G., Machmali-Kievitz, R. & Tapiro, S. (2015). Couples in the line of fire: Couple's resilience in preserving and enhancing their relationships. In D. Ajdukovic, S. Kimhi & M. Lahad. (Eds.), *Resiliency: Enhancing coping with crisis and terrorism* (pp. 155–78). Dordrecht: IOS Press, The NATO Science for Peace and Security Programme.

Sharlin, S. A. & Shamai, M. (2000). *Therapeutic intervention with poor, unorganized families: From distress to hope.* New York: Haworth Press.

Shin, M. L. & Handwerger, K. (2009). Is Posttraumatic Stress Disorder a stress-induced fear circuitry disorder? *Journal of Traumatic Stress, 22,* 409–15.

Shore, J. H., Tatum, E. L. & Vollmet, W. M. (1986). Evaluation of mental effect of disaster, Mount St. Helen's eruption. *American Journal of Public Health, 76,* 76–86.

Simon, J. B., Murphy, J. J. & Smith, S. M. (2005). Understanding and fostering family resilience. *The Family Journal, 13,* 427–36.

Sleeman, J. F. (1973). *The welfare state: Its aims. Benefits and costs.* London: George Allen & Unwin.

Solomon, Z. (1995). Men and women at war. In D. Meichenbaum (Ed.), *Coping with war-induced stress: The Gulf War and the Israeli response* (pp. 82–97). New York: Plenum Press.

Solomon, Z. & Dekel, R. (2007). Posttraumatic stress disorder and posttraumatic growth among Israeli ex-POWs. *Journal of Traumatic Stress, 20,* 303–12.

Solomon, Z., Waysman, M., Levy, G., Fried, B., Mikulincer, M., Benbenishty, R., Florian, V. & Bleich, A. (1992). From frontline to home front: A study of secondary traumatization. *Family Process, 31,* 289–302.

Somers, M. R. (1994). The narrative constitution of identity: A relational and network approach. *Theory and Society, 23,* 605–49.

Song, S. J., Tol, W. & de Jong, J. (2014). Indero: Intergenerational trauma and resilience between Burundian former child soldiers and their children. *Family Process, 53,* 239–251.

Sonn, C. & Fisher, A. (1998). Sense of community: Community resilient responses to oppression and change. *Journal of Community Psychology, 26,* 457–72.

Stamm, B. H. (Ed.) (1999). *Secondary traumatic stress: Self-care issues for clinicians, researchers, and educators.* Baltimore, MD: The Sidran Press.

Stamm, B. H. (2002). Measuring compassion satisfaction as well as fatigue: Developmental history of the Compassion Satisfaction and Fatigue Test. In C. R. Figley (Ed.), *Treating compassion fatigue* (pp. 107–19). New York: Brunner-Routledge.

Standing Bear, L. (1978). *The land of the spotted eagle.* Boston, MA: Houghton Mifflin (original edition published 1933).

Staub, E. (1989). *The roots of evil: The origin of genocide and other group violence.* New York: Cambridge University Press.

Stuart, R. B. (2004). *Helping couples change: A social learning approach.* New York: Guilford Press.

Summerfield, D. & Toser, L. (1991). Low intensity war and mental trauma: A study in a rural community. *Medicine and War, 7,* 84–99.

Sztompka, P. (2000). Cultural trauma: The other face of social change. *European Journal of Social Theory, 3,* 449–66.

Taft, C. T., Stafford, J., Watkins, L. E., Street, A. E. & Monson, C. M. (2011). Post-traumatic stress disorder and intimate relationships problems: A meta analysis. *Journal of Consulting and Clinical Psychology, 79,* 22–33.

Taner, A. (2006). *A shameful act: The Armenian genocide and the question of Turkish responsibility.* New York: Metropolitan Books.

Tedeschi, R. G. & Calhoun, L. G. (1995). *Trauma and transformation: Growing in the aftermath of suffering.* Thousand Oaks, CA: Sage.

Tedeschi, R. G. (1996). The posttraumatic growth inventory: Measuring the positive legacy of trauma. *Journal of Traumatic Stress, 9,* 455–71.

Tedeschi, R. G. (2004). The foundation of posttraumatic growth: New considerations. *Psychology Inquiry, 15,* 1–18.

Tennen, H. & Affleck, G. (1998). Personality and transformation in the face of adversity. In R. G. Tedeschi, C. L. Park & L. G. Calhoun (Eds.), *Posttraumatic growth: Positive change in the aftermath of crisis* (pp. 65–98). Mahwah, NJ: Lawrence Erlbaum Associates.

Terrell, F., Taylor, J., Menzise, J. & Barrett, R. K. (2008). Cultural mistrust: A core component of African American consciousness. In H. A. Neville, B. M. Tynes & S. O. Utsey (Eds.), *Handbook of African American Psychology* (pp. 299–309). Thousand Oaks, CA: Sage.

Thompson, C. (2003). Clinical experience as evidence in evidence-based practice. *Journal of Advanced Nursing, 43,* 230–37

Tierney, K., Bevc, C. & Kuligowski, E. (2006). Metaphors matter: Disaster myths, media, frames, and their consequences in Hurricane Katrina. *Annals of the American Academy of Political and Social Science, 604,* 57–81.

Titmus, R. M. (1958). *Essays on "The welfare state."* London: George Allen & Unwin.

Tobin, J. P. (2000). Observation on the mental health of a civilian population living under long-term hostility. *Psychiatric Bulletin, 24,* 69–70.

Tomich, P. L. & Helgeson, V. S. (2004). Is finding something good in the bad always good? Benefit finding among women with breast cancer. *Health Psychology, 23,* 16–23.

Towle, C. (1945). *Common human needs.* Washington, DC: National Association of Social Work.

Tuckey, M. R. (2007). Issues in the debriefing debate for the emergency services: Moving research outcomes forward. *Clinical Psychology: Science and Practice, 14,* 106–16

Turkel, G. (2002). Sudden solidarity and the rush to normalization: Toward alternative approach. *Sociological Focus, 35,* 73–9.

Turnbull, G. J. & McFarlane, A. C. (1996). Acute treatments. In B. van der Kolk, A. C. Alexander & L. Weisaeth (Eds.), *Traumatic stress: The effects of overwhelming experience on mind, body, and society* (pp. 480–90). New York: Guilford Press.

Turner, J. C., Hogg, M. A., Oakes, P. J., Reicher, S. D. & Wetherell, M. S. (1987). *Rediscovering the social group: A self-categorization theory.* Oxford: Blackwell

Turner, R. J., Wheaton, B. & Lloyd, L. A. (1995). The epidemiology of social stress. *American Sociological Review, 60,* 104–25.

Turner, V. (1967). *The forest of symbols: Aspect of Ndembo rituals.* Ithaca, NY: Cornell University Press.

Ungar, M. (2010). Families as navigators and negotiators: Facilitating culturally and contextually specific expressions of resilience. *Family Process, 49,* 421–35.

Ungar, M. (2011). Community resilience for youth and families: Facilitative physical and social capital in contexts of adversity. *Children and Youth Services Review, 33,* 1742–8.

Unger, S. (1977). *The destruction of American Indian families*. New York: Association of American Indian Affairs.

Usher, C. L. (2007). Trust and well-being in the African-American neighborhood. *City & Community, 6,* 367–87.

Van den Berg, J. H. (1972). *A different existence: Principles of phenomenological psychopathology*. Pittsburgh, PA: Duquesne University Press.

van der Kolk, B. A. & McFarlane, A. C. (1996). The black hole of trauma. In van der Kolk, B. A., McFarlane, A. C. & Weisaeth, L. (Eds.), *Traumatic stress* (pp. 3–23). New York: Guilford.

Veremis, T. (1998). The Kosovo puzzle. In T. Veremis & E. Kofos (Eds.), *Kosovo: Avoiding another Balkan war* (pp. 17–42). Athens: Hellenistic Foundation for European and Foreign Policy University of Athens.

Veremis, T. & Kofos, E. (Eds.), *Kosovo: Avoiding another Balkan war*. Athens: Hellenistic Foundation for European and Foreign Policy University of Athens.

Vicarcy, D., Searle, G. & Andrews, H. (2000). Assessment and intervention with Kosovar refugees: Design and management of a therapeutic team. *Australian Journal of Disaster and Trauma Studies, 2.* Retrieved from www.massey.ac-nzl-trauma/issues-2/vicarcy.htm.

Von-Bartalanffy, L. (1968). *General system theory*. New York: Braziller.

Wachtendorf, T. (1999). *Exploring the popular culture of disaster*. Newark, DE: Disaster Research Center, University of Delaware.

Walsh, F. (1996). The concept of family resilience: Crisis and challenge. *Family Process, 35,* 261–81.

Walsh, F. (1998). *Strengthening family resilience*. New York: Guilford.

Walsh, F. (1999). Religion and spirituality: Wellsprings for healing and resilience. In F. Walsh (Ed.), *Spiritual resources in family therapy* (pp. 3–27). New York: Guilford.

Walsh, F. (2007). Traumatic loss and major disasters: Strengthening family and community resilience. *Family Process, 46,* 207–28.

Walsh, F. (2009). Religion, spirituality, and the family: Multifaith perspectives. In F. Walsh (Ed.), *Spiritual resources in family therapy* (2nd edn., pp. 3–30). New York: Guilford.

Walsh, F. & McGoldrick, M. (2004). Loss and the family: A systemic perspective. In F. Walsh & M. McGoldrick (Eds.), *Living beyond loss: Death in the family* (2nd edn., pp. 3–26). New York: Norton.

WAVE (1999). *Injured . . . on that day*. Belfast: WAVE Trauma Centre Publications.

WAVE (2009). *That night in December*. Belfast: WAVE Trauma Centre Publications.

Waysman, M., Mikulincer, M., Solomon, Z. & Weisenberg, M. (1993). Secondary traumatization among wives of posttraumatic combat veterans: A family typology. *Journal of Family Psychology, 7,* 104–18.

Weaver, J. (1995). *Disasters: Mental health interventions*. Sarasota, FL: Professional Resource Press.

Webb, G. R. (2002). Sociology, disasters, and terrorism: Understanding threats of the new millennium. *Sociological Focus, 35,* 87–95.

Wee, D. F. & Myers, D. (2002). Stress responses of mental health workers following disaster: The Oklahoma City bombing. In C. R. Figley (Ed.), *Treating compassion fatigue* (pp. 57–84). New York: Brunner-Routledge.

Wegner, E. (2000). *Communities of practice: Learning, meaning, and identity.* Cambridge: Cambridge University Press.

Weiner, N. (1948). *Cybernetics or control and communication in the animal and machine.* Cambridge, MA: Technology Press.

Weiss, T. (2004). Correlates of posttraumatic growth in husbands of breast cancer survivors. *Psycho-oncology, 13,* 260–68.

White, M. & Epston, D. (1990). *Narrative means to therapeutic ends.* New York: Norton.

Wieling, E. & Mittal, M. (2008). Developing evidence-based systemic interventions for mass trauma. *Journal of Marital and Family Therapy, 34,* 127–31.

Wijkman, A. & Timberlake, L. (1998). *Natural disasters: Acts of God or acts of man?* Philadelphia, PA: New Society Publishers.

Wilson, J. P. (2004). PTSD and complex PTSD: Symptoms, syndromes and diagnoses. In J. P. Wilson & T. M. Keane (Eds.), *Assessing psychological trauma and PTSD* (pp. 1–46). New York: Guilford.

Wilson, J. P. (2006). Trauma archetypes and trauma complexes. In J. P. Wilson (Ed.), *The posttraumatic self* (pp. 157–210). New York: Routledge.

Wistrick, R. S. (1994). *Antisemitism, the longest hatred.* New York: Pantheon.

World Health Organization (2007). *International statistical classification of diseases and related health problems, 10th Revision.* Retrived from http://apps.who.int/classifications/apps/icd/icd10online/?gf60.htm+f62.

Wortman C. B. & Silver, R. C. (1989). The myth of coping with loss. *Journal of Consulting and Clinical Psychology, 57,* 349–57.

Wuthnow, R. (1991). *Acts of compassion.* Princeton, PA: Princeton University Press.

Yeomans, P. D. & Forman, E. M. (2008). Cultural factors in traumatic stress. In S. Eshun & R.A.R. Gurung (Eds.), *Culture and mental health* (pp. 221–44). Hoboken, NJ: Wiley-Blackwell Publishing.

Young, I. M. (2000). Five faces of oppression. In M. Adams (Ed.), *Readings for diversity and social justice* (pp. 35–49). New York: Routledge.

Zarit, S., Todd, P. A. & Zarit, J. M. (1986). Subjective burden of husbands and wives as caregivers: A longitudinal study. *The Gerontologist, 26,* 260–66.

Zinner, E. S. & Williams, M. B. (1999). *When a community weeps: Case studies in group survivorship.* London: Taylor & Francis.

Zukerman, Y. (1993). *A surplus of memory: Chronicle of the Warsaw ghetto uprising.* Berkeley, CA: University of California Press.

AUTHOR INDEX

SUBJECT INDEX